Introduction

to

Computer

Organization

YAOHAN CHU

Professor of Computer Science
University of Maryland

PRENTICE-HALL, INC.

Englewood Cliffs, New Jersey

Library of Congress Catalog Card No. 77-130352

Current Printing (last digit): 10 9 8 7 6 5 4 3 2 1

Printed in the United States of America

PRENTICE-HALL INTERNATIONAL, INC., *London*
PRENTICE-HALL OF AUSTRALIA, PTY. LTD., *Sydney*
PRENTICE-HALL OF CANADA, LTD., *Toronto*
PRENTICE-HALL OF INDIA PRIVATE LIMITED, *New Delhi*
PRENTICE-HALL OF JAPAN, INC., *Tokyo*

Preface

Computer organization, to put it simply, describes how a modern digital computer functions. It describes neither electronic circuits, modules, cabinets, cables, and the like of which a computer is made, nor interconnections of gates, flipflops, and memories by which the computer is implemented. It does describe number representation and digital arithmetic, instruction format and repertoire, computer elements and their functions, micro-operations and sequences by which the instructions are carried out, control and command logic, and so forth. In short, computer organization describes the functional organization and sequential operations of a digital computer.

Since electronic general-purpose digital computers became commercially available about 20 years ago, tens of thousands of digital computers have been put into operation, and more are being built and installed each year to meet the expanding needs. Other than those who design, fabricate, assemble, test, and install digital computers, there is need for even more people in programming, selling, experimenting, servicing, operating, and teaching the use of computers. In order that these people be confident and competent in their jobs, a thorough understanding of how a modern stored program computer works and of how it is programmed is needed.

This book consists of part of the material for the first course on computer organization which has been taught at the Computer Science Center of the University of Maryland. It is now prepared as a textbook for a course on introductory computer organization for undergraduates at universities and junior colleges who are interested in computer programming, computer engineering, or computer science. No knowledge of electronics is needed, but a good background in high school algebra and an exposure to a digital computer are required. Also, Chapter 5 requires some knowledge of Fortran programming.

The approach taken in this book is to describe in depth the organization of a commercially available digital computer especially designed for educational use. The organization is described in great detail, sequence by sequence and clock by clock, including the start-stop logic, switch logic, and input-output logic. Such a in-depth treatment gives the student a firm grasp of the subject matter. In teaching this subject, it has been the author's experience that for an introductory course the use of a real but simple computer is far more effective than the use of a hypothetical computer or parts of several computers.

This book is prepared with three objectives. The first is to teach students to understand thoroughly how a specific stored program digital computer works.

The second objective is to teach students a language by means of which computer organization and operations can be concisely and precisely described. The third objective is to introduce some concepts of machine language programming and symbolic programming.

There are 13 chapters and one appendix. Chapter 1 introduces the subjects of binary numbers and boolean algebra to the extent that they are needed in the succeeding chapters. Chapters 2, 3, and 4 present the topics of computer elements, microoperations and sequences by means of which the organization and sequences of a digital computer are described. This approach is unique not only in the way the material is organized but also in the manner in which the description is presented. Chapter 5 presents simulations of functional organizations and sequential operations by an algorithmic programming language as well as by a specially developed simulation language called the CDL. (The CDL Simulator has been available since the fall of 1968. Those who are interested in acquiring a copy of the Simulator may contact the author.) Chapters 6 through 13 show the description of the above-mentioned educational digital computer, the Bi-Tran Six computer. Since the digital computer is commerically available, the description is realistic and gives the students a genuine grasp of the subject matter. Chapter 6 describes the configuration, formats, instruction set, and characteristics of the computer. Chapter 7 introduces the use of the instruction set as well as some programming techniques. Description of program loading and operation of the simple computer is also shown in this chapter. Chapter 8 shows the generation of the timing and control signals of the computer. Chapter 9 describes the fetch sequence. Photographs showing sequential operations of the fetch sequence are shown in the Appendix. Chapters 10 through 13 describe the execution sequences. The addition and subtraction algorithms and sequences as well as the parallel adder are described in Chapter 10. The multiplication and division sequences are described in Chapter 11. Chapter 12 shows the logic of manual controls and the input and output sequences. Chapter 13 describes the other sequences.

This book can be used with or without the particular computer. If the computer is not available, it can be simulated. With the simulation background provided in Chapter 5, the student may undertake, as a term project throughout the course, the simulation of the Bi-Tran Six computer as the functional organization and sequential operations of this computer are being presented in the succeeding chapters. If the computer is available, the student may not only undertake the simulation project but also may verify the fetch and execution sequences on the computer as well as run the programs in Chapter 7 and his own programs. Observing the step-by-step and instruction-by-instruction operation of the computer offers an effective way to develop understanding of computer organization and operations.

The author is grateful to Fabri Tek, Inc. which permits the use of the design and description of the Bi-Tran Six computer and to Dr. Abe Franck, the designer of the computer, for their assistance. The author wishes to express his appreciation to his colleague, Mr. C. K. Mesztenyi, who developed the CDL Simulator, and to many of his students who read chapters of the manuscript, particularly Mr. Richard P. Glasspool.

Yaohan Chu

Chevy Chase, Maryland

Contents

8 Generation of Timing and Control Signals, 257

9 Fetch Sequence, 269

10 Addition and Subtraction Sequences, 277

11 Multiplication and Division Sequences, 303

12 Manual Controls and Input/output Sequences, 321

13 Other Sequences, 341

Appendix   Display of the Fetch-sequence Operation, 349

References, 369

Index, 373

1

Introduction

Because of the binary nature of its circuits and memories, a modern digital computer is commonly built to handle binary numbers. A major task of the digital computer is to perform arithmetic and other operations; these operations can be described by the algebra of logic. This chapter introduces the subjects of binary numbers, binary arithmetic, and boolean algebra to provide the background for studying the succeeding chapters.

1.1 BINARY NUMBERS

A decimal number can be represented in more than one form. Consider decimal number N, 1968.906, which has seven digits (four integral and three fractional digits). This number is represented above in the commonly used form. In this form, the decimal point demarcates the integral and fractional parts. This number may also be represented in the following form:

$$N = 1 \times 10^3 + 9 \times 10^2 + 6 \times 10^1 + 8 \times 10^0$$
$$+ 9 \times 10^{-1} + 0 \times 10^{-2} + 6 \times 10^{-3}$$

where symbols 1,9,6, . . . are called *digits.* For a decimal number system, there are ten digits: 0,1,2, . . ., 8,9. The number 10 in the above form is called the *base* or *radix* of the number system. A decimal number system has a base of 10. The exponents 3,2, . . ., -3 indicate the *weight* of each of the digits of the number.

For a binary number system, the base is 2 and digits are 0 and 1. Consider binary number B, 1011.01, where the point is called the *binary point.* This number may also be represented by the following form:

$$B = 1 \times 2^3 + 0 \times 2^2 + 1 \times 2^1 + 1 \times 2^0 + 0 \times 2^{-1} + 1 \times 2^{-2}$$

By adding these terms, we obtain 11.25 which is the decimal equivalent of the above binary number. The above binary number has six binary digits. Since the term binary digit occurs so frequently, it is abbreviated and denoted by *bit.*

Similarly, for an octal number system, the base is 8 and the digits are 0,1, . . ., 7. These three number systems—decimal, octal, and binary—are to be encountered in the succeeding chapters. As an example, the sixteen 4-bit binary integers together with the corresponding octal and decimal equivalents are shown in Table 1.1.

Table 1.1 Decimal, octal, and binary numbers

Binary	Octal	Decimal
0000	0	0
0001	1	1
0010	2	2
0011	3	3
0100	4	4
0101	5	5
0110	6	6
0111	7	7
1000	10	8
1001	11	9
1010	12	10
1011	13	11
1100	14	12
1101	15	13
1110	16	14
1111	17	15

When the system to which a number belongs is not apparent, a subscript may be employed to indicate the number system. For example, number 1234.56 can be a decimal number or an octal number. If it is a decimal number, it can be written as 1234.56_{10} . If it is an octal number, it can be written as 1234.56_8 . The subscript is omitted if the system of a number is apparent or otherwise stated.

1.1.1 Single-bit Arithmetic

Binary arithmetic is based on single-bit arithmetic. The addition of two single bits, an augend bit, and an addend bit, gives a sum bit and a carry bit. The rules of single-bit addition are shown below:

Augend bit		Addend bit		Carry bit	Sum bit
0	+	0	=	0	0
0	+	1	=	0	1
1	+	0	=	0	1
1	+	1	=	1	0

Note that the carry bit occurs only when both augend and addend bits are 1.

The subtraction of two bits, a subtrahend bit from a minuend bit, gives a difference bit and a borrow bit. The rules of single-bit subtraction are shown below:

Minuend bit		Subtrahend bit		Borrow bit	Difference bit
0	-	0	=	0	0
0	-	1	=	1	1
1	-	0	=	0	1
1	-	1	=	0	0

Note that the borrow bit occurs only when the subtrahend bit is larger than the minuend bit. Also note that the corresponding sum and difference bits in the above addition and subtraction rules are the same; only the carry and borrow bits are different.

The multiplication of two single bits, a multiplicand bit and a multiplier bit, gives a single-bit product. The rules of single-bit multiplication are shown below:

Multiplicand bit		Multiplier bit		Product bit
0	X	0	=	0
0	X	1	=	0
1	X	0	=	0
1	X	1	=	1

The product bit is 1 only when the multiplicand and multiplier bits are both 1.

The above rules of single-bit arithmetic are now applied to binary addition, subtraction, multiplication, and division.

1.1.2 Binary Addition

When two five-bit numbers are added, the sum is a five-bit or a six-bit number. When the sum is a six-bit number, the carry bit from the most significant bit position is called *overflow.* These two cases are illustrated by the following examples where the single-bit addition rules are applied. The flow chart in Figure 1.1 shows an algorithm for binary addition of unsigned binary numbers X^* and Y^*.

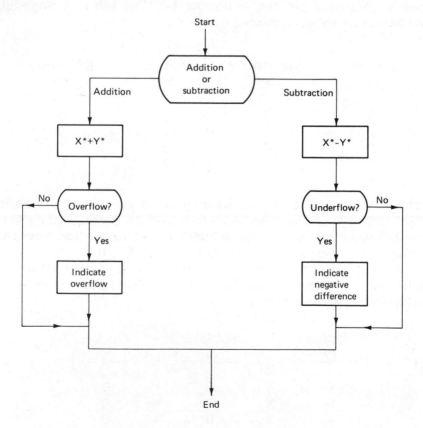

Fig. 1.1 Flow chart showing addition and subtraction of unsigned binary numbers X^* and Y^*

Example 1.1 Binary Addition with No Overflow

	Binary	*Decimal*
Augend	10001	17
Addend	+01001	+09
Digit sum	11000	26
Carry bits	+00001	
Sum	(0)11010 = 26_{10}	

No overflow bit

Example 1.2 Binary Addition with Overflow

	Binary	*Decimal*
Augend	10001	17
Addend	+10010	+18
Digit sum	00011	35
Carry bits	+10000	
	(1)00011 ≠ 35_{10}	

Overflow bit

Normally, there is no extra room in the computer to store this overflow bit for later use. As a result, the sum is 00011 (instead of 100011) which is incorrect. Although the above are additions of integers, the additions are similar if the numbers are fractional or mixed as long as the binary points of the two numbers are aligned.

1.1.3 Complements

For a given binary number, there are two associated numbers of importance; they are called the *2's complement* and the *1's complement* of the given binary number. The 2's complement of an n-bit binary number is obtained by subtracting the given n-bit binary number from n-bit zeros (with the borrow from the most significant bit being ignored). The 1's complement of an n-bit binary number is obtained by subtracting the given n-bit binary number from n-bit one's. An example of obtaining the 2's complement N2 and the 1's complement N1 of the given binary number N in this manner is shown on page 6.

Example 1.3 2's and 1's Complements of a Binary
Number

Let N be the given binary number
N1 be the 1's complement of N
N2 be the 2's complement of N

Given N = 00111

then N2 = 00000 − 00111 = 11001

and N1 = 11111 − 00111 = 11000

Let N22 be the 2's complement of N2
N11 be the 1's complement of N1

then N22 = 00000 − 11001 = 00111
N11 = 11111 − 11000 = 00111

In the above example, the 2's complement of the given binary
number N is larger than its 1's complement by one least significant
bit. Furthermore, the 2's complement of the 2's complement of a
binary number is the number itself (i.e., N22 = N). And the 1's
complement of the 1's complement of a binary number is also the
number itself (i.e., N11 = N). Note that the 2's complement of a
number is obtained by subtraction, while the 1's complement can be
obtained by 1's complement of each bit of the number. Thus, it is
easier in a computer to obtain the 1's complement of a binary
number than its 2's complement.

1.1.4 Binary Subtraction

When a number (subtrahend) is subtracted from another number
(minuend), the difference can be positive or negative. If the
subtrahend is smaller than (or equal to) the minuend, the difference
is positive (or zero). If the subtrahend is larger than the minuend, the
difference is negative. These two cases are illustrated by the
following examples, where the single-bit subtraction rules are
applied.

Example 1.4 Binary Subtraction with Positive
　　　　　　　　Difference

	Binary	*Decimal*
Minuend	10001	17
Subtrahend	−01010	−10
Digit diff.	▷ 11011	07
Borrow bits	−1010	
1st diff.	01111	
Borrow bits	−0100	
Difference	00111 = 7_{10}	

Example 1.5 Binary Subtraction with Negative
　　　　　　　　Difference

	Binary	*Decimal*
Minuend	01010	10
Subtrahend	−10001	−17
Digit diff.	11011	−07
Borrow bits	−10001	
Difference	(1)11001	

↑
Underflow

The above minuends and subtrahends are *unsigned* binary
numbers; they are regarded as positive binary numbers. In example
1.4, the difference is positive; difference 00111 is correct. In
example 1.5, the difference is negative, since difference 1100l is
regarded as a positive number and it could not be correct. However,
if one recognizes that 1100l is the 2's complement of 00111, then
difference 11001 is correct because the negative binary number in
this case is represented by the 2's complement. The existence of the
negative difference is indicated by the appearance of an underflow as
shown in example 1.5.

1.1.5 Subtraction by Addition of 2's Complement

Binary subtraction can be accomplished by addition of the 2's complement of the subtrahend. The rule for such a subtraction is as follows:

 a. Add the 2's complement of the subtrahend to the minuend.
 b. If there is no overflow, the result is negative and is in the 2's complement form.
 c. If there is an overflow, the result is positive and the overflow is ignored.

Subtraction by addition of 2's complement is illustrated by the following two examples.

Example 1.6 Binary Subtraction with Positive
　　　　　　　　Difference

	Binary	*Decimal*
Minuend	10001	17
Subtrahend	−01001	− 9
		8
Augend	10001	
Addend	+10111	
Sum	(1)01000 = 8_{10}	

↑
Overflow

In the above, the minuend becomes the augend and the addend is the 2's complement of the subtrahend. Since there is an overflow, the difference is positive. The overflow is ignored and the difference is 01000.

Example 1.7 Binary Subtraction with Negative
　　　　　　　　Difference

	Binary	*Decimal*
Minuend	01001	9
Subtrahend	− 10001	− 17
		− 8
Augend	01001	
Addend	+01111	
Sum	11000	

In the above, the addend is again the 2's complement of the subtrahend. Since there is no overflow, the result is negative and the difference 11000 is in the 2's complement form. Note that the 2's complement of 11000 is 8_{10}. That the difference is negative is expected since the subtrahend is larger than the minuend.

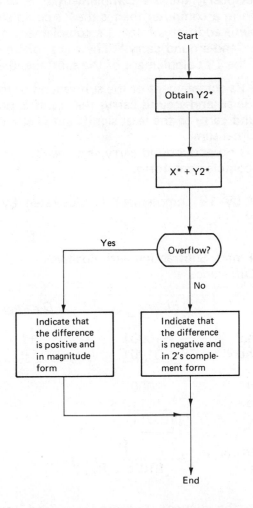

Fig. 1.2 Flow chart showing subtraction of unsigned binary numbers X* and Y* by addition of 2's complement of Y* (i.e., Y2*)

The flow chart in Figure 1.2 shows an algorithm for subtraction of unsigned binary numbers X* and Y* by addition of 2's complement of subtrahend Y*.

1.1.6 Subtraction by Addition of 1's Complement of Subtrahend

Binary subtraction can be accomplished by addition of the 1's complement of the subtrahend. Addition of the 1's complement is sometimes preferred to addition of the 2's complement because, as mentioned previously, the 1's complement of a binary number is easier to obtain in a computer than is the 2's complement. However, as will be shown, addition of the 1's complement may require the addition of an "end-around carry." The rules for binary subtraction by addition of the 1's complement of the subtrahend are:

    a. Add the 1's complement of the subtrahend to the minuend.
    b. If there is an end-around carry, the result is positive. Add the end-around carry to the least significant position of the sum to give the final sum.
    c. If there is no end-around carry, the result is negative and is in the 1's complement form.

Subtraction by 1's complement is illustrated by the following examples.

Example 1.8 Binary Subtraction with Positive
               Difference

	Binary	*Decimal*
Minuend	10001	17
Subtrahend	−01001	− 9
		8
Augend	10001	
Addend	+10110	
Sum	(1)00111	
Add end-around carry	+ 1	
Final sum	01000 $= 8_{10}$	

In the above, the minuend becomes the augend, and the addend is the 1's complement of the subtrahend. The end-around carry appears as an overflow; but, this is not an overflow because overflow does not exist in a subtraction. Since the end-around carry occurs, the result is positive. Add the end-around carry to the sum 00111; this gives the final sum (or rather difference) **01000** or **8**.

Example 1.9 Binary Subtraction with Negative
Difference

	Binary	*Decimal*
Minuend	01001	9
Subtrahend	- 10001	- 17
		- 8
Augend	01001	
Addend	+01110	
Sum	10111	

In the above, the addend is again the 1's complement of the
subtrahend. Since there is no end-around carry, the result is negative
and difference 10111 is in the 1's complement form. Note that the
1's complement of 10111 is 01000 or 8.

Example 1.10 Binary Subtraction with Zero
Difference

	Binary	*Decimal*
Minuend	01001	9
Subtrahend	- 01001	-9
		0
Augend	01001	
Addend	+10110	
Sum	11111	

In the above, the addend is again the 1's complement of the
subtrahend. Since there is no end-around carry, the difference 11111
is in the 1's complement form. Note that the 1's complement of
11111 is 00000 or zero.

The flow chart in Figure 1.3 shows an algorithm for subtraction
of unsigned binary numbers X^* and Y^* by addition of 1's
complement of subtrahend Y^*.

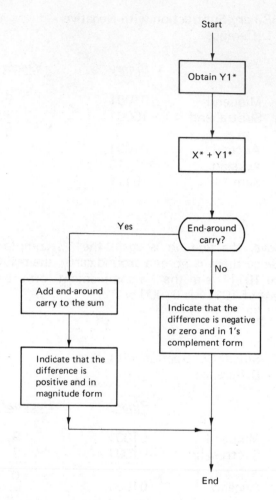

Fig. 1.3 Flow chart showing subtraction of unsigned binary numbers X* and Y* by addition of 1's complement of Y* (i.e., Y1*)

1.1.7 Binary Multiplication

Let X* be the multiplicand, Y* the multiplier, and P* be the product. All are unsigned binary numbers. Binary multiplication can be described as follows:

Let $X^* = x_n \cdot 2^n + \cdots + x_i \cdot 2^i + \cdots + x_0 \cdot 2^0$
$\qquad Y^* = y_n \cdot 2^n + \cdots + y_i \cdot 2^i + \cdots + y_0 \cdot 2^0$
Then $P^* = X^* \cdot Y^*$
Assume $X^* = 10001 \qquad$ or $\qquad X_4 = 1, X_3 = 0, X_2 = 0, X_1 = 0,$
$\qquad\qquad\qquad\qquad\qquad\qquad\qquad\qquad\qquad X_0 = 1$

$$Y^* = 01001 \quad \text{or} \quad Y_4 = 0, Y_3 = 1, Y_2 = 0, Y_1 = 0,$$
$$Y_0 = 1$$

When $n = 4$

$$\text{Then } P^* = 0 \cdot X^* \cdot 2^4 + 1 \cdot X^* \cdot 2^3 + 0 \cdot X^* \cdot 2^2$$
$$+ 0 \cdot X^* \cdot 2^1 + 1 \cdot X^* \cdot 2^0$$

The above equation shows that product P^* is the sum of the "shifted" multiplicands and that, when a multiplier bit is 0, no addition of the multiplicand is required. Instead of adding these terms simultaneously as one usually does with paper and pencil, the computer adds one term at a time to form a partial product repeatedly. Because of the repeated formation of a partial product by addition, this method of multiplication is known as the *repeated addition method.* The flow chart in Figure 1.4 shows an algorithm for multiplication of the above unsigned binary numbers X^* and Y^*. In Figure 1.4, i and p_i represent the index and the ith partial product respectively. An example of multiplication by repeated addition is shown below.

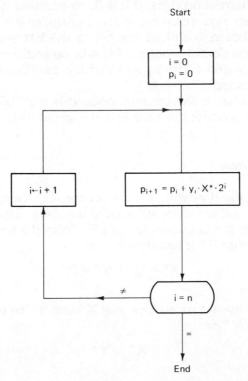

Fig. 1.4 Flow chart showing multiplication of unsigned binary numbers X^* and Y^*

Example 1.11 Binary Multiplication

$$10001 = \text{multiplicand}$$
$$\underline{\times\ 01001} = \text{multiplier}$$

$$10001 = 1 \cdot X \cdot 2^0, \text{ first partial product}$$
$$\underline{00000\ } = 0 \cdot X \cdot 2^1$$

$$010001 = \text{second partial product}$$
$$\underline{000000\ } = 0 \cdot X \cdot 2^2$$

$$0010001 = \text{third partial product}$$
$$\underline{10001\ \ \ } = 1 \cdot X \cdot 2^3$$

$$10011001 = \text{fourth partial product}$$
$$\underline{00000\ \ \ \ } = 0 \cdot X \cdot 2^4$$

$$010011001 = 153_{10}, \text{ final product}$$

In the above multiplication, the least significant bit of the multiplier is first examined. If it is 1, the multiplicand is added to form the first partial product; if it is 0, no addition is required. Then, the second least significant bit of the multiplier is examined. If it is 1, the multiplicand is shifted one bit to the left and then added to form the second partial product; if it is 0, no addition is needed. This process of repeated addition and shifting continues until the final product is obtained.

Note that when a five-bit multiplicand is multiplied by a five-bit multiplier, the product can have as many as ten bits.

1.1.8 Binary Division

Let X^* be the dividend, Y^* the divisor, Q^* the quotient, and R^* the remainder; all are unsigned binary numbers. Binary division is a process to find the unknown Q^* and R^* from the known X^* and Y^* in such a way that R^* is less then Y^*, or

$$X^* = Q^* \cdot Y^* + R^* \tag{1.1}$$

where $R^* < Y^*$

For simplicity, let us assume that X^* and Y^* be integers and that X^* is less than Y^* or

$$X^* < Y^* \tag{1.2}$$

This inequality or one similar to this one is needed because the value of Y^* must be limited; otherwise, quotient Q^* can become very large or even infinite. With the above conditions, quotient Q^* is a fraction, or

$$Q^* = q_1 2^{-1} + q_2 2^{-2} + \ldots + q_n 2^{-n}$$

$$= \sum_{i=1}^{n} q_i 2^{-i} \tag{1.3}$$

where q_i are quotient bits.

Remainder R^* can be expressed as

$$R^* = X^* - Q^* \cdot Y^* \tag{1.4}$$

If we assume, as an example, X^* and Y^* are five-bit integers and Q^* is a five-bit fraction (i.e., $n = 5$), we then have

$$R^* = X^* - Y^* (q_1 2^{-1} + q_2 2^{-2} + \ldots + q_5 2^{-5}) \tag{1.5}$$

Let $r_0, r_1, r_2, \ldots, r_5$, be the initial, first, second, $\ldots$, fifth partial remainder, respectively, or

$$\begin{aligned}
r_0 &= X^* \\
r_1 &= r_0 - q_1 \cdot Y^* \cdot 2^{-1} \\
r_2 &= r_1 - q_2 \cdot Y^* \cdot 2^{-2} \\
r_3 &= r_2 - q_3 \cdot Y^* \cdot 2^{-3} \\
r_4 &= r_3 - q_4 \cdot Y^* \cdot 2^{-4} \\
r_5 &= r_4 - q_5 \cdot Y^* \cdot 2^{-5}
\end{aligned} \tag{1.6}$$

Then,
$$\begin{aligned}
R^* &= r_0 - q_1 Y^* 2^{-1} - q_2 Y^* 2^{-2} - q_3 Y^* 2^{-3} - q_4 Y^* 2^{-4} - q_5 Y^* 2^{-5} \\
&= r_1 - q_2 Y^* 2^{-2} - q_3 Y^* 2^{-3} - q_4 Y^* 2^{-4} - q_5 Y^* 2^{-5} \\
&= r_2 - q_3 Y^* 2^{-3} - q_4 Y^* 2^{-4} - q_5 Y^* 2^{-5} \\
&= r_3 - q_4 Y^* 2^{-4} - q_5 Y^* 2^{-5} \\
&= r_4 - q_5 Y^* 2^{-5} \\
&= r_5
\end{aligned} \tag{1.7}$$

It is possible to formulate an algorithm for division of unsigned binary numbers from the above relation (1.7) by repeatedly finding partial remainder r_i. This algorithm is shown by the flow chart in Figure 1.5 where the arrowhead means "is replaced by." It is assumed in Figure 1.5 that the above inequality (1.2) is fulfilled. The flow chart shows that the ith partial remainder is compared with the divisor which has been shifted $(i + 1)$ bit positions to the right. If the partial remainder is greater than or equal to the shifted divisor, quotient bit q_{i+1} is 1 and the shifted divisor is subtracted from the ith partial remainder to give the $(i + 1)$th partial remainder. Otherwise, quotient bit q_{i+1} is 0 and the $(i + 1)$th partial remainder is the same as the ith partial remainder as there is no subtraction.

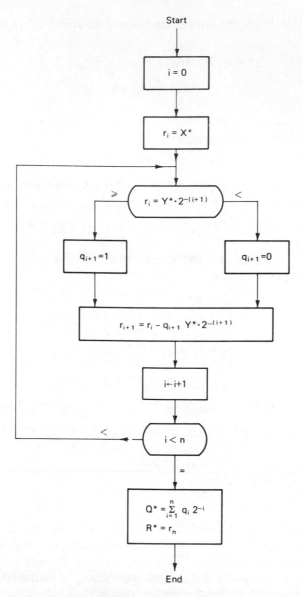

Fig. 1.5 Flow chart showing division of unsigned binary numbers X^* by Y^* (assume $X^* < Y^*$)

After the partial remainder is repeatedly obtained for n times, quotient Q^* of the division is obtained from quotient bits q_i and the remainder of the division R^* is the nth partial remainder.

An example illustrating binary division of unsigned binary numbers X^* by Y^* by the algorithm in Figure 1.5 is shown below.

Example 1.12 Binary Division

$$\text{Let } X = \text{dividend} = 10001 = 17_{10}$$
$$Y = \text{divisor} = 10101 = 21_{10}$$
$$Q = \frac{X}{Y} = .809523\ldots$$

```
                    .11001 = quotient
        10101/10001.00000
               1010 1
               0110 10
                101 01
                001 010
                 00 000
                 01 0100
                  0 0000
                  1 01000
                    10101
                    10011 = Remainder
```

The above quotient .11001 is decimally equivalent to .78125 which is significantly different from the correct quotient of .809523. ... This means that many more bits are required to represent the dividend, divisor, and quotient more accurately.

The comparison between the divisor and the partial remainder in the above division is apparent, but it is not so in a machine. Different methods of comparison result in different algorithms for division.

1.2 SIGNED BINARY NUMBERS

Up to now, the binary numbers considered were unsigned binary numbers; they were regarded as positive numbers. In practical applications, binary numbers can be positive or negative; therefore, the sign must be represented and the resulting numbers are called *signed binary numbers.*

1.2.1 Three Representations

Signed binary numbers have one bit (usually the leftmost bit) to denote the sign; 0 and 1 are normally chosen to denote the positive and negative signs, respectively. The other bits of the signed binary numbers are called *number bits.* There are three representations of signed binary numbers that are commonly used:

a. the signed magnitude representation,
b. the signed 2's complement representation,
c. the signed 1's complement representation.

When the numbers are positive, the three representations are the same. When the numbers are negative, the number bits in the signed magnitude representation represent the magnitude (i.e., the absolute value), the number bits in the signed 2's complement representation represent the 2's complement of the magnitude, and the number bits in the 1's complement representation represent the 1's complement of the magnitude. The following example illustrates the three representations.

Example 1.13 Three Representations of a Signed
Binary Number

Signed magnitude representation

$$0,10001 = +17_{10}$$
$$1,10001 = -17_{10}$$

Signed 2's complement representation

$$0,10001 = +17_{10}$$
$$1,01111 = -17_{10}$$

Signed 1's complement representation

$$0,10001 = +17_{10}$$
$$1,01110 = -17_{10}$$

The above signed binary numbers represent either $+17_{10}$ or -17_{10}. The leftmost bits of the above numbers are the sign bits with 0 denoting the positive sign and 1 the negative sign. The commas indicate the sign bits, but they are not actually required. Notice that the representations of the positive numbers are all the same.

1.2.2 Negative Zeros

Consider a 3-bit number. If the eight possible binary numbers consisting of 3 bits are listed,

$$0,11 = +3$$
$$0,10 = +2$$
$$0,01 = +1$$
$$0,00 = +0$$
$$1,00 = -0$$
$$1,01 = -1$$
$$1,10 = -2$$
$$1,11 = -3$$

we can identify them as signed binary numbers in the signed magnitude representation. As shown above, they are +3, . . ., 0, . . ., −3. Furthermore, we have the number 1,00 which, if interpreted according to the rule of number representation, is negative zero. We can also identify these eight binary numbers as signed binary numbers in the signed 2's complement representation as shown below,

$$0,11 = +3$$
$$0,10 = +2$$
$$0,01 = +1$$
$$0,00 = +0$$
$$1,00 = -0 \text{ or } -4$$
$$1,11 = -1$$
$$1,10 = -2$$
$$1,01 = -3$$

Again, we have number 1,00 which could be interpreted as negative zero or −4. We can further identify these eight binary numbers as signed binary numbers in the signed 1's complement representation as shown below,

$$0,11 = +3$$
$$0,10 = +2$$
$$0,01 = +1$$
$$0,00 = +0$$
$$1,11 = -0$$
$$1,10 = -1$$
$$1,01 = -2$$
$$1,00 = -3$$

Again, we have number 1,11 which is interpreted as a negative zero. Therefore, in representing signed binary numbers, there exists the superfluous representation of negative zero. Most of the today's computers automatically change the negative zero to positive zero when negative zero occurs.

1.2.3 Signed Binary Addition

Binary arithmetic of signed binary numbers requires determination of both the number bits and the sign bit. The rules of binary arithmetic for signed binary numbers are different for different representations of signed binary numbers. Here, the rules of binary addition for numbers in the signed magnitude representation are shown.

Let x_0 and X^* be, respectively, the sign bit and the number bits of the augend, y_0 and Y^* be, respectively, the sign bit and the number bits of the addend, z_0 and Z^* be, respectively, the sign bit and the number bits of the sum, and w_0 be the overflow bit (i.e., the carry from the most significant bit). Binary addition determines both z_0 and Z^*. The rules are:

1. When the signs of the two binary numbers are the same, perform the addition $Z^*=X^*+Y^*$ and set $z_0=x_0$. If w_0 is 0, then the result is correct. If w_0 is 1, then overflow occurs and the result is incorrect. (See examples 1.14 and 1.15.)
2. When the signs of the two numbers are different, perform the subtraction $Z^*=X^*-Y^*$ and (a) if w_0 is 0, set $z_0=x_0$ or (b) if w_0 is 1, set $z_0 = y_0$ and replace Z^* by its 2's complement (i.e., $Z2^*$). (See examples 1.16 and 1.17.)
3. The sum after addition if not overflown or the difference after subtraction if not underflown is tested for zero. If it is zero, the result is set to positive zero.

The flow chart which describes addition of binary numbers in the signed magnitude representation by these rules is shown in Figure 1.6. Examples of such binary additions are shown below.

Example 1.14 Signed Binary Addition with No
Overflow

	Binary	*Decimal*
Augend	+10001	17
Addend	+01001	+ 9
Sum	+11010	26

$$w_0 = 0$$
$$x_0 = y_0$$
$$z_0 = x_0 = +$$
$$Z^* = 11010 = 26_{10}$$

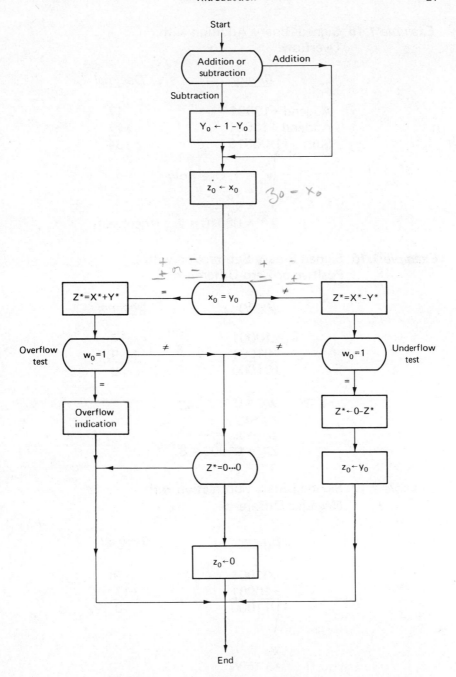

Fig. 1.6 Flow chart showing addition and subtraction of two signed binary numbers in the signed magnitude representation

Example 1.15 Signed Binary Addition with Overflow

	Binary	*Decimal*
Augend	+10001	17
Addend	+10001	+17
Sum	(1)00010	34

$w_0 = 1$, Overflow
$x_0 = y_0$
$z_0 = x_0 = +$
$Z^* = 00010 = 2_{10}$ (Incorrect)

Example 1.16 Signed Binary Subtraction with Positive or Zero Difference

Binary	*Decimal*
+10001	17
–01001	+(–9)
+01000	8

$w_0 = 0$
$x_0 \neq y_0$
$z_0 = x_0 = +$
$Z^* = 01000 = 8_{10}$

Example 1.17 Signed Binary Subtraction with Negative Difference

Binary	*Decimal*
-01001	(-9)
+10001	+17
(1)11000	8

$w_0 = 1$,
$x_0 \neq y_0$
$z_0 = y_0 = +$
$Z^* = 00000 - 11000$
$\quad = 01000 = 8_{10}$

Note that 2's complement of 11000 is required in order to obtain the correct result 01000.

The subtraction required in the above rule (2) can be replaced by addition of 2's complement of the subtrahend or by addition of 1's complement of the subtrahend. An application of subtraction by addition of 1's complement of the subtrahend will be shown in a later chapter.

1.2.4 Signed Binary Subtraction

Binary subtraction for numbers in the signed magnitude representation can readily be accomplished by applying the rules for binary addition for numbers in the signed magnitude representation, if the sign of the subtrahend is first changed into minus if it is plus or into plus if it is minus. The flow chart which describes subtraction of binary numbers in the signed magnitude representation by these rules is also shown in Figure 1.6. An example of such binary subtraction is shown below.

Example 1.18 Signed Binary Subtraction

	Binary	*Decimal*
Minuend	+10001	17
Subtrahend	+01001	- 9
		8

Change the sign of the subtrahend and then follow the rule for signed binary addition. Since the sign bits are now different, rule (2) which calls for a subtraction is applied.

Minuend	+10001
Subtrahend	-01001
	+01000

$$w_0 = 0$$
$$x_0 \neq y_0$$
$$z_0 = x_0 = +$$
$$Z^* = 01000 = 8_{10}$$

1.2.5 Subtraction by Addition of 1's Complements

Binary addition and subtraction shown in the flow chart of Figure 1.6 require both a parallel adder and a parallel subtracter; this is not practical. Normally, there is only one parallel adder or one parallel subtracter. Use of only a parallel adder can be accomplished if subtraction is performed by addition of 1's complement of subtrahend.

Figure 1.7 is a flow chart which shows binary addition and

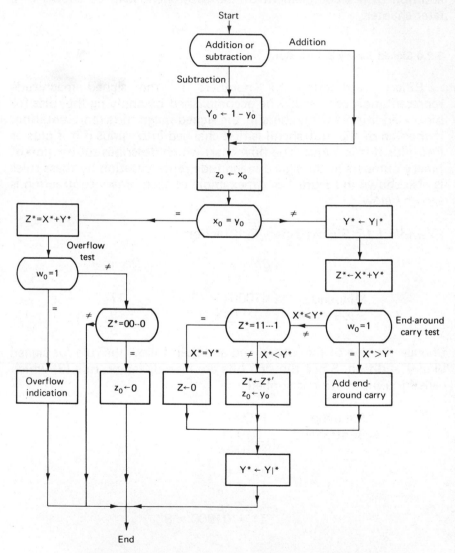

Fig. 1.7 Flow chart showing addition and subtraction of two signed binary numbers in the signed magnitude representation where subtraction is performed by addition of 1's complement of subtrahend

subtraction of two signed binary numbers in the signed magnitude representation where subtraction is performed by addition of 1's complement of subtrahend. The algorithm in this flow chart is essentially the flow chart in Figure 1.6 in which the algorithm in Figure 1.3 is incorporated. When signs x_0 and y_0 are the same, the addition process in Figure 1.7 is the same as that in Figure 1.6. When they are not the same, magnitude Y^* is first 1's complemented before it is added to magnitude X^* and is later restored by being 1's complemented once more. End-around carry occurs if carry w_0 is 1; in this case, magnitude X^* is greater than magnitude Y^* and the end-around carry is added to magnitude Z^*. End-around carry does not occur if carry w_0 is 0; in this case, the magnitude of the sum Z^* is tested for all 1's. If Z^* consists of all 1's, X^* is equal to Y^* and sum Z should consist of all 0's. If Z^* does not consist of all 1's, X^* is less than Y^* and sum Z^* is in the 1's complement form; therefore, Z^* is again 1's complemented to give sum Z^* in the magnitude form in addition to using sign y_0 as sign z_0.

1.2.6 Signed Binary Multiplication

The rules of binary multiplication for numbers in the signed magnitude representation are the same as those for unsigned binary numbers except, in the case of signed binary numbers, the sign bit of the product must also be determined. The rule for determining the sign of the product is: the sign of the product is positive if the signs of the multiplicand and multiplier are the same; otherwise, the sign of the product is negative. The flow chart for multiplication of signed binary numbers can be readily extended from that shown in Figure 1.4.

1.2.7 Signed Binary Division

The rules of binary division for numbers in the signed magnitude representation are the same as those for unsigned binary numbers except the sign of the quotient must also be determined. The rule for determining the sign of the quotient is: the sign of the quotient is positive if the signs of the dividend and divisor are the same; otherwise, the sign of the quotient is negative. The flow chart for division of signed binary numbers can be readily extended from that shown in Figure 1.5.

1.3 BOOLEAN ALGEBRA

Boolean algebra, the algebra of logic, is a symbolic method of studying logical relations. It was originated by George Boole (1815-1864), an English mathematician, who published his book *An Investigation of the Laws of Thought* in 1854. Boolean algebra is now widely applied to the description of digital computer designs because digital computers of today employ devices and circuits whose signals and states are represented by two values.

1.3.1 Boolean Variables

A boolean variable is a quantity which may, at different times, have one of two possible values. The existence of only two values in boolean algebra is the important difference between boolean algebra and ordinary algebra where a variable may have many values. A boolean variable is thus a binary variable. Boolean variables are represented by capital letters such as A,B,X,Z, etc. The two values of a binary variable are denoted by "true" and "false" or by 1 and 0; they are called *truth values* or *logical constants.* In electronic circuits and memories, these two values are represented by two voltage levels, or by the presence or absence of a pulse, or by two physical states.

1.3.2 Logical Operators

Like the operators x (multiplication) and ÷ (division) in ordinary algebra, there are boolean or logical operators which specify logical operations on boolean variables and/or logical constants. Six logical operators whose names and symbols are shown in Table 1.2 are now introduced.

· **Table 1.2** Logical operators

Names	Symbols	Examples
logical EQUAL	=	A = B
logical NOT (1)	′	A′
logical OR (2)	+	A + B
logical AND	·,*	A · B or A * B or AB
logical EXOR (3)	⊕	A ⊕ B
logical COIN (4)	⊙	A ⊙ B

Note 1, also called complement operator
Note 2, also called inclusive-or operator
Note 3, also called exclusive-or operator
Note 4, also called coincidence operator

Logical EQUAL

Given a boolean variable A, consider a new variable B. Variable A can have a value of 1 or 0. If the truth value of variable B is always the same as the truth value of variable A, B is said to be logically equal to A. This logical equality can be described by the table of truth values of variables A and B as shown in Table 1.3. The first column in Table 1.3 shows all the possible truth values of variable A and the second column shows the corresponding truth values of variable B. As shown in the table, when A is 0, B is 0; when A is 1, B is 1. Therefore, variable B is equal to variable A

$$B = A$$

and vice versa.

Table 1.3 Truth table for logical EQUAL

A	B
0	0
1	1

Logical NOT

Given a boolean variable A, consider a new variable A' which is the logical NOT of A (or logical complement of A). The truth values of variables A and A' are shown in Table 1.4. As shown, when variable A is 0, variable A' is 1; when A is 1, A' is 0. Thus, the truth value of A' is always the complement of the truth value of A; or conversely, the truth value of A is always the complement of the truth value of A'.

Also, Table 1.4 describes the following relations,

$$0 = 1'$$
$$1 = 0'$$

(1.8)

Table 1.4 Truth table for logical NOT

A	A'
0	1
1	0

Logical OR

Given two boolean variables A and B, consider a new variable A + B which is the logical OR of variables A and B. The truth values of variables A, B and A + B are shown in Table 1.5. As shown in Table 1.5, when both variables A and B are 0, the new variable A + B is also 0. When either A or B or both is 1, the new variable A + B is 1. Table 1.5 thus states that

$$0 + 0 = 0,$$
$$0 + 1 = 1,$$
$$1 + 0 = 1, \qquad (1.9)$$
$$1 + 1 = 1.$$

Table 1.5 Truth table for logical OR

A	B	A + B
0	0	0
0	1	1
1	0	1
1	1	1

The logical OR operation is also known as the logical sum operation.

Logical AND

Given two boolean variables A and B, consider a new variable A * B (or A·B or, if no ambiguity exists, AB) which is the logical AND of variables A and B. The truth values of A, B and A * B are shown in Table 1.6. This table shows that, when either variable A or variable B is 0, the new variable A * B is 0. When both variables A and B are 1, then the new variable A * B is 1. In other words, Table 1.6 states that

$$0 * 0 = 0,$$
$$0 * 1 = 0,$$
$$1 * 0 = 0, \qquad (1.10)$$
$$1 * 1 = 1.$$

The logical AND operation is also known as the logical multiplication operation.

Table 1.6 Truth table for logical AND

A	B	A * B
0	0	0
0	1	0
1	0	0
1	1	1

Logical EXOR

Given two boolean variables A and B, consider a new variable $A \oplus B$ which is the logical EXOR (exclusive-or) of variables A and B. Table 1.7 shows the truth values of variables A, B and $A \oplus B$. As shown in Table 1.7, when variable A is 1 and variable B is 0 or when A is 0 and B is 1, the new variable $A \oplus B$ is 1. Otherwise, the new variable is 0. Table 1.7 thus shows that

$$\begin{aligned} 0 \oplus 0 &= 0, \\ 0 \oplus 1 &= 1, \\ 1 \oplus 0 &= 1, \\ 1 \oplus 1 &= 0. \end{aligned} \qquad (1.11)$$

Table 1.7 Truth table for logical EXOR

A	B	A ⊕ B
0	0	0
0	1	1
1	0	1
1	1	0

Logical EXOR operation means logical exclusive-or operation, while logical OR means logical inclusive-or operation.

Logical COIN

Given two boolean variables A and B, consider a new variable $A \odot B$ which is the logical COIN (coincidence) of variables A and B. The truth values of A, B, and $A \odot B$ are shown in Table 1.8. As shown, when variables A and B are both 0 or both 1, the new variable $A \odot B$ is

1. Otherwise, the new variable is 0. Table 1.8 also establishes that

$$0 \odot 0 = 1,$$
$$0 \odot 1 = 0,$$
$$0 \odot 0 = 0, \qquad\qquad (1.12)$$
$$0 \odot 1 = 1.$$

Logical COIN of variables A and B means logical coincidence of the two variables.

Table 1.8 Truth table for logical COIN

A	B	A ⊙ B
0	0	1
0	1	0
1	0	0
1	1	1

1.3.3 Truth Tables

Tables 1.3 through 1.8 are called *truth tables* because each table shows the truth values of the given boolean variables and the new variable. The truth table must have as many rows as the number of possible combinations of the truth values of the *given* boolean variables. The given variable in Tables 1.3 and 1.4 is A. Tables 1.3 and 1.4 have two rows because there are two possible truth values for variable A. The given variables in Table 1.5 (also in Tables 1.6 through 1.8) are A and B. Table 1.5 has four rows because there are four possible combinations of truth values for the two given variables A and B. If there are three (or four or five) given variables, the truth table will have 8 (or 16 or 32) rows because of 8 (or 16 or 32) possible combinations of the truth values for three (or four or five) variables. For this reason, a truth table is also called a *table of combinations.* Truth tables 1.3 through 1.8 have been employed to define the six logical operators in Table 1.2.

1.3.4 Boolean Function

A boolean function of one or more variables shows the logical relation of these variables. The boolean function itself is also a boolean variable. Let F represent a boolean function of two boolean variables A and B as follows,

$$F(A,B) = A' * B + A * B' \qquad (1.13)$$

The quantity $A' * B$, or $A * B'$, is called a *term* which is the logical AND of two or more variables. Each variable in a term is either in the true form, such as A and B, or in the complemented form, such as A' and B'. The above boolean function is a logical OR of two terms. The truth value of a boolean function depends on the truth values of the boolean variables of the function. The truth values of variables A and B can be arbitrarily chosen because these variables are independent variables, while the truth value of the boolean function F must be evaluated because F is a dependent variable. If the truth values of variables A and B are both chosen to be 0, then $F(A,B)$ or simply F is,

$$F = 0' * 0 + 0 * 0'$$

By relation (1.1), F becomes

$$F = 1 * 0 + 0 * 1$$

By relation (1.3), F becomes

$$F = 0 + 0$$

By relation (1.2), F finally becomes

$$F = 0 \qquad (1.14)$$

If the truth value of A is 0 and that of B is 1, then F becomes

$$F = 0' * 1 + 0 * 1'$$

By relations (1.1) through (1.3), F finally becomes

$$F = 1 + 0 = 1 \qquad (1.15)$$

If the truth value of A is 1 and that of B is 0, then F becomes

$$F = 1' * 0 + 1 * 0' = 0 + 1 = 1 \qquad (1.16)$$

If the truth values of both A and B are 1, then F becomes

$$F = 1' * 1 + 1 * 1' = 0 + 0 = 0 \qquad (1.17)$$

A truth table can now be constructed for the four possible combinations of the truth values of A and B and the corresponding truth values of the boolean function F in (1.14) through (1.17). This

Table 1.9 Truth table for a boolean function

A	B	F(A,B)
0	0	0
0	1	1
1	0	1
1	1	0

truth table is shown in Table 1.9. Thus, a truth table can be constructed from a boolean function.

Conversely, a boolean function can be obtained from a truth table. Consider the truth table of Table 1.9, which states that the truth value of boolean function F is 1,

when	$A = 0$ and $B = 1$
or when	$A = 1$ and $B = 0$

By relation (1.8), these conditions can be rewritten as

when	$A' = 1$ and $B = 1$
or when	$A = 1$ and $B' = 1$

The above conditions state that function F is 1 when both A' and B are 1 or when both A and B' are 1. By relation (1.10), these conditions can be rewritten as

when	$A' * B = 1$
or when	$A * B' = 1$

The above conditions state that function F is 1 when term $A' * B$ is 1 or when term $A * B'$ is 1. By means of relation (1.9), function F is then a logical OR of these two terms as shown below,

$$F = A' * B + A * B' \qquad (1.18)$$

This expression is the boolean function obtained from the truth table. It is the same as the previous function (1.13) as it should be. Thus, a boolean function can be obtained from a truth table.

The above steps for obtaining a boolean function from a truth table is too lengthy and impractical for later applications. The following set of rules is formulated so that the boolean function can be obtained directly from the truth table.

a. For each row where the truth value of F is 1, form a term for that row. (e.g., Form a term for each of the second and third rows in Table 1.9 where F has a value of 1.)

b. Each term is a logical AND of all the given independent variables in a row of the truth table. Each of these variables is in the true form when the truth value of the variable in that row is 1 or in the complemented form when the truth value of the variable is 0.
c. The boolean function is a logical OR of these terms (e.g., function 1.18).

There exists only one term for each row of the truth table. For a truth table of two or three variables, there are, respectively, four or eight possible terms. The four or eight possible terms for a truth table of two or three variables are shown, respectively, in Tables 1.10 and 1.11. The terms in these tables are formed according to the above rule (c). For example, in the first row of Table 1.10, both A and B are 0; therefore, the term is a logical AND of A' and B'.

Notice that the truth values of the boolean function F in Table 1.9 are the same as the truth values of variable $A \oplus B$ in Table 1.7. Thus, we have incidentally shown that

$$A \oplus B = A' * B + A * B' \qquad (1.19)$$

Table 1.10 Terms of boolean function of two variables

A	B	Terms
0	0	A' * B'
0	1	A' * B
1	0	A * B'
1	1	A * B

Table 1.11 Terms of boolean function of three variables

A	B	C	Terms
0	0	0	A' * B' * C'
0	0	1	A' * B' * C
0	1	0	A' * B * C'
0	1	1	A' * B * C
1	0	0	A * B' * C'
1	0	1	A * B' * C
1	1	0	A * B * C'
1	1	1	A * B * C

which shows the relation between operator $\oplus$ and operators +, *, and '. Similarly, we can show that

$$A \odot B = A' * B' + A * B \qquad (1.20)$$

1.3.5 Block Representation

As has been shown, a boolean function can be represented by a truth table. A boolean function may also be represented by a diagram of blocks with each block representing a logical operator. Block representations of the logical operators in Table 1.2 are shown in Figure 1.8. Each operator is represented by a square block with a symbol inside the block to designate the particular operator.

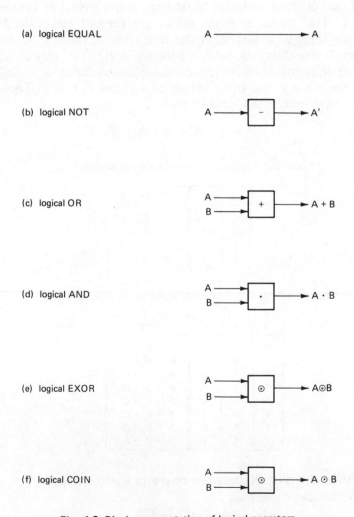

Fig. 1.8 Block representation of logical operators

Symbols $-$, $+$, $\cdot$, $\oplus$ and $\odot$ are chosen to designate operators NOT, OR, AND, EXOR, and COIN, respectively. Notice that operator logical EQUAL is represented by a line and requires no block. Inputs and outputs of the blocks are shown by arrowheaded lines. For each block, there are one or more inputs but there is only one output. Since each block may represent a logic circuit, the block diagram representing a boolean function is often called a *logic diagram.* A logic diagram may represent a network of logic circuits.

The complexity of the block representation of a boolean function is sometimes expressed in terms of levels. Consider the boolean function

$$F(A,B,C,D) = A + B + C + D \qquad (1.21)$$

where the block representation is shown in Figure 1.9(a). Since the signals from the input to the output go through only one block, the logic in the diagram is said to be one-level. This function may be rewritten as below

$$F(A,B,C,D) = (A + B) + (C + D) \qquad (1.22)$$

where the two pairs of parentheses indicate the *precedence* of logical operations. Block representation of this function is shown in Figure 1.9(b). In this diagram, a signal from the input to the output may go through two blocks; the logic in this diagram is said to be two-level. Boolean functions (1.21) and (1.22) are logically equal, but they may differ in circuit implementation.

1541933

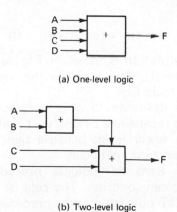

(a) One-level logic

(b) Two-level logic

Fig. 1.9 Logic diagrams

If the boolean function (1.13) is represented by a logic diagram (shown in Figure 1.10), it gives a two-level logic. Since the first level is logical AND and the second level is logical OR, it is called AND-OR logic.

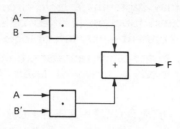

Fig. 1.10 A logic diagram (AND-OR logic)

A boolean function may have a logical relation of more than two levels. Consider the boolean function

$$F(A,B,C) = (A * C' + A' * B) * (A + B) \qquad (1.23)$$

whose block representation is shown in Figure 1.11(a). Some signals go from the input to the output through three blocks; thus, the logic in the diagram is a three-level AND-OR-AND logic. Consider boolean function

$$F(A,B,C,D,E) = (D' * E + A * C) * (B' + D) + A * E \qquad (1.24)$$

whose block representation is shown in Figure 1.11(b). Some signals go through four levels. The logic in this diagram is a four-level AND-OR-AND-OR logic.

In general, it is desirable to have a logic network with fewer blocks, which often means less circuitry. It is also desirable to have a logic network with fewer levels because signals thereby encounter less attenuation, distortion, and delay.

Parentheses are used to indicate precedence of the logical operations in a boolean function. The rule is: if no parentheses are used, the logical NOT operation takes precedence over logical AND operation, and the logical AND operation takes precedence over the logical OR operation. Boolean functions (1.23) and (1.24) are examples of this rule.

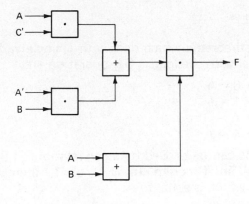

(a) AND-OR-AND logic

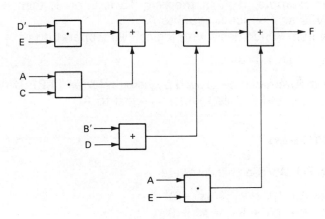

(b) AND-OR-AND-OR logic

Fig. 1.11 Logic diagrams

1.3.6 Theorems of Boolean Algebra

The theorems described below are rules by which a boolean function may be factored, expanded, complemented, manipulated, and simplified. Application of these rules will be shown in the next section.

Single Variable Theorems

There are nine theorems which deal with a single variable. Four theorems which deal with the logical OR operation are:

Theorem 1a, $A + 0 = A$
        2a, $A + 1 = 1$
        3a, $A + A' = 1$
        4a, $A + A = A$

The above theorems can be proved by using relations (1.8) and 1.9). For example, if A in Theorem 1a is 0 or 1, then $A + 0$ is, respectively, 0 or 1 which is equal to A.

Four theorems which deal with the logical AND operation are:

Theorem 1b, $A * 1 = A$
        2b, $A * 0 = 0$
        3b, $A * A' = 0$
        4b, $A * A = A$

The above theorems can be proved by using relations (1.8) and (1.10). For example, if A in theorem 1b is 0 or 1, then $A * 1$ is, respectively, 0 or 1 which is equal to A.

One theorem which deals with logical NOT operation is:

Theorem 5, $(A')' = A$

The above theorem can be proved by using relation (1.8). If A is 0 or 1, then $(0')'$ is 0 and $(1')'$ is 1 which is equal to A.

De Morgan's Theorems

The two De Morgan theorems are:

Theorem 6a, $(A + B)' = A' * B'$
        6b, $(A * B)' = A' + B'$

De Morgan's theorems are useful when a boolean function is complemented. They can be stated in terms of a simple rule: replace all operators + by *, all operators * by +, all variables in the true form by the complemented form, and all variables in the complemented form by the true form. An example in applying this rule is to be shown.

Theorems on Commutation, Association, and Distribution

Theorems 7, 8, and 9 are, respectively, the theorems on commutation, on association, and on distribution.

Theorems 7a, $A + B = B + A$
7b, $A * B = B * A$
8a, $A + (B + C) = (A + B) + C$
8b, $A * (B * C) = (A * B) * C$
9a, $A + B * C = (A + B) * (A + C)$
9b, $A * (B + C) = A * B + A * C$

Theorem 7 allows exchange of terms or factors in a boolean function. Theorem 8 allows use of terms and factors without parentheses. Theorem 9 allows direct expansion of a term or a factor. These theorems can be readily proved by using truth tables.

Simplification Theorems

The following theorems are useful for simplification of boolean functions. They can be readily proved by using truth tables or the above theorems.

Theorems 10a, $A * B + A * B' = A$
10b, $(A + B) * (A + B') = A$
11a, $A + A * B = A$
11b, $A * (A + B) = A$
12a, $A + A' * B = A + B$
12b, $A * (A' + B) = A * B$

Theorem 10 shows that variable B is redundant and can be removed. Theorem 11a shows term $A * B$, and theorem 11b shows factor $(A + B)$, can be eliminated. Theorem 12 shows variable A' can be replaced by 1.

Duality

The above theorems are numbered in pairs, because there exists a *duality* between constants 1 and 0 and between operators * and +. Each pair of the theorems forms a *dual*. In one theorem of a pair of the above theorems, if operator * is replaced by operator + and operator + by operator *, and if constant 1 is replaced by 0 and constant 0 by 1, the result is the other theorem of the pair. Theorem 5 is a dual of itself.

For example, consider De Morgan theorem 6a,

$$(A + B)' = A' * B'$$

If operator + is replaced by * and operator * is replaced by +, we have

$$(A * B)' = A' + B'$$

which is theorem 6b.

Because of the duality of boolean theorems, if a new theorem is proved, a dual theorem exists and can be obtained by applying the above duality with no need of further proof.

1.3.7 Applying the Theorems

In order to illustrate the use of these theorems, factoring, expanding, complementing, manipulation, and simplification of boolean functions are now shown.

Factoring

The following example shows the use of Theorems 7a and 9b for factoring.

Example 1.19

$$
\begin{aligned}
F(A,B,C,D,E) &= A * B * D + B * C * (D + E) + A * B * E \\
&= A * B * (D + E) \\
&\quad + B * C * (D + E) && \text{Th(7a), Th(9b)} \\
&= (A * B + B * C) * (D + E) && \text{Th(9b)} \\
&= B * (A + C) * (D + E) && \text{Th(7a), Th(9b)}
\end{aligned}
$$

Expanding

The following example shows the use of Theorems 1b, 3a, and 9b for expanding a boolean function.

Example 1.20

$$
\begin{aligned}
F(A,B,C) &= A * (B' + B * C) \\
&= A * B' + A * B * C && \text{Th(9b)} \\
&= A * B' * 1 + A * B * C && \text{Th(1b)} \\
&= A * B' * (C + C') + A * B * C && \text{Th(3a)} \\
&= A * B' * C + A * B' * C' + A * B * C && \text{Th(9b)}
\end{aligned}
$$

Notice that this expansion has resulted in terms corresponding to those that would be obtained from a truth table.

Complementing

The following example shows the use of De Morgan's theorems for complementing a boolean function.

Example 1.21

$$F(A,B,C) = (A * B + B' * C')'$$
$$= (A * B)' * (B' * C')' \qquad Th(6a)$$
$$= (A' + B') * (B + C) \qquad Th(6b)$$

Each step is actually obtained by applying the previously described simple rule derived from De Morgan's theorems. It is simpler to remember the rule than the theorems themselves.

Manipulating

The following example shows the use of theorems 7a and 9b for changing a boolean function in the AND-OR logic into one in the OR-AND logic.

Example 1.22

$$F(A,B,C,D) = A * B + C * D$$
$$= (A * B + C) * (A * B + D) \qquad Th(9a)$$
$$= (C + A * B) * (D + A * B) \qquad Th(7a)$$
$$= (C + A) * (C + B) * (D + A) * (D + B) \qquad Th(9b)$$

Simplification

Three examples are shown below to illustrate simplification of functions.

Example 1.23

$$F(A,B,C) = A' * B * C + A * B' * C + A * B * C' + A * B * C$$
$$= A' * B * C + A * B' * C + A * B * C' + A * B * C$$
$$+ A * B * C + A * B * C$$
$$= (A' * B * C + A * B * C) + (A * B' * C + A * B * C)$$
$$+ (A * B * C' + A * B * C)$$
$$= B * C + C * A + A * B$$

Example 1.24

Show $(A \oplus B)' = A \odot B$
let F1 = $A \oplus B$
    F2 = $A \odot B$

From the truth table in Table 1.7, we obtain

$$F1 = A' * B + A * B'$$

From the truth table in Table 1.8, we obtain

$$F2 = A' * B' + A * B$$

The given problem now becomes to show $(F1)' = F2$

$$
\begin{aligned}
(F1)' &= (A' * B + A * B')' \\
      &= (A' * B)' * (A * B')' & \text{Th(6a)} \\
      &= (A + B') * (A' + B) & \text{Th(6b)} \\
      &= A * A' + B' * A' + A * B + B' * B & \text{Th(9b)} \\
      &= 0 + B' * A' + A * B + 0 & \text{Th(3b)} \\
      &= B' * A' + A * B & \text{Th(1a)} \\
      &= F2 & \therefore \text{ Q.E.D.}
\end{aligned}
$$

Example 1.25

$$
\begin{aligned}
F(A,B,C) &= A' * B' * C + A' * B * C' + A * B' * C' + A * B * C \\
         &= A' * (B' * C + B * C') + A * (B' * C' + B * C) \\
         &= A' * (B \oplus C) + A * (B \odot C) \\
         &= A' * (B \oplus C) + A * (B \oplus C)' \\
         &= A \oplus (B \oplus C) \\
         &= A \oplus B \oplus C
\end{aligned}
$$

In this example, the result in example 1.24 is used.

1.4 APPLICATION OF BOOLEAN ALGEBRA

A boolean function describes a logic model for implementation by logic circuits. To implement a digital function, one needs only to specify the digital function by boolean functions. There are five steps by which the logic model for a digital function can be obtained:

1. describe the digital function,
2. express the function into a truth table,
3. write the boolean functions from the truth table,
4. simplify the boolean functions, and
5. draw a logic diagram from the boolean functions.

The logic models of a number of simple digital functions are worked out below to illustrate these steps.

1.4.1 A Single-bit Comparator

Step 1. A single-bit comparator compares two bits X and Y. When the two bits are the same, output Z is 1; otherwise, output Z is 0. Block diagram of the comparator is shown in Figure 1.12.

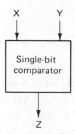

Fig. 1.12 A single-bit comparator

Step 2. A truth table is constructed with X and Y as the given boolean variables and with Z as the output variable. There are four rows for the two given variables. When X and Y are both 0's and 1's, output Z has the value of 1; otherwise, Z has the value of 0. The truth table is shown in Table 1.12.

Table 1.12 Truth table for the single-bit comparator

X	Y	C
0	0	1
0	1	0
1	0	0
1	1	1

Step 3. The boolean function for output Z can be obtained from the truth table. We thus have

$$Z = X' * Y' + X * Y = X \odot Y$$

Step 4. Function Z cannot be further simplified.

Step 5. The single-bit comparator is the logical COIN operator shown in Figure 1.8(f).

1.4.2 A Single-bit Half Adder

Step 1. A single-bit half adder performs addition of two bits X and Y, giving as outputs sum bit S and carry bit C. Block diagram of the half adder is shown in Figure 1.13.

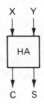

Fig. 1.13 A single-bit half adder

Step 2. A truth table is constructed with X and Y as the given boolean variables and with C and S as the output variables. The truth table is shown in Table 1.13. The values of C and S are taken from the previous addition result of single-bit arithmetic.

Table 1.13 Truth table for the half adder

X	Y	C	S
0	0	0	0
0	1	0	1
1	0	0	1
1	1	1	0

Step 3. The two boolean functions are

$$S = A' * B + A * B' = A \oplus B$$
$$C = X * Y$$

Step 4. Functions S and C cannot be further simplified.

Step 5. The logic diagram consists of two blocks, one for logical EXOR operator and the other for logical AND operator.

1.4.3 A Single-bit Full Adder

Step 1. A single-bit full adder performs addition of three input bits, giving two output bits. The input bits are augend bit X, addend bit Y, and input carry bit C_i; the output bits are sum bit S_i and output carry bit C_o. Block diagram of the full adder is shown in Fig. 1.14.

Fig. 1.14 A single-bit full adder

Step 2. A truth table is constructed with X, Y, and C_i as the given boolean variables and with C_o and S as the output variables. The truth table is shown in Table 1.14. The values of C_o and S in each row are obtained by adding the values of X, Y, and C_i of the corresponding row. For example, for the second row, we have

$$0 + 0 + 1 = 01$$

For the fourth row, we have

$$0 + 1 + 1 = 10$$

Table 1.14 Truth table for the full adder

X	Y	C_i	C_o	S
0	0	0	0	0
0	0	1	0	1
0	1	0	0	1
0	1	1	1	0
1	0	0	0	1
1	0	1	1	0
1	1	0	1	0
1	1	1	1	1

Step 3. The two boolean functions are

$$S = X' * Y' * C_i + X' * Y * C_i' + X * Y' * C_i' + X * Y * C_i$$

$$C_o = X' * Y * C_i + X * Y' * C_i + X * Y * C_i' + X * Y * C_i$$

Step 4. By using the result in Example 1.25 we have

$$S = X \oplus Y \oplus C_i$$

By using the result in Example 1.23 we have

$$C_o = X * Y + Y * C_i + C_i * X = X * Y + C_i * (X + Y)$$

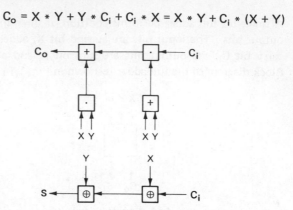

Fig. 1.15 Logic diagram of the single-bit full adder

Step 5. The logic diagram for the single-bit full adder is shown in Figure 1.15

1.4.4 A Two-bit Multiplier

Step 1. A two-bit multiplier performs multiplication of two multiplicand bits X_1 and X_2 by two multiplier bits Y_1 and Y_2 and produces four output bits P_1, P_2, P_3, and P_4. Block diagram of the two-bit multiplier is shown in Figure 1.16.

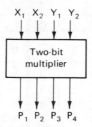

Fig. 1.16 A two-bit multiplier

Step 2. A truth table is constructed with X_1, X_2, Y_1, and Y_2 as the given boolean variables and with P_1, P_2, P_3, and P_4 as the output variables. The truth table is shown in Table 1.15 where there are 16 rows. The values of the four-bit output are the product of two-bit multiplicand and two-bit multiplier. For example, for the twelfth row we have

$$10 \times 11 = 0110$$

and for the sixteenth row we have

$$11 \times 11 = 1001$$

Table 1.15 Truth table for the two-bit multiplier

X_1	X_2	Y_1	Y_2	P_1	P_2	P_3	P_4
0	0	0	0	0	0	0	0
0	0	0	1	0	0	0	0
0	0	1	0	0	0	0	0
0	0	1	1	0	0	0	0
0	1	0	0	0	0	0	0
0	1	0	1	0	0	0	1
0	1	1	0	0	0	1	0
0	1	1	1	0	0	1	1
1	0	0	0	0	0	0	0
1	0	0	1	0	0	1	0
1	0	1	0	0	1	0	0
1	0	1	1	0	1	1	0
1	1	0	0	0	0	0	0
1	1	0	1	0	0	1	1
1	1	1	0	0	1	1	0
1	1	1	1	1	0	0	1

Step 3. The boolean functions are

$$P_1 = X_1 * X_2 * Y_1 * Y_2$$

$$P_2 = X_1 * X_2' * Y_1 * Y_2' + X_1 * X_2' * Y_1 * Y_2 + X_1 * X_2 * Y_1 * Y_2'$$

$$P_3 = X_1' * X_2 * Y_1 * Y_2' + X_1' * X_2 * Y_1 * Y_2 + X_1 * X_2' * Y_1' * Y_2$$

$$+ X_1 * X_2' * Y_1 * Y_2 + X_1 * X_2 * Y_1' * Y_2 + X_1 * X_2 * Y_1 * Y_2'$$

$$P_4 = X_1' * X_2 * Y_1' * Y_2 + X_1' * X_2 * Y_1 * Y_2 + X_1 * X_2 * Y_1' * Y_2$$

$$+ X_1 * X_2 * Y_1 * Y_2$$

Step 4. The boolean functions can be simplified by means of the previous theorems and the results are shown below,

$$P_1 = X_1 * X_2 * Y_1 * Y_2$$

$$P_2 = X_1 * Y_1 * (X_2' + Y_2')$$

$$P_3 = (X_1 * Y_2) \oplus (X_2 * Y_1)$$

$$P_4 = X_2 * Y_2$$

Step 5. The logic diagram for the two-bit multiplier is shown in Figure 1.17.

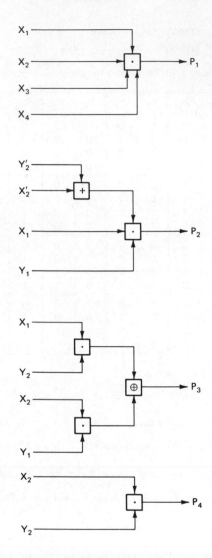

Fig. 1.17 Logic diagram of the two-bit multiplier

PROBLEMS

1.1   Compute the following arithmetic expressions
      (a) 10101 + 01001
      (b) 10011 + 11000
      (c) 10101 − 01001
      (d) 10011 − 11000
      (e) 10101 × 01001

    (f) 10011 × 11000
    (g) 01001 ÷ 10011
    (h) 11000 ÷ 10011

1.2   Repeat Prob. 1.1(c) and (d)
    (a) by addition of 2's complement
    (b) by addition of 1's complement

1.3   Represent the following decimal numbers by the three representations of signed binary numbers
    (a) +101
    (b) −55
    (c) −89

1.4   Given signed binary numbers X = 0,10111 and Y = 1,01010, compute
    (a) X + Y
    (b) X − Y
    (c) X · Y
    (d) X ÷ Y

1.5   Repeat Prob. 1.4(b)
    (a) by addition of 2's complement
    (b) by addition of 1's complement

1.6   Draw a flow chart which shows an algorithm for multiplication of two signed binary numbers in the signed magnitude representation.

1.7   Draw a flow chart which shows an algorithm for division of two signed binary numbers in the signed magnitude representation.

1.8   Construct a truth table for each of the following boolean functions

$$\text{(a)}\quad F(A,B,C) = A * (A' + C) * (B + C)$$

$$\text{(b)}\quad F(A,B,C) = (A + B') * (B + C')$$

$$\text{(c)}\quad F(A,B) \;\;= A \oplus B \oplus (A * B)$$

$$\text{(d)}\quad F(A,B) \;\;= A \odot B \odot (A * B)$$

1.9   Table 1.16 is a truth table of four given boolean variables A,B,C, and D and four output variables W,X,Y, and Z. Find the boolean function
    (a) W(A,B,C,D)
    (b) X(A,B,C,D)
    (c) Y(A,B,C,D)
    (d) Z(A,B,C,D)

1.10 Draw a logic diagram for each of the following boolean functions
    (a) F(A,B,C,D) = D + B * (C + D' * (A + C))
    (b) F(A,B,C,D) = ((B * C' + A' * D) * (A * B' + C * D'))'
    (c) F(A,B,C) = (A * B + B * C + C * A) + (A * B' + B * C' + C' * A)

1.11 Draw the logic diagram for functions W,X,Y, and Z in Prob. 1.9

1.12 Find the dual for each of the following boolean functions
    (a) F(A,B,C) = A + B' * C + A' * B * C
    (b) F(A,B,C) = A * B + B * C + C * D + D * A

1.13 Factor the following boolean functions
    (a) F(A,B,C) = A * B * C + A * B + A
    (b) F(A,B,C,D) = A' * B * C' * D + A' * B * C * D + A * B * C' * D + A * B * C * D

Table 1.16 A truth table

A	B	C	D	W	X	Y	Z
0	0	0	0	0	0	1	1
0	0	0	1	0	0	0	1
0	0	1	0	0	1	0	0
0	0	1	1	0	0	0	1
0	1	0	0	0	1	0	1
0	1	0	1	1	0	0	1
0	1	1	0	0	0	1	0
0	1	1	1	0	1	1	0
1	0	0	0	0	1	0	1
1	0	0	1	0	0	1	1
1	0	1	0	0	1	0	1
1	0	1	1	1	0	0	0
1	1	0	0	1	0	0	1
1	1	0	1	0	1	1	1
1	1	1	0	1	0	0	1
1	1	1	1	0	0	1	1

1.14 Expand
    (a) $F(A,B,C,D) = (A + B) * (B + C) * (C + D)$
    (b) $F(A,B,C,D) = A * B + C * D$

1.15 Complement the functions in Prob. 1.14

1.16 Simplify
    (a) $F(A,B,C) = A' * B' * C' + A' * B' * C + A' * B * C' + A' * B * C + A * B' * C' + A * B' * C + A * B * C' + A * B * C$
    (b) $F(A,B,C) = A * (A' + C) * (A' * B + C')$

1.17 Find the boolean functions and draw the logic diagram for a single-bit half subtracter. A single-bit half subtracter subtracts bit Y from bit X and produces a difference bit D and a borrow bit B.

1.18 Find the boolean functions and draw the logic diagram of a single-bit full subtracter. A single-bit full subtracter performs $(X - Y - B_i)$ and produces a difference bit D and an output borrow bit B_o where X, Y, and B_i are respectively the minuend bit, subtrahend bit, and input borrow bit.

1.19 Find the boolean functions and draw the logic diagram of a two-bit adder. A two-bit adder adds a two-bit augend to a two-bit addend and produces a two-bit sum and one-bit carry.

2

Computer

Elements

This chapter describes the functions of some basic computer elements. The operations that are performed by these elements will be described in Chapter 3, and the sequencing of these operations will be described in Chapter 4. Both block and statement representations are to be used in these chapters. For describing the computer elements in this chapter, nine statements are presented. They are the delay, register, subregister, casregister, memory, switch, light, terminal, and decoder statements.

2.1 DELAYS

Delay is an element which accepts a binary signal at the input, holds it for a fixed period of time, and produces it at the output. Thus, delay is a storage element for a limited period of time. A *delay statement* declares one or more types of delay elements and the amount of delay in each type. For example, the following delay statement,

$$\text{Delay, D, } \Delta=15 \tag{2.1}$$

declares two types of delay elements. The first type is named D with an unspecified amount of delay D; thus, D represents both the type of delay element and an unspecified amount of delay. The second type is named Δ with a specified amount of delay of 15 microseconds; thus Δ represents the second type of delay element and the amount of delay of 15 micro-seconds. Block representation of delay element Δ is shown in Figure 2.1(a).

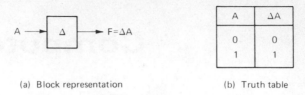

A	ΔA
0	0
1	1

(a) Block representation   (b) Truth table

Fig. 2.1 A delay element

The function of a delay element may be described by a truth table. Consider the following expression,

$$F = \Delta A \qquad (2.2)$$

where F and A are, respectively, the output and input of delay element Δ. The truth table in Figure 2.1(b) describes the above function F. It states that when input A is 0 or 1, output F is also 0 or 1, respectively, after a delay Δ.

Delays may be used in conjunction with the previously described logical operators. Consider the following functions,

$$F1 = \Delta(A*B)$$
$$F2 = \Delta(A\oplus B) \qquad (2.3)$$

where Δ represents the delay element. These functions describe the delayed logical AND and the delayed logical EXOR operations of boolean variables A and B. Block representations of these two delayed operations are shown in Figure 2.2.

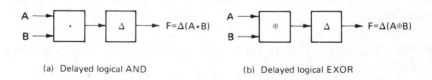

(a) Delayed logical AND   (b) Delayed logical EXOR

Fig. 2.2 Two delayed operations

Delays may be cascaded. Figure 2.3(a) shows a cascade of four delays which can be described by the following boolean function:

$$F = 4\Delta A \qquad (2.4)$$

This cascade of delays can temporarily store one bit for four Δ

delays. If the output from the rightmost delay element is fed back through a logical OR block to the input of the leftmost delay element as shown in Figure 2.3(b), this cascade of delays can be described by the following boolean function,

$$F = 4\Delta(A+F) \tag{2.5}$$

This cascade can circulate and thus store four bits continuously.

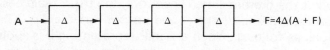

(a) Cascaded delays with no feedback

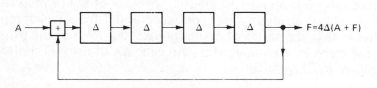

(b) Cascaded delays with feedback

Fig. 2.3 Cascaded delays

2.2 FLIPFLOPS

A basic storage element in a digital computer is the flipflop. It is a binary storage element. A binary storage element stores two states, false and true, to be represented by 0 and 1, respectively.

A flipflop is given a symbolic name such as A, JOE, OV, or B_1. Figure 2.4(a) is the block representation of a flipflop named A. The flipflop is represented by a square and its two outputs by two lines. The output indicated by A is the normal (or true) output and that by A' is the complemented (or false) output. The state of the flipflop is accessed at the normal output, and the complemented state of the flipflop at the complemented output.

Each flipflop has one or more inputs. By means of these inputs, binary information is transferred to the flipflop. The flipflop is commonly implemented with very fast electronic components; thus, this information transfer can be performed very rapidly. At the current state of technology, it is possible to make such a transfer in a matter of a few nanoseconds. (A nanosecond is one billionth of a second.) The flipflop transfer time is an important characteristic of logic circuits.

There are many types of flipflops, differing mostly in the number and logic of the inputs. Only one type is introduced here. This type is called *D flipflop* whose block representation has been shown in Figure 2.4(a). It has two imputs c and d (c denotes control and d denotes data). The input logic is described in the truth table of Figure 2.4(b). The state of the flipflop at delay Δ later depends on the states of inputs c and d at present time as well as the state of the flipflop at the present time. Therefore, the truth table has three given boolean variables c, d, and A and output variable ΔA. The D flipflop functions as follows. When a signal representing 0 is applied at input c, the state of the flipflop remains unchanged regardless of whether the signal at input d is 0 or 1. (Note that the states of A and ΔA in the first four rows of the truth table are the same.) When a signal representing 1 is applied to input c, the state of the flipflop becomes 1 if the signal at input d is 1, or becomes 0 if the signal at input d is 0. (Note that the states of ΔA in the last four rows of the truth table are the same as the values of d.) An example of using D flipflops will be shown in Chapter 9.

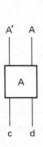

c	d	A	ΔA
0	0	0	0
0	0	1	1
0	1	0	0
0	1	1	1
1	0	0	0
1	0	1	0
1	1	0	1
1	1	1	1

(a) Block representation   (b) Truth table

Fig. 2.4 D flipflop

2.3 REGISTERS

A *binary word* is a series of bits which represents a binary number, a decimal number, a special symbol, a number of characters, etc. For example, binary words 01101 and 01011 may represent decimal numbers 13 and 11, respectively. Binary words 0011 and 1001 may represent decimal digits 3 and 9, respectively. Binary words

010000 and 001011 may represent symbols + and =, respectively.

A *register* is a group of flipflops arranged to store a binary word. A register is given a symbolic name such as DATA, MQ, or LZ, and each flipflop of the register is specified by a subscript. For example, a register named B may include five flipflops specified as B_1, B_2, B_3, B_4, and B_5, or, alternatively, as $B(1), B(2), B(3), B(4)$, and $B(5)$. The block representation of this register is shown in Figure 2.5(a). As generally drawn, the input and output lines of each flipflop are not shown.

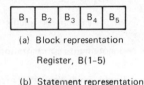

(a) Block representation

Register, B(1–5)

(b) Statement representation

Fig. 2.5 Block and statement representations of a register

A register may also be represented by a register statement. The register statement for the above register B is

$$\text{Register, B(1–5)} \tag{2.6}$$

as indicated in Figure 2.5(b). It is important to recognize that the statement representation is equivalent to the block representation; the former representation is concise, while the latter is pictorial. Similarly, the statement

$$\text{Register, P(3–0)} \tag{2.7}$$

represents a register named P, and the names of the flipflops are P(3), P(2), P(1), and P(0), or alternatively P_3, P_2, P_1, and P_0. The block and the statement representations of this register are shown in Figure 2.6. It should be noted that the subscripts are a sequence of decimal numbers in an ascending order in Figure 2.5(a) and in descending order in Figure 2.6(a), and the subscript specification for each statement consists of the first and the last subscripts interposed by a hyphen.

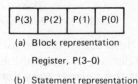

(a) Block representation

Register, P(3–0)

(b) Statement representation

Fig. 2.6 Block and statement representations of a register

Figure 2.7 shows the block and the statement representations of register LZ which consists of only one flipflop. To denote such a register, no subscript specification is used. Note the absence of the subscript specification in the register statement in Figure 2.7(b).

(a) Block representation

Register, LZ

(b) Statement representation

Fig. 2.7 Block and statement representations of a register

Figure 2.8 shows the block and the statement representations of register A which uses a symbolic name and decimal numbers as subscripts. The symbolic subscript S (denoting the sign bit of the register) refers to the left flipflop of the register A, and the decimal subscripts refer to the remaining flipflops.

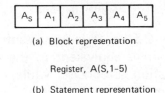

(a) Block representation

Register, A(S,1-5)

(b) Statement representation

Fig. 2.8 Block and statement representations of a register

A register statement may specify more than one register. For example, the statements in Figures (2.5) through (2.8) may be combined and specified in one statement as

$$\text{Register, } B(1\text{-}5), P(3\text{-}0), LZ, A(S, 1\text{-}5) \qquad (2.8)$$

An alternative form for specifying a number of registers is

Register, B(1-5), $buffer register
        P(3-0), $program register   (2.9)
        LZ, $logical zero indicator
        A(S,1-5) $accumulator

This form may include descriptive comments. As indicated above, a dollar sign ($) is used to denote the beginning of a comment.

Since the contents of the register may vary, a register represents a variable. Thus, the name of a register is a variable name. Similarly, the name of each flipflop of the register is the name of a binary variable.

2.3.1 Subregisters

A *subregister* is a part of a register and, for convenience, a *subregister statement* is used to declare a symbolic subscript to this part. For example, consider the two statements

> Register, A(0–5)
>
> Subregister, A(S)=A(0), A(M)=A(1–5)   (2.10)

The first statement indicates that register A has six bits. The second statement specifies subscript S for flipflop A(0) because the sign bit is stored in this flipflop. The second statement also specifies that the other flipflops of register A(1–5) be given a symbolic subscript M, because the magnitude bits are stored in these flipflops. The subregisters of this register A are indicated in Figure 2.9.

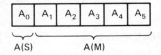

Fig. 2.9 An example showing subregisters A(S) and A(M)

The use of a subregister makes it easier to identify a part of a register which, in turn, usually provides a meaningful indication of the function that the part of a register performs. Compare the symbolic subscript S of register A in the statement in Figure 2.8(b) with the symbolic subscripts for the subregisters in the statement (2.10). The former denotes only one bit, while the latter denotes one or more bits.

2.3.2 Casregister

A *casregister,* abbreviated from "cascaded register," is a register combined from one or more registers and subregisters. A *casregister statement* gives the combined register a name and a subscript specification. For example, consider the statements

> Register, A(0–5), Q(0–5)
>
> Casregister, AQ(0–10)=A–Q(1–5)   (2.11)

The first statement specifies registers A and Q. The second statement specifies a combined register named AQ with subscripts from 0 to 10 which are the six bits of the register A and the rightmost five bits of the register Q. The hyphen used between A and Q(1–5) denotes the cascade. A block representation of cascaded register AQ is shown in Figure 2.10.

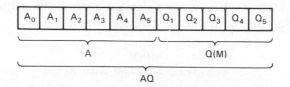

Fig. 2.10 An example showing casregister AQ

The use of the casregister offers a simple method of identifying combinations of registers and subregisters. Like the subregister statement, the casregister statement also provides a meaningful indication of the function that the combined register performs.

2.4 RANDOM ACCESS MEMORIES

A memory in a digital computer can be regarded as an array of registers which is capable of storing a large number of binary words each of which can be accessed. These registers are often referred to as the *locations* of the memory. When each location of the memory can be arbitrarily chosen for access, the memory is called a *random access memory.* In a random access memory, an address is associated with each location and usually only one word can be transferred into or out of the memory at one time. Practical random access memories are commonly made of magnetic cores instead of flipflops, often because of cost and other considerations.

There are two registers associated with a random access memory: a buffer register and an address register. The buffer register accepts the word read out of the memory during a read operation and holds the word to be stored into the memory during a write operation. The address register contains the address of the memory location while the location is being accessed.

For example, consider a random access memory named M. It is capable of storing 64 words consisting of 6 bits each. A block representation of the memory is shown in Figure 2.11. The block

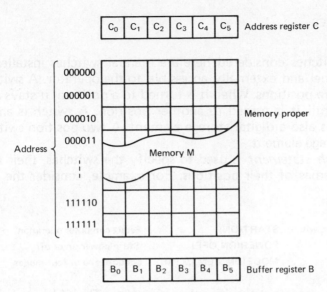

Fig. 2.11 Block representation of a random access memory

with 384 squares is the memory proper where each square represents a binary storage element. Since each word consists of 6 bits, the buffer register named B also has 6 bits. To address the 64 words, a 6-bit address is required; thus, the address register named C has 6 bits. The addresses are binary numbers 000000, 000001,. . ., 111110, and 111111. Practical high-speed magnetic core memories may have a capacity of hundreds of thousands of words or more, and a word length of 64 bits or more.

Instead of the block representation, the above memory may also be described by the statements

$$\text{Register,} \quad B(0-5), C(0-5)$$
$$\text{Memory,} \quad M(C)=M(0-63,0-5) \tag{2.12}$$

The first statement describes the buffer and address registers, while the second statement is a *memory statement* which specifies the memory proper. A register may be regarded as a one dimensional array and requires one subscript. A memory is a two dimensional array and needs two subscripts. In the memory statement, $M(C)$ specifies M as the name of the memory and C as the name of the address register. $M(0-63,0-5)$ specifies the two memory subscripts. The first subscript specification $0-63$ denotes that there are 64 words with their addresses being from 000000 to 111111. And the second subscript specification $0-5$ indicates that each word has 6 bits with the bit positions being from 0 to 5.

2.5 SWITCHES

The switches considered here are manual switches installed on a control panel and externally accessible to the operator. A switch has one or more positions. When it is turned to a position, it stays at that position until it is turned to another position. A switch is an input device. It is also a digital storage element. A two position switch is a binary storage element.

A *switch statement* is used to specify the switches, their names, and the names of their positions. For example, consider the switch statement

$$
\begin{array}{lll}
\text{Switch,} & \text{START(ON)} & \text{\$start computer operation} \\
& \text{POWER(ON,OFF)} & \text{\$turn power on or off} \qquad (2.13) \\
& \text{MODE(DM,AEM,IM,PM)} & \text{\$choose one of four modes}
\end{array}
$$

The above statement specifies three switches. Their block representations are shown in Figure 2.12. Switch START has one position named ON. As named, it is used to start the operation of the computer. A switch with one position generates a pulse when it is turned to the ON position (i.e., it sets to state 1 for a short duration). It produces no further action if it is kept at the ON position. Thus, a one position switch can store a bit lasting only for a short duration. Switch POWER has two positions, ON and OFF. It is used to turn the computer power on or off. Switch MODE has four positions, DM, AEM, IM, and PM. It is used to choose one of four computer operation modes. The above switch statement does not specify the types of switches (i.e., push-down type, rotary type, or the other types). This is not needed since the type of switch merely facilitates the operation and is not functionally important.

For a row or an array of switches, one or two subscripts may be used to simplify their specifications. For example, consider switch statement

$$
\begin{array}{ll}
\text{Switch,} & \text{SWQ(0–5) (ON),} \\
& \text{BICON(1–2,0–7) (ON)} \qquad\qquad\qquad (2.14)
\end{array}
$$

Switch SWQ is the name for a row of six one position switches. These 6 switches are named SWQ(0),. . .,SWQ(5), and their positions are all named ON. Switch BICON is the name for an array of one position switches consisting of two rows, each row having eight switches. These 16 switches are named BICON(1,0),. . . . . . ,

BICON(1,7),BICON(2,0), ... ,BICON(2,7), and their positions are all named ON.

(a) Switch START with one position named ON

(b) Switch POWER with two positions named ON and OFF

(c) Switch MODE with four positions named DM, AEM, IM, and PM

Fig. 2.12 Block representations of switches

2.6 LIGHTS

The lights considered here are those indicators installed on a control panel and visible to the operator. A light can have one or more light conditions. When it is turned on, it illuminates and remains so until it is turned to another condition. A light is an output device. It is also a digital storage element. A two-condition light is a binary storage element.

The *light statement* is used to specify the lights, their names, and the names of their light conditions. For example, consider the light statement

$$
\begin{aligned}
&\text{Light,}\quad \text{ALARM(ON)}\\
&\qquad\quad \text{LTSIGN(ON,OFF)}\\
&\qquad\quad \text{COLOR(RED,BLUE,GREEN,OFF)}\qquad\qquad (2.15)\\
&\qquad\quad \text{LTQ(0–5) (ON,OFF),}\\
&\qquad\quad \text{LTBICON(1–2,0–7) (ON,OFF)}
\end{aligned}
$$

The above statement specifies five lights. Block representations of these lights are shown in Figure 2.13. Light ALARM has one condition named ON. When it is turned to the ON condition, it gives a flash. Light LTSIGN has two conditions: ON and OFF. When it is turned to ON, it illuminates. Light COLOR has four conditions:

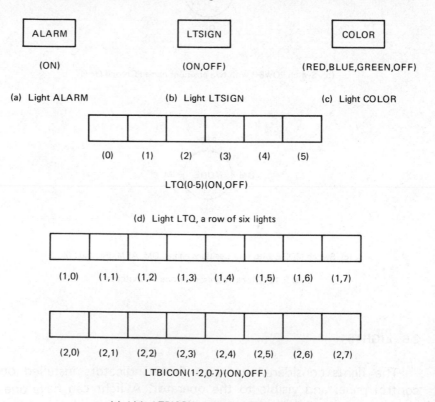

(a) Light ALARM   (b) Light LTSIGN   (c) Light COLOR

LTQ(0-5)(ON,OFF)

(d) Light LTQ, a row of six lights

LTBICON(1-2,0-7)(ON,OFF)

(e) Light LTBICON, an array of sixteen lights

Fig. 2.13 Block representations of lights

RED, BLUE, GREEN, and OFF. When it is turned to RED, BLUE, or GREEN condition, it may, for example, give a red, blue, or green light. Light LTQ is a row of two condition lights. These six lights are named LTQ(0), ... ,LTQ(5), and their two conditions are all named ON and OFF. Light LTBICON is an array of two-condition lights consisting of two rows, each having eight lights. These sixteen lights are named LTBICON(1,0), ... ,LTBICON(1,7),LTBICON (2,0), ... ,LTBICON(2,7), and their two conditions are all named ON and OFF.

2.7 LOGIC NETWORKS

A *logic network* is an aggregate of interconnected logic blocks to implement a functional operation. The block representation of a logic network is shown in Figure 2.14. When signals are applied to the input terminals, signals appear instantly at the output terminals. There are no storage elements in a logic network. Such a logic network is also known as a *combinational circuit.*

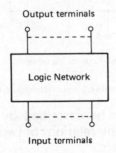

Fig. 2.14 Block representation of a logic network

A logic network is described by a *terminal statement.* Terminal statements which describe a complementer, a decoder, and a comparator are shown below to illustrate their use.

2.7.1 A Complementer

A complementer considered here is a logic network where there are as many output terminals as input terminals. The state at each output terminal is the complemented state of its respective input terminal. The block representation of the complementer is shown in

Figure 2.15(a). Figure 2.15(b) shows the logic diagram of the complementer; there are only three logical NOT blocks.

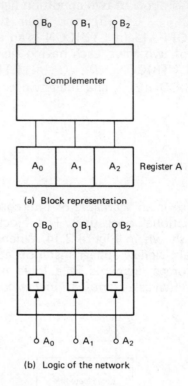

(a) Block representation

(b) Logic of the network

Fig. 2.15 An example of logic network, a complementer

This logic network can be described by the following terminal statement which specifies the relations between the input and output terminals

$$\text{Register, } A(0\text{--}2) \tag{2.16}$$

$$\text{Terminal}, B0 = A(0)',$$

$$B1 = A(1)', \tag{2.17}$$

$$B2 = A(2)'$$

The input terminals in the above terminal statement are specified by the above register statement. In case the source of the input terminals is not known, this case can be described as follows

$$\text{Terminal, } B0 = A0',$$

$$B1 = A1',$$

$$B2 = A2', \tag{2.18}$$

$$A0,$$
$$A1,$$
$$A2$$

where A0, A1, and A2 (not defined) are understood to be input terminals. The above descriptions become too long if register A has many bits. Subscripted terminals may be used to give a concise terminal statement. By using subscripted terminals, statements (2.16) and (2.17) become

$$\text{Register,} \quad A(0\text{–}2) \tag{2.19}$$

$$\text{Terminal,} \quad B(0\text{–}2)=A(0\text{–}2)' \tag{2.20}$$

2.7.2 A Decoder

A decoder is a logic network which translates each value of the contents of a register to one and only one of the outputs. For a register of n bits, there can be as many as 2^n outputs. The block representation of a decoder for a three-bit register is shown in Figure 2.16(a). Figure 2.16(b) shows the logic diagram of the decoder which employs only four logical AND blocks.

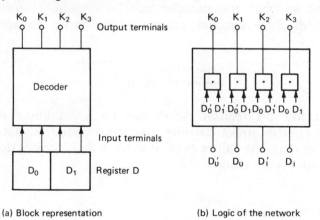

(a) Block representation   (b) Logic of the network

Fig. 2.16 An example of logic network, a decoder

This logic network can be described by the following terminal statement

$$\text{Register,} \quad D(0\text{–}1) \tag{2.21}$$

$$\text{Terminal,} \quad K0=D_0{}'*D_1{}',$$

$$K1=D_0{}'*D_1, \tag{2.22}$$

$$K2=D_0*D_1{}',$$

$$K3=D_0*D_1$$

For a two-bit register D, there can be only four values in register D; thus, there are at most four output terminals K0, ... ,K3. The logic of the decoder is described in the truth table of Table 2.1. As shown in Table 2.1, for each pair of the values at the input terminals, there is only one output terminal whose state becomes 1. Therefore, the boolean expressions for the four output terminals are respectively $D_0' * D_1'$, $D_0' * D_1$, $D_0 * D_1'$, and $D_0 * D_1$.

Table 2.1 Truth table of a decoder

D_0	D_1	K_0	K_1	K_2	K_3
0	0	1	0	0	0
0	1	0	1	0	0
1	0	0	0	1	0
1	1	0	0	0	1

As the number of bits of the register increases, the number of the output terminals grows exponentially and it becomes too cumbersome to describe the decoder. Therefore, a *decoder statement* is created so that the decoder can be concisely and conveniently specified. By a decoder statement, the above decoder description becomes

$$\text{Register, D(0–3)} \qquad (2.23)$$
$$\text{Decoder, K(1–12)=D} \qquad (2.24)$$

For a four-bit register, there can be a maximum of 16 values. However, the above decoder statement specifies that the decoder decodes only the values ranging from 1 to 12; this is done by having subscript specification 1–12.

2.7.3 A Comparator

The comparator considered here compares the contents of the corresponding bits of two registers for equality, and produces as many outputs as the number of bits of the registers. The comparison of the corresponding bits is performed simultaneously. The block representation of the comparator is shown in Figure 2.17(a). Figure 2.17(b) shows the logic diagram of the comparator which requires only three logical COIN blocks.

This logic network can be described by the statements

$$\text{Register, } A(0-2), B(0-2) \tag{2.25}$$
$$\text{Terminal, } C(0-2) = A(0-2) \odot B(0-2) \tag{2.26}$$

As shown, the output terminals of the comparators are named $C(0), \ldots, C(2)$. If the number of the bits of the registers A and B increases, the terminal statement remains unchanged except the subscript specification which needs a change.

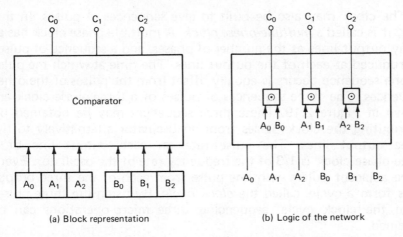

(a) Block representation   (b) Logic of the network

Fig. 2.17 An example of logic network, a comparator

2.8 CLOCKS

In a digital computer, there is an electronic oscillator, called the *clock,* which generates a sequence of electrical pulses. As shown in Figure 2.18, these pulses occur at a fixed interval of time. The clock rate (or pulse rate) on most of today's digital computers ranges from 1 to 100 megacycles per second. The time between two adjacent pulses is called a *clock period.* The memory cycle time of the random access memory in a computer is usually a multiple of the clock period.

The clock pulse initiates information transfers among the registers, and each micro-operation is completed in one or several clock periods. When the computer operates in this way, it is called *synchronous,* because the information transfers are in synchronism with the clock pulses. If a computer operates asynchronously, no clock is required. Each operation instead takes a time interval required, and completion of one operation initiates the next operation. Most parts of a digital computer operate synchronously because of ease of design, reliability and economy.

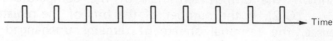

Fig. 2.18 Clock pulses

The clock may also be built to give sequences of pulses. In this case, it is called a *multiple-phase clock.* A multiple-phase clock has as many output lines as the number of phases, and a sequence of pulses is produced at each of the output lines. The time at which the pulse of one sequence occurs is equally offset from the pulses of the other sequences. The three sequences of pulses of a three-phase clock are shown in Figure 2.19. These three sequences may be obtained by distributing the clock pulses from an oscillator alternatively to the three output lines. The pulse rate on each output line of a three-phase clock is 1/3 of the frequency rate of the oscillator. Every three adjacent pulses with one pulse from each of the three output lines form a cycle, called the *clock cycle.* By using the three pulses from the clock cycle, sequencing three micro-operations can be obtained.

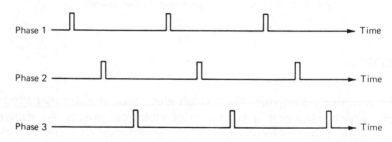

Fig. 2.19 Pulses from a three-phase clock

Since the clock is often needed, a *clock statement* is created to specify the above described clocks. The following clock statement,

$$\text{Clock, P} \tag{2.27}$$

specifies a single-phase clock. P is the name of the pulses; it becomes 1 when the pulse occurs and 0 at any other time. The following clock statement specifies a three-phase clock,

$$\text{Clock, CP(1-3)} \tag{2.28}$$

CP(1), CP(2), and CP(3) are the names of the pulses of the three phases.

A multiple-phase clock may also be obtained from a single-phase clock by means of delays. Figure 2.20 shows the block diagram of generating a three-phase clock. The first phase, CP(1), comes directly from the single-phase clock. The other two phases, CP(2) and CP(3), are obtained by means of suitable delays. To be specific, the three-phase clock is described as below,

Clock,	P
Delay,	Δ
Terminal,	$CP(1)=P$
	$CP(2)=\Delta CP(1) = \Delta P$
	$CP(3)=\Delta CP(2) = 2\Delta P$

(2.29)

If n is the number of the clock phases and T is the clock cycle time, then the amount of delay Δ should be,

$$\Delta \leqslant T/n$$

When Δ is equal to T/n, the pulse periods within the clock cycle are all equal; this is the most widely used case.

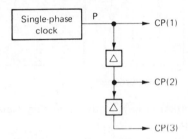

Fig. 2.20 Generation of a three-phase clock

PROBLEMS

2.1 Draw the truth table for boolean functions (2.2) and (2.3).

2.2 Flipflop A has two inputs j and k, whose input logic is described by the truth table in Table 2.2.
   (a) Describe the operation of this flipflop, and
   (b) Compare its operation with the operation of D flipflop.

2.3 Flipflop A has two inputs r and s, whose input logic is described by the truth table in Table 2.3.
   (a) Describe the operation of this flipflop, and
   (b) Compare its operation with the operations of JK flipflop and D flipflop.

Table 2.2 Truth table of JK flipflop

k	j	A	ΔA
0	0	0	0
0	0	1	1
0	1	0	1
0	1	1	1
1	0	0	0
1	0	1	0
1	1	0	1
1	1	1	0

Table 2.3 Truth table of rs flipflop

r	s	A	ΔA
0	0	0	0
0	0	1	1
0	1	0	0
0	1	1	1
1	0	0	0
1	0	1	0
1	1	0	*
1	1	1	*

*Undetermined

2.4 Show the block representations of the following registers and indicate the name of each flipflop,

Register,   A(10–2),Q(1–3,P,4–6)
Subregister,   A(M)=A(1–3),Q(N)=(4–6)
Casregister,   AQ(1–12)=A(10–2)–Q(1–3)

2.5 For the following memory statement which describes a random access memory

Memory, MEM(M) = MEM(0 – 4095,0 – 35)

(a) Complete the description of the memory by providing a register statement, and
(b) Draw a block representation of the memory.

2.6 Given the following statements

Register, A(0–5)
Switch,   SWX(0–5)(ON),   SWXM(OFF)
Light,   LTX(0–5) (ON,OFF)

(a) Draw a block representation of the register, switches, and lights, and
(b) Suggest a logic relation among them (i.e., What do these lights indicate? What is the purpose of these switches? etc.)

2.7 Use a terminal statement to describe each of the following logic networks,
   (a) the single-bit comparator,
   (b) the single-bit half adder
   (c) the single-bit full adder
   (d) the two-bit multiplier
   These logic networks are described in Chapter 1.

2.8 A logic network is described by the following statements,

$$\text{Register, } D(0-3)$$
$$\text{Decoder, } DT(0-15)=D$$
$$\text{Terminal, } TO,$$
$$DP(0-15)=TO*DT(0-15)$$

   where TO is an input terminal.
   (a) Show the logic of the network and the register by a block diagram, and
   (b) Explain what function this network performs.

3

Micro-operations

A micro-operation is an elementary, functional operation physically built into a digital computer. Examples of micro-operations are: clear the register, set the register to a particular binary constant, shift the contents of the register one bit to the left (or right), increment or decrement the number in the register by one bit, generate an odd (or even) parity for the binary word in the register, transfer the contents of one register to the other, add (or subtract) the two binary numbers in the two registers, and the like. These micro-operations perform simple functions from which more complex functions can be obtained. In this chapter, the process of realizing a micro-operation as well as those commonly encountered micro-operations are described.

3.1 REALIZATION OF MICRO-OPERATIONS

A *micro-operation* transfers the contents of one (or two) register to another register during which a function is performed. This process of realizing a micro-operation is illustrated by the block diagram in Figure 3.1. Registers A and R are operand and result registers respectively, and the logic network performs the function. A micro-operation is usually elementary, because it is partly limited by the complexity of the logic network and partly by the need of flexibility to form various complex functions from a small number of elementary functions. Because of the physical nature of the logic circuitry, a micro-operation requires a register transfer. In fact, data transfer between the registers is the basic principle by which digital operations are implemented.

3.1.1 Delays in a Transfer

The transfer from the register A to register R in Figure 3.1 is physically not instantaneous. A finite amount of time for signal propagation is required. This amount of time is known as propagation delay. For today's circuitry, this delay ranges from a few nanoseconds to a fraction of a microsecond, depending on the complexity of the logic network.

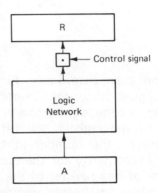

Fig. 3.1 Configuration for realizing a micro-operation

For certain micro-operations such as shift and count, it is often more practical to combine the registers A and R in Figure 3.1 into one register; this is shown in Figure 3.2. Now a definite amount of delay in the data path is required for storing the information temporarily. For this reason, delays are inserted in Figure 3.2. These delays can be inserted at the inputs or at the outputs of the logic network. In Figure 3.2(a), the original information in the register A is held temporarily while the contents of A are being changed. In Figure 3.2(b), the new information is being held temporarily while A is being changed. These delays usually are not separate circuits as indicated in Figure 3.2; they are rather a part of the flipflops of the register.

In Figure 3.2, a logical AND block is placed before the data enter the register A. This block allows the control of the transfer by a control signal. The transfer takes place only when the control signal appears. The description and application of the control signal is deferred to the next chapter.

3.1.2 Micro-statements

Instead of the block diagram, a micro-operation may be described

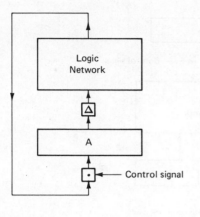 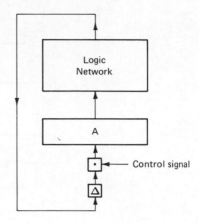

(a) Delays at the output side
of the register

(b) Delays at the input side
of the register

Fig. 3.2 Delays in the path of a register transfer

by a statement, called a *micro-statement.* A micro-statement is symbolized by an arrowhead to denote the transfer. The micro-statement for describing the micro-operation shown in Figure 3.1 is

$$R \leftarrow opr\ A \tag{3.1}$$

where opr denotes an operator whose operation is performed by the logic network. A and R are, respectively, the operand register and result register. For the block representation in Figure 3.2, the micro-statement is

$$A \leftarrow opr\ A$$

If a micro-operation requires two operand registers as illustrated by the block diagram in Figure 3.3(a), the micro-statement is

$$R \leftarrow A\ opr\ B \tag{3.3}$$

or

$$R \leftarrow B\ opr\ A \tag{3.4}$$

Micro-operations

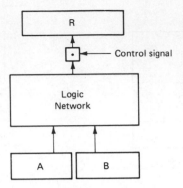

(a) With a separate result register

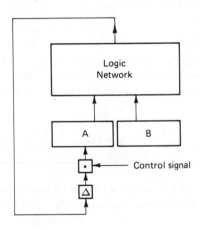

(b) Without a separate result register

Fig. 3.3 Configuration for a micro-operation with two operand registers

Should the register A in Figure 3.3(a) be combined with the register R, the resulting configuration is shown in Figure 3.3(b); the micro-statement becomes

$$A \leftarrow A \text{ opr } B \qquad\qquad (3.5)$$

If a micro-operation involves only a transfer, the logic network in Figure 3.1 becomes trivial and the corresponding micro-statement becomes

$$R \leftarrow A \qquad (3.6)$$

If a micro-operation requires no operand register but, instead, a constant, the block diagram of Figure 3.1 becomes that in Figure 3.4, and the micro-statement becomes

$$R \leftarrow K \qquad (3.7)$$

where K represents a constant. If R is less than three bits, K is binary; otherwise, K is octal. In either case, the number of bits or octal digits of K agrees with the number of bits of the register R except the case where K is 0. In this case, a single 0 is regarded as adequate.

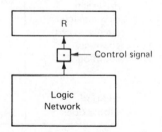

Fig. 3.4 Configuration of a micro-operation with no operand register

3.1.3 Operators and Expressions

An *operator* is a symbol which represents the function to be performed by the logic network during one clock period. Operators whose functions are frequently encountered are established as basic operators. Some basic operators are listed in Table 3.1. They are classified into logical, functional, and arithmetical operators. Some operators are unary such as countup; a unary operator requires one operand. Some operators are binary such as + and add; a binary operator requires two operands. Unless otherwise stated, the symbol of an operator is either a special character such as + or * or a combination of *small* letters such as shr, while the name of a computer element such as START and MQ employs *capital* letters.

Table 3.1 Basic operators

Type	Name	Symbol
Logical		
	logical NOT	'
	logical OR	+
	logical AND	*
	logical EXOR	⊕
	logical COIN	⊙
Functional		
	shift-left	shl
	shift-right	shr
	circulate-left	cil
	circulate-right	cir
	count-up	countup
	count-down	countdn
Arithmetical		
	addition	add
	subtraction	sub

An *expression* is a formatted combination of constants, operators, and/or operands to describe a part of a micro-statement. It represents the function that a micro-operation performs before the transfer in the micro-operation takes place. An expression can be a constant, an operand, a unary operator with one operand, or a binary operator with two operands. The values of an expression represent the signals at the output terminals of a logic network.

The basic unary and binary operators are defined in Tables 3.2 and 3.3 respectively. As will be shown subsequently, these expressions form logical, functional, and arithmetical micro-operations.

Table 3.2 Definitions of the basic unary operators

Expression	Definition*
A$'$	logical NOT of each bit of A.
shl A	shift A one bit to the left and insert a 0 at the right end.
shr A	shift A one bit to the right and insert a 0 at the left end.
cil A	circulate A one bit to the left.
cir A	circulate A one bit to the right.
countup A	increment A by one.
countdn A	decrement A by one.

*A refers to register A.

Table 3.3 Definition of the basic binary operators

Expressions	Definition*
A + R	logical OR of the respective bits of A and R.
A * R	logical AND of the respective bits of A and R.
A ⊕ R	logical EXOR of the respective bits of A and R.
A ⊙ R	logical COIN of the respective bits of A and R.
A add R	add unsigned binary number in R to that in A.
A sub R	subtract unsigned binary number in R from that in A.
k shl A	shift A k-bits to the left and insert 0's at the right end.
k shr A	shift A k-bits to the right and insert 0's at the left end.
k cil A	circulate A k bits to the left.
k cir A	circulate A k bits to the right.

*R and A are registers, and k is a constant.

3.2 REGISTER TRANSFERS

A register transfer is the transfer of the contents of one register to another register or registers. It is a simple micro-operation. Some forms of register transfers are now described.

3.2.1 Bit Transfers

Consider two one-bit registers A and R. Bit transfer from R to A transfers the contents of register R to register A. Figures 3.5(a) and (b) show, respectively, the contents of registers A and R before and after the transfer. After the transfer, register R retains but register A loses its original information.

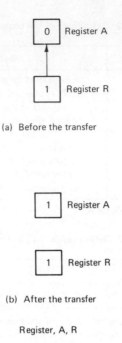

(a) Before the transfer

(b) After the transfer

Register, A, R

A ← R

(c) Statement representation

Fig. 3.5 Bit transfer

The bit transfer in Figure 3.5 may be described by a micro-statement. Consider the following two statements,

Register, A,R

$$A \leftarrow R \qquad\qquad (3.8)$$

As has been shown, the register statement describes the two one-bit registers A and R, while the micro-statement describes the transfer from register R to register A.

The line indicating the transfer in Figure 3.5(a) as well as the lines in Figures 3.6(a) through 3.9(a) are called the *data paths.* These data paths require actual, physical wiring.

3.2.2 Direct Transfers

A direct transfer between two registers is the bit transfer of all the bits in one register to the respective bits in the other register. Figures 3.6(a) and (b) show, respectively, the contents of registers A and R before and after the transfer. The direct transfer in Figure 3.6 is described by the following statements,

Register, A(0–5), R(0–5)

$$A \leftarrow R \qquad (3.9)$$

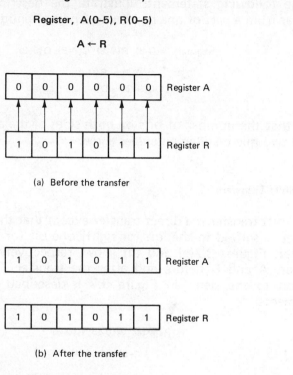

(a) Before the transfer

(b) After the transfer

Register, A(0–5), R(0–5)

$$A \leftarrow R$$

(c) Statement representation

Fig. 3.6 Direct transfer

The micro-statement for a direct transfer in (3.9) appears to be the same as that for a bit transfer in (3.8). However, the former means the following set of micro-statements,

$$A(0) \leftarrow R(0),$$
$$A(1) \leftarrow R(1),$$
$$------------, \qquad (3.10)$$
$$A(5) \leftarrow R(5)$$

This difference is due to the number of bits of the registers specified by the register statements in (3.8) and (3.9). In statement (3.8), one bit is transferred; in statement (3.9), six bits are transferred. In any case, the number of bits in the two registers must agree.

The following statements illustrate the description of a direct transfer from a part of one register to a part of another register,

$$\text{Register, } A(0–5), R(0–5), C(0–5), D(0–2)$$

$$A(0–4) \leftarrow R(0–4) \tag{3.11}$$
$$C(0–2) \leftarrow D$$

Note that the number of bits on both sides of the arrowheads of the above two micro-statements does agree.

3.2.3 Shift Transfers

A shift transfer is a direct transfer except that the contents of one register is shifted to the left (or right) one bit (or more) during the transfer. Figures 3.7(a) and (b) show, respectively, the contents of registers A and R before and after the transfer. The shift transfer, one bit to the right, in Figure 3.7 is described by the following statements,

$$\text{Register, } A(0–5), R(0–5)$$
$$A(1–5) \leftarrow R(0–4) \tag{3.12}$$

The above micro-statement again means the following group of bit transfers,

$$A(1) \leftarrow R(0)$$
$$A(2) \leftarrow R(1)$$
$$\text{- - - - - - - - - - - - -}$$
$$A(5) \leftarrow R(4) \tag{3.13}$$

Note that the contents of bit A(0) are not changed. If they are to be changed, another micro-statement is required. Similarly, the shift transfer, one bit to the left, is described by the following three statements,

$$\text{Register, } A(0–5), R(0–5)$$
$$A(0–4) \leftarrow R(1–5) \tag{3.14}$$
$$A(5) \leftarrow 0$$

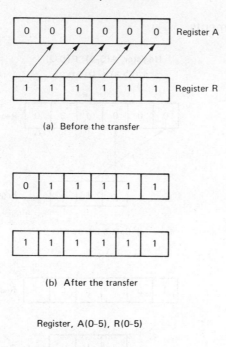

(a) Before the transfer

(b) After the transfer

Register, A(0-5), R(0-5)

$$A(1-5) \leftarrow R(0-4)$$

Fig. 3.7 Shift right transfer

In this case, bit A(5) is set to 0 by the third statement.

Instead of using two micro-statements, one micro-statement may be used if a cascaded register is used as shown below,

$$A \leftarrow R(1-5)-0 \qquad (3.15)$$

The above casregister is cascaded with a binary constant (0 in this case); it is different from that described in Chapter 2. This extension of the casregister to constants makes possible the more concise description of some transfers.

3.2.4 Scatter Transfers

A scatter transfer distributes the contents of some bits of one register to the bit positions of another register. Figures 3.8(a) and (b) show, respectively, the contents of registers A and R before and after the transfer. The scatter transfer in Figure 3.8 is described by the following statements,

$$\text{Register, } A(0-5), R(0-2)$$
$$A(0,2,5) \leftarrow R(1,0,2)$$ (3.16)

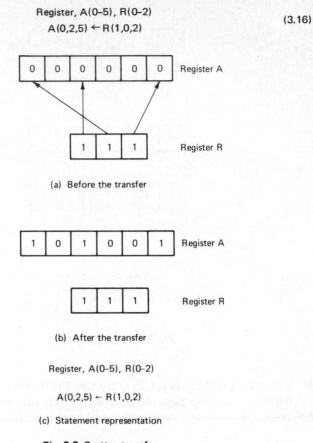

(a) Before the transfer

(b) After the transfer

Register, A(0–5), R(0–2)

$$A(0,2,5) \leftarrow R(1,0,2)$$

(c) Statement representation

Fig. 3.8 Scatter transfer

The above micro-statement means the following three bit transfers,

$$A(0) \leftarrow R(1),$$
$$A(2) \leftarrow R(0),$$ (3.17)
$$A(5) \leftarrow R(2)$$

3.2.5 Collect Transfers

A collect transfer assembles the contents of one register from the scattered bits of another register. A collect transfer is the reverse process of a scatter transfer. Figures 3.9(a) and (b) show,

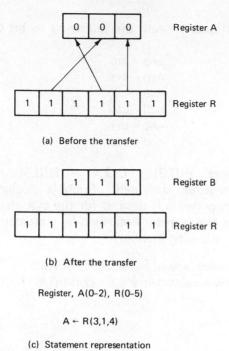

(a) Before the transfer

(b) After the transfer

Register, A(0–2), R(0–5)

A ← R(3,1,4)

(c) Statement representation

Fig. 3.9 Collect transfer

respectively, the contents of registers A and B before and after the transfer. The collect transfer in Figure 3.9 can be described by the following statements,

$$\begin{aligned} &\text{Register, A(0–2), R(0–5)}\\ &\quad A \leftarrow R(3,1,4) \end{aligned} \qquad (3.18)$$

The above micro-statement means the following three bit transfers,

$$\begin{aligned} A(0) &\leftarrow R(3),\\ A(1) &\leftarrow R(1),\\ A(2) &\leftarrow R(4) \end{aligned} \qquad (3.19)$$

If a collect transfer assembles the contents of one register from more than one register, a cascaded register may be used. Consider the following transfer,

$$\begin{aligned} &\text{Register, A(0–5), B(0–5), C(0–5), D(0–5)}\\ &\quad A \leftarrow B(0,3)–C(2,4)–D(1,5) \end{aligned} \qquad (3.20)$$

The above micro-statement means the following six bit transfers,

$$A(0) \leftarrow B(0),$$
$$A(1) \leftarrow B(3),$$
$$A(2) \leftarrow C(2),$$
$$A(3) \leftarrow C(4),$$
$$A(4) \leftarrow D(1),$$
$$A(5) \leftarrow D(5)$$

(3.21)

The cascaded register, B(0,3) – C(2,4) – D(0,5), has not been declared in a casregister statement. Such a declaration is not necessary unless a new name is desired for the cascaded register. If a new name is desired, the transfer described by statements (3.20) may be described in the following manner,

Register, A(0–5), B(0–5), C(0–5), D(0–5)

Casregister, W(0–5)=B(0,3)–C(2,4)–D(1,5)   (3.22)

A ← W

3.3 BUS TRANSFER

So far, we have described the transfer of the contents of one register to another register. If the transfer is from one register in one group of registers to one in another group of registers, the transfers may use a bus register or a bus.

3.3.1 Transfer Through a Bus Register

Consider one group of registers named A, B, and C and another named X, Y, and Z, as shown in Figure 3.10. The transfer may occur from register X to register A, B, or C. There are nine (i.e., 3^2) data paths. If each register consists of 36 bits, there are nine groups of 36 lines or a total of 324 lines. As the number of registers increases, the number of lines increases exponentially.

If, at one time, there is only one transfer from one register in one group to one in the other group, the number of the data paths can be reduced by transferring through a bus register. This is shown in Figure 3.11 where the bus register is the one named BUS. The bus register serves as a traffic center through which the transfer must pass. For example, for a transfer from register X to register A, the

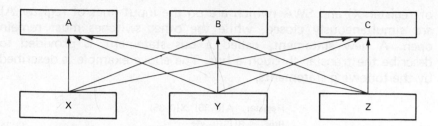

Fig. 3.10 Transfer between one group of register to another group

transfer must go through two steps: from X to the bus register and from the bus register to A. In micro-statements, the transfers are,

Step 1, BUS ← X

Step 1, A ← BUS (3.23)

The reduction in the data paths is obtained at the price of limiting one transfer at one time.

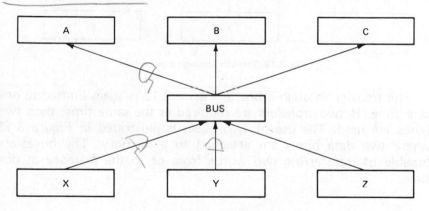

Fig. 3.11 Transfer through a bus register

3.3.2 Transfer Through a Bus

Instead of using a bus register, one may use a bus. A bus is a group of wires through which a binary word can be transferred. For a parallel transfer, the number of wires in the bus is equal to the number of flipflops in the register. Each output or input line of the flipflop is connected through an electronic switch to a wire in the bus; this is illustrated in Figure 3.12. All these switches are normally open, until a transfer is required. For a transfer from register X to register A, for example, switches SWX (which are on the output lines of register X) and SWA (which are on the input lines of register A) are simultaneously closed, while the other switches must remain open. A new statement, called a bus statement, is provided to describe the transfer through a bus. The above example is described by the following statements,

Register, A(0–35), X(0–35)
Bus,   BUS(0–35)   (3.24)
         A←BUS, BUS←X

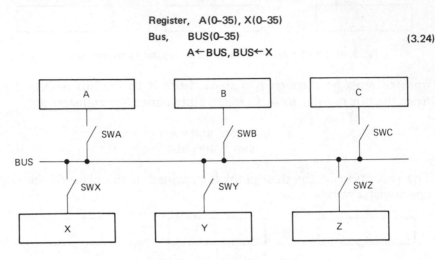

Fig. 3.12 Transfer through a single bus

The transfer through a bus in Figure 3.12 is again limited to one at a time. If two transfers are required at the same time, then two buses are used. The use of two buses is illustrated in Figure 3.13 where two data buses are attached to a memory. The buses are capable of transferring two words from or to the memory at one time.

3.4 MEMORY TRANSFERS

Most of today's random access memories are magnetic core memories of the coincident current type. This type of memory operates on a memory cycle during which the complete task to read a binary word out of the memory or to write a word into the memory is performed. The time for completing a memory cycle is called the *memory cycle time.* The memory cycle time, an important characteristic of the magnetic core memory, is at present closely related to the speed of a modern digital computer. Typical memory cycle time ranges from a few microseconds to less than 100

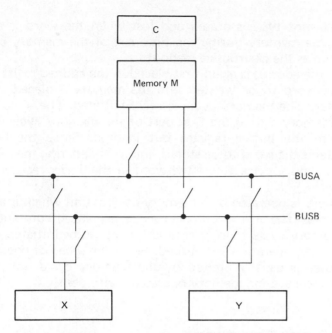

Fig. 3.13 Transfer through two buses

nanoseconds. The memory cycle time is much longer than the flipflop transfer time. The ratio of the memory cycle time to the flipflop transfer time is an important parameter, because it significantly influences the computer organization.

The coincident current magnetic-core memory, in reading a word out of the memory, produces the word in the buffer register before reaching the end of the memory cycle. The time when the word becomes available in the buffer register is known as the *access time.* The access time ranges approximately from 0.3 to 0.7 of the memory cycle time.

3.4.1 Memory Operations

There are two memory transfer operations: to read a word out of and to write a word into the memory. To read, the address is first transferred to the address register, and the memory cycle is then initiated. During the first part of the memory cycle, the word is read out of the memory and stored in the buffer register. During the second part of the memory cycle, the word in the buffer register is stored into the memory proper. This re-store operation is required because the stored word in a magnetic core memory of the coincident current type is erased and lost when the word is being read out of the memory during the first part of the memory cycle. (This is known as the destructive readout.)

To write, the address is again first placed in the address register; in addition, the word to be written into the memory is placed in the buffer register. The memory cycle is again initiated. The word read out of the memory during the first part of the memory cycle is not transferred to the buffer register but ignored. Since the buffer register contains the word to be stored, the writing during the second part of the memory cycle stores the word in the buffer register into the memory.

The memory is operated by a memory control unit which is a part of the memory. The memory cycle can be sequenced continuously (i.e., one memory cycle follows another), or it can be initiated when a read or a write operation is required. Since the speed of operation of a computer is usually limited by the memory cycle time, it is advantageous to have the memory operated continuously.

3.4.2 Memory Transfer Micro-statements

Consider the following random access memory,

$$\text{Register, } B(0\text{--}5), C(0\text{--}5), R. W, P(0\text{--}5)$$
$$\text{Memory, } M(C)=M(0\text{--}63,0\text{--}5) \tag{3.25}$$

where B and C are, respectively, the buffer and address registers, R and W are two one-bit registers for initiating a read or write operation, respectively, and P is the register where the desired memory address is stored. For a read operation, the following steps are necessary,

$$\text{Step 1, } C \leftarrow P$$
$$\text{Step 2, } R \leftarrow 1 \tag{3.26}$$
$$\text{Step 3, } B \leftarrow M(C)$$

The desired address is first transferred to the address register C. Register R is next set to 1. Then, the word is read out of the memory. (R is reset to 0 by the memory.) The time between steps 2 and 3 should be no less than the previously mentioned memory access time. Similarly, the steps for a write operation are,

Step 1, C ← P
Step 2, W ← 1   (3.27)
Step 3, M(C) ← B

In this write operation, the word to be stored into the memory has already been transferred to buffer register B. Registers R and W are reset to 0 by the memory control unit when the read or write operation is completed. The re-store operation of the memory is automatic and no micro-statement is required.

In some memories, the initiation of a read or a write operation is also automatic after an address is transferred to the address register. In this case, the above step 2 can be omitted.

If the memory transfer is through a bus as that shown in Figure 3.13, the micro-statements in describing such a write operation, for example, are,

Register, C(0–11), X(0–35)
Memory,   M(C)=(0–4095,0–35)
Bus,   BUSA(0–35), BUSB(0–35)   (3.28)
Step 1,   C ← P
Step 2,   BUSA ← X, M(C) ← BUSA

The above description assumes that the memory cycle is automatically initiated.

3.5 CONDITIONAL MICRO-STATEMENTS

A micro-statement describes a micro-operation. If the micro-operation is carried out conditionally, it is described by a conditional micro-statement. In a conditional micro-statement, the condition which is symbolized by character = or ≠ represents a test logic network; this fact is shown by the block diagram in Figure 3.14. If the output terminal of the network gives a signal representing 1, the micro-operation is executed; otherwise, the micro-operation is ignored.

For example, the following statements describe the micro-operation of clearing the register P upon the condition that the bit B(0) is 1,

Register, R(0–5), B(0–5)
IF (B(0)=1) THEN (R ← 0)   (3.29)

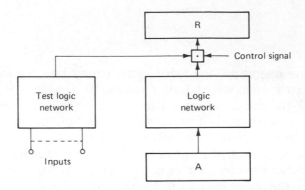

Fig. 3.14 Configuration for realizing a conditional micro-operation

The above IF statement is a conditional micro-statement which is characterized by the words IF and THEN. The quantity, $B(0) = 1$, between these two words is the condition. The test logic network represented by the condition is in this case trivial. If the condition is satisfied, the value of the condition is 1 and register R is cleared; otherwise, the value of the condition is 0 and no action is taken.

The conditional statement has another form which is characterized by three words IF, THEN, and ELSE. Consider the micro-operation to clear register R when the condition of $B(0)$ being 1 is true; but register R is cleared instead if $B(0)$ is 0. For this conditional operation, the statements are,

$$\text{Register, } P(0\text{--}5),\ R(0\text{--}5),\ B(0\text{--}5)$$
$$\text{IF}(B(0)=1) \text{ THEN } (R \leftarrow 0) \text{ ELSE } (P \leftarrow 0) \tag{3.30}$$

Since $B(0)$ must be either 1 or 0, either P or R is cleared. Instead of the above one conditional micro-statement, two conditional micro-statements may be used as shown below,

$$\text{IF } (B(0)=1) \text{ THEN } (R \leftarrow 0),$$
$$\text{IF } (B(0)=0) \text{ THEN } (P \leftarrow 0) \tag{3.31}$$

If the condition in the above micro-statement becomes that bit $B(0)$ is not equal to bit $X(0)$, then we have,

$$\text{Register, } P(0\text{--}5),\ R(0\text{--}5),\ A(0\text{--}5),\ X(0\text{--}5)$$
$$\text{IF}(B(0) \neq X(0)) \text{ THEN } (R \leftarrow 0) \text{ ELSE } (P \leftarrow 0) \tag{3.32}$$

The conditional micro-statement may also be used to describe the switch logic. The following statements,

```
Switch,   POWER(ON,OFF)
Light,    RED(ON,OFF)                                          (3.33)
          IF (POWER=ON) THEN (RED ← ON) ELSE (RED ← OFF)
```

specify that the light RED is turned to the ON condition, when switch POWER is turned to the ON position; otherwise, to the OFF condition.

3.5.1 Multiple-bit Conditions

In the above conditional micro-statements, all are single-bit test conditions. The condition can be of multiple bits. The multiple-bit condition may test the contents of a register, the positions of a row of switches, or the conditions of a row of lights. Consider the following example,

```
Register,  C(0–5), D(0–4)                                      (3.34)
           IF (C≠77) THEN (D ← 13)
```

Register C is a six-bit counter. When the contents of the counter is not equal to octal 77, register D is set to octal 13. The following statements give another example,

```
Register,     A(0–5), P(0–5)
Subregister,  A(M)=A(1–5)
Light,        TOPAZ(ON,OFF)                                    (3.35)
              IF (A(M)≠0) THEN (P ← 0, TOPAZ ← ON)
```

Subregister A(M) stores the five-bit magnitude of the number in register A. If this magnitude is not equal to 0 (this means binary number 00000), register P is cleared and light TOPAZ is turned to the ON condition.

3.5.2 Conditions with Logical Operators

In all the above conditional statements, the value of the condition is either 1 (true) or 0 (false). For this reason, logical operators may be used to form a conditional expression. For example, if the condition is that bit A(0) is 1 and bit B(1) is 0, the conditional expression is,

$$\text{IF } (((A(0)=1)*(B(1)=0))=1) \text{ THEN } (\dots\dots) \qquad (3.36)$$

If the condition is that A(0) bit is 1 and B(1) bit is not 1 and C(2) bit is 1 or that D(3) is not 1 and switch STOP is ON, the conditional expression is

IF (((A(0)=1*(B(1)≠1)*(C(2)=1)+(D(3)≠1)*(STOP=ON))=1) THEN (. . . . .)   (3.37)

It is apparent that the conditional expression becomes lengthy and awkward. Simplification of these conditional expressions can be readily achieved if each condition is converted into a boolean quantity. For example,

$$A(0)=1 \quad or \quad A(0)≠0 \quad \text{is substituted by } A(0),$$
$$A(0)=0 \quad or \quad A(0)≠1 \quad \text{is substituted by } A(0)'. \quad (3.38)$$

The condition for the switch is rewritten as below,

STOP=ON   is substituted by STOP(ON).   (3.39)

With these substitutions, micro-statement (3.36) becomes

IF (A(0)*B(1)') THEN (. . . . .)   (3.40)

and micro-statement (3.37) becomes

IF (A(0)*B(1)'*C(2)+D(3)'*STOP(ON)) THEN (. . . . .)   (3.41)

These conditional expressions now become concise and readable.

If the condition is not a comparison of a single bit with 1 or 0, but instead a comparison between the single-bit variables or a comparison of a multiple-bit variable with another multiple-bit variable or with a multiple-bit constant such as,

$$A(0)≠X(0),$$
$$C≠77, \quad (3.42)$$
$$A(M)=X(M)$$

conversion of these conditions into boolean expressions is not desirable.

3.5.3 Nesting of Conditional Micro-statements

A conditional micro-statement can be of the form,

IF (condition expression) THEN (micro-statement,. . . . .)   (3.43) or of the form,

IF (cond. expr.) THEN (micro-statement,. . . .) ELSE (micro-statement,. . .)   (3.44)

If one of the above micro-statements is a conditional micro-state-ment, it is called *nesting*. For example, the following is a nested, conditional micro-statement,

Register, A,B,R(0–1)
    IF (A=0) THEN (IF (B=0) THEN (R← 0) ELSE (R← 1))
        ELSE (IF (B=0) THEN (R←1) ELSE (R←2))   (3.45)

This nested statement specifies the numerical addition of the bit in A to the bit in B and the storing of the sum in register R. The nesting in a conditional micro-statement can be avoided by using additional, conditional micro-statements. For example, the above nested micro-statement is equivalent to the following set of four conditional micro-statements,

IF (A'∗B') THEN (R←0),
IF (A'∗B) THEN (R←1),
IF (A∗B') THEN (R←1),
IF (A∗B)   THEN (R←2)   (3.46)

These statements describe the truth table for a single-bit addition where A and B are the augend bit and addend bit respectively, and R(0) and R(1) are the carry bit and sum bit, respectively.

As another example of nested, conditional micro-statement, we have the following nested micro-statement which specifies that P is set to 17,37,57, or 77 when A is 0, 1, 2, or 3, respectively:

Register, A(0–1), P(0–5)
    IF (A=0) THEN (P← 17)
        ELSE (IF (A=1) THEN (P← 37)   (3.47)
        ELSE (IF (A=2) THEN (P ←57)
        ELSE (P← 77)))

Note that the above conditions are of multiple bits, because register A is of two bits. The above nested statement can be rewritten into the equivalent set of the following four conditional micro-statements,

IF (A=0) THEN (P ←17),
IF (A=1) THEN (P ←37),
IF (A=2) THEN (P ←57),
IF (A=3) THEN (P ←77)   (3.48)

3.6 LOGICAL MICRO-OPERATIONS

Logical micro-operations are those which employ logical operators. Five basic logical operators $'$, $+$, $*$, $\oplus$, and $\odot$ have been shown in Table 3.1, and their definitions have been shown in Tables 3.2 and 3.3. These operators perform logical NOT, OR, AND, EXOR, and COIN operations. Logical NOT is a unary operator, while the other four are binary operators.

3.6.1 Operands

The operands for these and other basic operators can be one bit, a part of a register, or an entire register. The following micro-statements illustrate the logical micro-operations when the logical operators are applied to single-bit operands,

$$\begin{aligned}
&\text{Register, } A(0\text{--}5), B(0\text{--}5) \\
&\quad A(1) \leftarrow A(1)', \\
&\quad A(1) \leftarrow A(1)+B(1), \\
&\quad A(1) \leftarrow A(1)*B(1), \\
&\quad A(1) \leftarrow A(1)\oplus B(1), \\
&\quad A(1) \leftarrow A(1)\odot B(1)
\end{aligned} \tag{3.49}$$

When the logical operators are applied to a part of a register, some examples are,

$$\begin{aligned}
&\text{Register, } A(0\text{--}5), B(0\text{--}5) \\
&\quad A(1\text{--}3) \leftarrow A(1\text{--}3)', \\
&\quad A(1\text{--}3) \leftarrow A(1\text{--}3)+B(1\text{--}3), \\
&\quad A(1\text{--}3) \leftarrow A(1\text{--}3)*B(1\text{--}3), \\
&\quad A(1\text{--}3) \leftarrow A(1\text{--}3)\oplus B(1\text{--}3), \\
&\quad A(1\text{--}3) \leftarrow A(1\text{--}3)\odot B(1\text{--}3)
\end{aligned} \tag{3.50}$$

When the logical operators are applied to an entire register, some examples are shown below,

$$\begin{aligned}
&\text{Register, } A(0\text{--}5), B(0\text{--}5) \\
&\quad A \leftarrow A', \\
&\quad A \leftarrow A+B, \\
&\quad A \leftarrow A*B, \\
&\quad A \leftarrow A\oplus B, \\
&\quad A \leftarrow A\odot B
\end{aligned} \tag{3.51}$$

A logical micro-statement may have more than one logical operator. For example, consider registers A and B. If one wishes to know whether the contents of these two registers are equal and wishes to have the equality indicated by setting flipflop EQ to 1, this comparison and indication can be described by the following logical micro-operation,

Register, A(1–3), B(1–3), EQ

$$EQ \leftarrow (A(1) \odot B(1)) * (A(2) \odot B(2)) * (A(3) \odot B(3)) \qquad (3.52)$$

There are five logical operators in the above logical micro-statement.

3.6.2 Description of Logical Operations

In Chapter 1, five basic logical operations have been described by the truth table. Instead of the truth tables, they can be described by conditional micro-statements.

Let A and F be two single-bit registers, and their logical relation be specified by the conditional micro-statement,

$$\text{IF } (A=0) \text{ THEN } (F \leftarrow 1) \text{ ELSE } (F \leftarrow 0) \qquad (3.53)$$

This statement states that if A is 0, F is 1 and if A is 1, F is 0. A truth table can be constructed from this statement, and the truth table is shown in Table 3.4. This table shows a logical NOT relation

$$F = A'$$

It is thus shown that statement (3.53) describes the logical NOT operation of variable A.

Table 3.4 Truth table for logical NOT operation

A	F
0	1
1	0

Let A, B, and F be three single-bit registers and their logical relation be specified by the conditional micro-statement,

$$(3.54)$$

This statement states that if A is 0, F is 0, and if A is 1, it depends on

B. In this latter case, if B is 0, F is 0; if B is 1, F is 1. Again, a truth table can be constructed from this statement and the truth table is shown in Table 3.5. This table shows a logical AND relation

$$F = A*B$$

Table 3.5 Truth table for logical AND operation

A	B	F
0	0	0
0	1	0
1	0	0
1	1	1

It is thus shown that statement (3.54) describes the logical AND operation of variables A and B. Similarly, the conditional micro-statement

$$\text{IF } (A=0) \text{ THEN } (F \leftarrow B) \text{ ELSE } (F \leftarrow 1) \tag{3.55}$$

describes the logical OR operation of variables A and B. And the conditional micro-statements

$$\text{IF } (A=0) \text{ THEN } (F \leftarrow B) \text{ ELSE } (F \leftarrow B') \tag{3.56}$$
$$\text{IF } (A=0) \text{ THEN } (F \leftarrow B') \text{ ELSE } (F \leftarrow B) \tag{3.57}$$

describe the logical EXOR and COIN operations of variables A and B.

3.6.3 A Description of the Full Adder

The above descriptions of logical operations demonstrate that the logic in a truth table can be described by conditional micro-statements. As a final example, the logic of the single-bit full adder described by the truth table 1.14 of Chapter 1 is now described. Let X, Y, C_i, and C_o and S be single-bit registers. The logic for the sum bit S from the truth table 1.14 is,

$$\text{IF } (C_i=0) \text{ THEN } (S \leftarrow X \oplus Y) \text{ ELSE } (S \leftarrow X \odot Y) \tag{3.58}$$

This statement specifies: if the input carry bit C_i is 0, the sum bit S is 1 when either the augend bit X is 1 or the addend bit Y is 1; if C_i is 1, the sum bit is 1 when X and Y are both 0 or both 1. The logic for the output carry bit C_o from the truth table 1.14 is,

$$\text{IF } (C_i=0) \text{ THEN } (C_o \leftarrow X * Y) \text{ ELSE } (\bar{C_o} \leftarrow X + Y) \tag{3.59}$$

This statement states that if input carry bit C_i is 0, output carry bit C_o is 1 when both X and Y are 1; if C_i is 1, C_o is 1 when either X or Y is 1.

3.7 FUNCTIONAL MICRO-OPERATIONS

Functional micro-operations are those which employ functional operators. As shown in Table 3.1, there are six basic functional operators: shl, shr, cil, cir, countup, and countdn; their definitions are given in Tables 3.2 and 3.3. They perform shift, circulate, and count micro-operations.

3.7.1 Shift Micro-operations

The two basic shift operators (shl and shr) can be either unary or binary. When they are unary, they shift the contents of a register one bit to the left or right and insert a 0 at the right or left end respectively. When they are binary, they shift k bits instead of one bit where k is an octal constant. The following micro-statements are examples of describing the basic shift micro-operations,

$$\begin{aligned} &A \leftarrow shl \ A, \\ &A \leftarrow shr \ A, \\ &A \leftarrow k \ shl \ A, \\ &A \leftarrow k \ shr \ A \end{aligned} \tag{3.60}$$

Although the shift micro-operations can alternately be described by previously shown shift transfer micro-statements, the use of the basic operators whenever possible makes the micro-statement more readable and thus preferred.

The shifting of the contents of a register (say, A) may be accomplished by using a slave register (say, R). As an example, the following statements,

$$\begin{aligned} &\text{Register, } A(0-5), R(0-5) \\ &\text{Step 1,} \quad R \leftarrow 0 \\ &\text{Step 2,} \quad R \leftarrow shl \ A \\ &\text{Step 3,} \quad A \leftarrow R \end{aligned} \tag{3.61}$$

describe the three steps of the left shift. The slave register R is first cleared. The shift transfer from register A to R is next performed. And then the direct transfer from register R to A completes the left shift. The configuration of using master register A and slave register R is identical to that in Figure 3.1 except the additional logic network to transfer the data in R to A. The use of master and slave registers allows a high-speed operation, because no delays are needed in the data paths. The speed of operation is essentially limited by the flipflop transfer time.

3.7.2 Circulate Micro-operations

The two basic circulate operators (cil and cir) can be either unary or binary. When they are unary, they circulate the contents of a register one bit to the left or right. When they are binary, they shift k bits instead of one bit. The following micro-statements are examples of describing the basic circulate micro-operations,

$$
\begin{aligned}
&A \leftarrow \text{cil } A, \\
&A \leftarrow \text{cir } A, \\
&A \leftarrow k \text{ cil } A, \\
&A \leftarrow k \text{ cir } A
\end{aligned}
\tag{3.62}
$$

Again, these micro-operations can alternatively be described by shift transfer micro-statements. Since a circulate micro-operation is essentially a shift micro-operation, it may also be accomplished by means of a pair of master-slave registers.

3.7.3 Count Micro-operations

The two basic count operations (countup and countdn) increment or decrement the contents of a register by one. The following micro-statements are examples of describing the basic count micro-operations,

$$
\begin{aligned}
&A \leftarrow \text{countup } A \\
&R \leftarrow \text{countdn } R
\end{aligned}
\tag{3.63}
$$

The above micro-statements specify that A is a binary *up-counter* and R a binary *down-counter*. A counter increments or decrements its contents according to a particular sequence. A two-bit binary up-counter counts the sequence 0-1-2-3-0-1-2-3- - - -, while a two-bit binary down-counter counts the sequence 3-2-1-0-3-2-1-0- - - - . These numbers (0,1,2, and 3) which represent the contents of the counter are called the *states* of the counter. The count sequence may be described by showing the states in a diagram, called the *state diagram.* The state diagrams for a binary up-counter and a down-counter are shown in Figure 3.15. Each circle represents one state of the counter and it has one input and one output indicated by the arrowheads. The state diagram describes the operation of the counter.

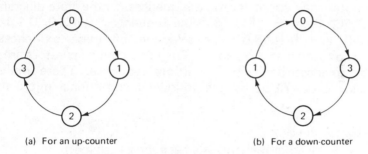

(a) For an up-counter   (b) For a down-counter

Fig. 3.15 State diagrams for binary counters

The count micro-operation may alternatively be described by conditional micro-statements. Let C be a two-bit register. If C is required to count according to the states in the state diagram of Figure 3.15(a), the operation of this counter is described by the following conditional micro-statements,

$$
\begin{aligned}
&\text{IF } (C=0) \text{ THEN } (C \leftarrow 1), \\
&\text{IF } (C=1) \text{ THEN } (C \leftarrow 2), \\
&\text{IF } (C=2) \text{ THEN } (C \leftarrow 3), \\
&\text{IF } (C=3) \text{ THEN } (C \leftarrow 0)
\end{aligned}
\tag{3.64}
$$

Each of the above micro-statements describes one state in the diagram. The four states result in four micro-statements. If the number of the bits of the counter increases, the above description becomes lengthy and unmanageable. One way to reduce it is to use a nested, conditional micro-statement as shown below,

$$
\begin{aligned}
&\text{Register, } C(0\text{-}1) \\
&\quad \text{IF } (C(1)=0) \text{ THEN } (C(1) \leftarrow 1) \\
&\quad\quad\quad \text{ELSE (IF } (C(0)=0) \text{ THEN } (C \leftarrow 2) \\
&\quad\quad\quad\quad\quad\quad\quad \text{ELSE } (C \leftarrow 0))
\end{aligned}
\tag{3.65}
$$

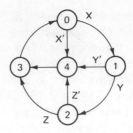

Fig. 3.16 State diagram of a multiple-sequence counter

A counter may count multiple sequences. In the state diagram of Figure 3.16, there are four possible sequences: 0-4-3-0, 0-1-4-3-0, 0-1-2-4-3-0 and 0-1-2-3-0. The selection of these sequences is controlled by variables X,Y, and Z. The basic count operators are not adequate to describe such a multiple sequence. These multiple sequences are described by the following conditional micro-statements,

> Register, C(0–2), X,Y,Z
>
> IF (C=0) THEN (IF (X=0) THEN (C←4) ELSE (C←1)),
>
> IF (C=1) THEN (If (Y=0) THEN (C←4) ELSE (C←2)),
>
> IF (C=2) THEN (IF (Z=0) THEN (C←4) ELSE (C←3)),   (3.66)
>
> IF (C=3) THEN (C←0),
>
> IF (C=4) THEN (C←3)

Again, one state is represented by one conditional micro-statement. States 5, 6, and 7 of the counter are undetermined; they should not occur.

A special counter, called the *ring counter,* is now described. It is a register with its ends "brought together to form a ring." At all times, only one bit of the register contains a 1; all the other bits contain 0's. For each count, the register circulates its contents one bit clockwise (or counterclockwise); thus, the bit position which contains the 1 moves one bit. An example of a four-bit ring counter is described below,

> Register, A(1–4)
>
> Step 1,   A← 10_8
>
> Step 2,   A← cir A
>
> Step 3,   A← cir A   (3.67a)
>
> Step 4,   A← cir A
>
> Step 5,   A← cir A

Step 1 sets Register A to contain 1000_2. Step 2 circulates

Register A to the right to give 0100_2. Step 3 circulates A again and gives 0010_2. Step 4 gives 0001_2. After Step 5, Register A contains 1000_2 again.

The above description may also be described by the following conditional micro-statements.

Comment, register A initially contains 10_8
Register, AC(1–4)

$$\text{IF } (A(1)=1) \text{ THEN } (A(1,2) \leftarrow 01),$$
$$\text{IF } (A(2)=1) \text{ THEN } (A(2,3) \leftarrow 01),$$
$$\text{IF } (A(3)=1) \text{ THEN } (A(3,4) \leftarrow 01),$$
$$\text{IF } (A(4)=1) \text{ THEN } (A(4,1) \leftarrow 01),$$

(3.67b)

The above conditional micro-statements specify that, for each count, the flipflop which contains 1 is reset to 0 and the flipflop on its right is set to 1. Thus, the above two descriptions of ring counter A are equivalent.

3.8 ARITHMETIC MICRO-OPERATIONS

Arithmetic micro-operations are those which employ arithmetic operators. Table 3.1 shows the two basic arithmetic operators, add and sub, which are described in Table 3.3. Both are binary operators. Although addition and subtraction are for unsigned binary numbers, these operators can be used to describe addition and subtraction of signed binary numbers.

3.8.1 Add and Subtract Micro-operations

The basic operator, add, adds the contents of one register to those of another register with the same number of bits. The basic operator, sub, subtracts the contents of one register from those of another register. Both registers should have the same number of bits. The following statements are examples of describing addition and subtraction micro-operations,

Register, A(0–35), X(0–35)
$$A \leftarrow A \text{ add } X,$$
$$A \leftarrow \text{sub } X$$

(3.68)

The register which performs addition and/or subtraction and stores the result is often called an *accumulator.* The accumulator may use two registers, called a *double-rank register* or a *master-slave register.* If A1 and A2 are the chosen names of the double-rank register, the addition micro-operation may be described as below,

3.8.2 A Parallel Adder

A parallel adder is a logic network which adds two binary numbers and produces the sum by adding the respective bits of the two numbers in parallel. This parallel operation is illustrated by the block diagram in Figure 3.17. The inputs to the add logic network are the augend bits A(1-5) and the addend bits X(1-5), and the outputs are the sum bits S(1-5).

Register, A1(0–35), A2(0–35), X(0–35)
Step 1,   A2 ← A1 add X
Step 2,   A1 ← A2

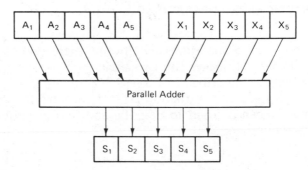

Fig. 3.17 Block diagram showing input and output terminals of a parallel adder

By means of the single-bit full adder described in Chapter 1, a parallel adder for the basic add operator can be realized. Figure 3.18 shows such a parallel adder for adding two 5-bit numbers. The parallel adder consists of five full adders with the output carry of one full adder connected to the input carry of the adjacent full adder.

The single-bit full adder, as shown in Chapter 1, is described by the following boolean functions,

$$S = X \oplus Y \oplus C_i$$
$$C_o = X*Y + Y*C_i + C_i*X \tag{3.70}$$

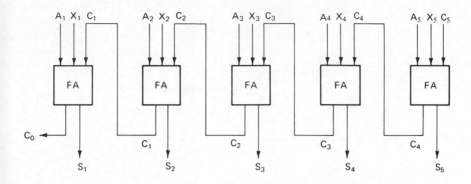

Fig. 3.18 A parallel adder by connecting single-bit full adders (FA means full adder.)

where X and Y are, respectively, the augend and addend bits, C_i and C_o, are respectively the input and the output carry bits, and S is the sum bit. In order to identify the five single-bit adders in Figure 3.18, subscripts in the manner shown in Figure 3.18 are adopted. With these subscripts, the parallel adder can now be described by the statements,

> Register, A(1–5), X(1–5)
> Terminal, $S(1–5) = A(1–5) \oplus X(1–5) \oplus C(1–5)$,
> $\quad\quad\quad C(0–4) = X(1–5) * A(1–5) + A(1–5) * C(1–5) + C(1–5) * X(1–5),$ (3.71)
> $\quad\quad\quad C(5) = 0$

The above terminal statement specifies eleven boolean functions. Carry C(5) is specified to be 0 as it does not exist; one can alternatively simplify boolean functions S(5) and C(4) by substituting 0 for C(5). Carry C(0) indicates the overflow of the sum.

By using the boolean functions in the above terminal statement, the logic diagram of the parallel adder can be constructed and is shown in Figure 3.19. Notice that the diagram in Figure 3.19 shows the details of the diagram in Figure 3.18.

If augend 11111 is added to addend 00001, carry C(4) is generated and in turn causes carry C(3) to appear. This process continues until carry C(0) appears. It is called the *carry propagation*. The top line in the logic diagram of Figure 3.18 is the line where the carry propagates. As shown, the carry may have to propagate a pair of AND-OR blocks (or gates) for each bit. For this reason, the parallel adder in Figure 3.18 is a parallel adder with the *gated carry*.

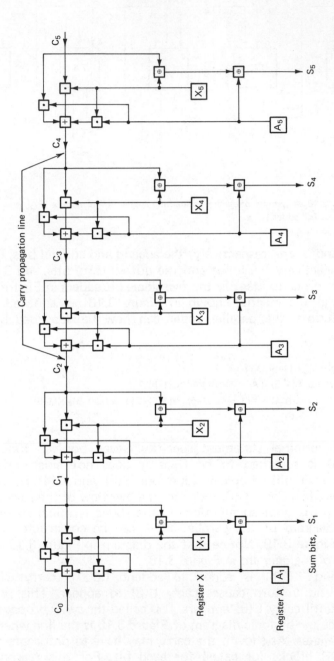

Fig. 3.19 Logic diagram of a parallel adder with the gated carry

3.8.3 Group Carries

As illustrated in Figure 3.19, the carry propagates through a series of AND-OR blocks when two binary numbers are added in a parallel adder. To propagate through these AND-OR blocks requires a finite amount of time because the logic circuits which implement the AND-OR blocks are not ideal and perfect. This finite time is called the *carry propagation time.* The carry propagation time increases with the increase of the number of bits of the augend and addend. An addition is not completed until the carry propagation is completed. Therefore, the addition time of a parallel adder depends on the carry propagation time. It is important that the propagation time in a parallel adder be reduced.

The propagation time of a parallel adder with the gated carry is often too long when the binary number has many bits. One approach often resorted to is to break the propagation line and provide group carries. An example is shown in the logic diagram of Figure 3.20, where G_1 and G_3 are group carries. In Figure 3.20, every two bits of the parallel adder form a group (bits 4 and 5 form one group, bits 2 and 3 form one group, and bit 1 alone forms a group). Within the group, the carry propagates with the gated carry as described above. The problem is then how the group carries G_1 and G_3 are generated.

A group carry of the parallel adder is an input carry for a group of bits. It is a function of augend and addend bits and other group carries; but it is independent of the other carries. Derivation of the group carries G_1 and G_3 is now shown below.

From the terminal statement in description (3.71), carries C_5, C_4, and C_3 are

$$C_5 = 0 \tag{3.72}$$
$$C_4 = A_5 X_5 + X_5 C_5 + C_5 A_5 \tag{3.73}$$
$$C_3 = A_4 X_4 + X_4 C_4 + C_4 A_4 \tag{3.74}$$

As mentioned in Section 1.3.2, symbol ∗ in the terms such as $A_5 X_5$ is omitted for the sake of simplicity. By definition, G_3 is C_3 or,

$$G_3 = C_3 \tag{3.75}$$

By substituting (3.72) into (3.73), we have,

$$C_4 = A_5 X_5 \tag{3.76}$$

By combining (3.74), (3.75), and (3.76), we have,

$$G_3 = A_4 X_4 + X_4 X_5 A_5 + X_5 A_4 A_5 \tag{3.77}$$

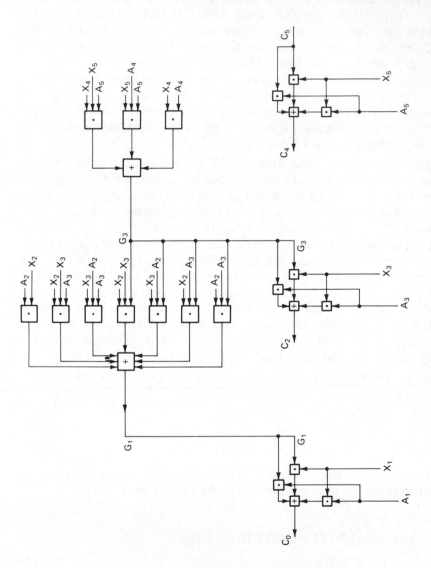

Fig. 3.20 Logic diagram of the group carries for a parallel adder

Again from the description (3.71), carries C_2 and C_1 are,

$$C_2 = A_3X_3 + X_3G_3 + A_3G_3 \qquad (3.78)$$
$$C_1 = A_2X_2 + X_2C_2 + C_2A_2 \qquad (3.79)$$

By definition, G_1 is C_1 or,

$$G_1 = C_1 \qquad (3.80)$$

By combining (3.78), (3.79), and (3.80), we have,

$$G_1 = A_2X_2 + X_2X_3A_3 + X_3A_2A_3 + X_2X_3G_3 \\ + X_3A_2G_3 + X_2A_3G_3 + A_2A_3G_3 \qquad (3.81)$$

In comparison of the parallel adder with the group carry in Figure 3.20 to the parallel adder with the gated carry in Figure 3.19, both adders add two unsigned binary numbers and produce a sum. Carries C_3 and C_1 in Figure 3.19 may have to propagate through two and four AND-OR blocks, respectively. Carries G_3 and G_1 in Figure 3.20 may have to propagate through one and two AND-OR blocks, respectively. Therefore, the carry propagation time and the addition time of the parallel adder in Figure 3.20 are shorter than those in Figure 3.19. The shorter carry propagation times of carries G_3 and G_1 are due to the fact that carry C_4 does not appear in boolean function (3.77) for G_3 and carry C_2 is not in boolean function (3.81) for G_1.

PROBLEMS

3.1 Given registers $A(5-1)$ and $R(5-9)$, write a micro-statement and draw a block diagram showing the transfer for,
 (a) a direct transfer from R to A,
 (b) a complement transfer from R to A,
 (c) an example of a scatter transfer,
 (d) an example of a collect transfer,
 (e) a two-bit leftshift transfer.

3.2 Repeat problem 3.1 for the registers $A(S,1-9)$ and $R(9-5,P,4-1)$.

3.3 A floating-point number is stored in register $A(0-35)$. The floating point number consists of a signed fraction and a characteristic. The signed fraction has its sign stored in $A(0)$ and its fraction stored in $A(9-35)$. The characteristic is stored in $A(1-8)$.
 (a) Define three subregisters for the sign, fraction, and characteristic.
 (b) If three registers are given to store the sign, fraction, and characteristic, define a casregister from the three registers to store the floating-point number properly.

3.4   A memory named MEM which has 128 six-bit words is given together with buffer register X(0–5), address register M(6–0), and two single-bit registers READ and WRITE.

(a) Describe by the micro-statements the memory read transfer for the word at address 0 and the write transfer for the word at address 137.

(b) If bus DATA(0–5) is also given, repeat part (a).

3.5   Given the following register, switches, and lights,

Register, X(0–5),
Switch,   SWXM(OFF), SWX(0–5)(ON),
Light,   LTX(0–5)(ON,OFF)

describe the following switch logic in English,

IF (SWXM(OFF)) THEN (X ← 0, LTX(0–5) ← OFF),
IF (SWX(0–5)(ON)) THEN (X(0–5) ← 1, LTX(0–5) ← ON)

3.6   Describe the register, switches, lights, and switch logic in problem 3.5 by an algorithmic programming language of your choice (such as Fortran, Algol, Mad, Snobol, PL/1, etc.)

3.7   Given a four-position switch MODE(DM,AEM,IM,PM) and four lights LTDM(ON,OFF), LTAEM(ON,OFF), LTIM(ON,OFF) and LTPM(ON, OFF), write conditional micro-statements to describe the logic: the light LTDM, LTAEM, LTIM, or LTPM is turned to the ON position when the MODE switch is turned to the DM, AEM, IM, or PM position respectively.

3.8   Given the truth table in Table 3.6,

Table 3.6 A truth table

A_1	A_2	A_3	A_4	Z_1	Z_2	Z_3	Z_4
0	0	0	0	0	0	1	1
0	0	0	1	0	0	0	1
0	0	1	0	0	1	0	0
0	0	1	1	0	0	0	1
0	1	0	0	0	1	0	1
0	1	0	1	1	0	0	1
0	1	1	0	0	0	1	0
0	1	1	1	0	1	1	0
1	0	0	0	0	1	0	1
1	0	0	1	0	0	1	1
1	0	1	0	0	1	0	1
1	0	1	1	1	0	0	0
1	1	0	0	1	0	0	1
1	1	0	1	0	1	1	1
1	1	1	0	1	0	0	1
1	1	1	1	0	0	1	1

(a) write one or more conditional micro-statements (not nested) to describe the truth table,

(b) write one or more nested, conditional micro-statements to describe the table,

(c) what function does the truth table describe?

3.9 Given a register C(0-5), write a nested, conditional micro-statement for a six-bit binary up-counter.

3.10 Given M1(5-0) and M2(5-0) as a double-rank register, describe the basic cil and countup micro-operations by using these registers.

3.11 Construct one truth table each for the conditional micro-statements (3.55), (3.56), and (3.57).

3.12 Given the following micro-statements,

(a) IF (Q=1) THEN (T←0) ELSE (T←5)

(b) IF (Q=1) THEN (A←shl A)

ELSE (IF (Q=2) THEN (A←cil A)

ELSE (IF (Q=0) THEN (A←A$'$)

ELSE (A←countup)))

draw for each micro-statement a block diagram to describe the micro-operation. The logic network should be included in each diagram.

3.13 Draw the state diagram of the ring counter described in statements (3.71).

3.14 Revise the statements (3.71) for a ring counter for a clockwise circulation and draw the state diagram.

3.15 Given a nine-bit parallel adder where every three bits form a group,

(a) find the boolean functions representing the group carries, and

(b) draw a logic diagram of the parallel adder including the group carry logic network.

3.16 From the boolean function for a single-bit subtracter,

(a) describe a five-bit parallel subtracter that can realize the basic sub operator, and

(b) draw the logic diagram in which the carry propagation line is shown.

4

Sequences

A micro-operation performs a simple function. If a number of micro-operations are performed in succession to form a sequence, a more complex function can be achieved. For example, a single-bit comparator compares two bits and determines whether the two bits are equal or not. If a sequence of such one-bit comparisons is performed on the bits of two words, it can determine whether these two words are equal or not. Similarly, by means of sequencing micro-operations, a word can be shifted by a single-bit shifter for as many bit positions as desired, two numbers can be added by a sequence of single-bit addition, and two numbers can be multiplied by a sequence of as many parallel additions as the number of bits in the numbers.

In a digital computer, there are many instructions, each of which performs a function (such as add, shift, or load) and is implemented by a sequence of micro-operations. A series of instructions forms a program which may compute the solution of a problem. Execution of the program results in the execution of each instruction, and execution of each instruction results in the execution of a sequence of micro-operations. Thus, sequences are functional units upon which a digital computer is organized.

In this chapter are described control signals which form the label of an execution statement, the execution statement for describing a controlled micro-operation (or micro-operations), the control sequence for sequencing the execution statements, and examples which show that a more complex function can be achieved by a sequence of micro-operations.

4.1 EXECUTION STATEMENTS

A micro-statement, conditional or not, may describe a micro-operation, but it does not specify when the micro-operation occurs. Since a micro-operation is activated by a control signal as shown in Figure 3.1, the control signal must be represented and included in the description. An execution statement is formed to describe execution of one or more micro-operations.

An *execution statement* consists of a label and one or more micro-statements. Because of the label, it may also be called a *labeled statement.* The label which represents the control signal is a logical variable. When the logical value of the label is 1, the micro-operation or micro-operations described by the micro-statement or micro-statements are all carried out at the same time. If the logical value is 0, these micro-operations are all ignored.

As an example, consider the following statements:

$$
\begin{array}{ll}
\text{Register,} & A(0\text{--}5), R(0\text{--}5), T \\
\text{Clock} & P \\
/T*P/ & R \leftarrow A
\end{array}
\tag{4.1}
$$

In the above, T is a control flipflop. The third statement is the execution statement where the quality enclosed by two slashes, $T*P$, is the label. When the label $T*P$ has a logical value of 1 (i.e., when the next clock pulse occurs after T is set to 1), the direct transfer from register A to register R occurs, and the micro-operation is completed during the clock period. Otherwise, this micro-operation of direct transfer is ignored.

It is important to note that an execution statement may describe more than one micro-statement. This is the way that parallel operation of micro-operations is described. As an example, consider the following statements:

$$
\begin{array}{ll}
\text{Register,} & A(0\text{--}5), R(0\text{--}5), C(0\text{--}5), B(1\text{--}3), T(0\text{--}1) \\
\text{Decoder,} & K(0\text{--}3) = T \\
\text{Clock,} & P \\
/K(1)*P/ & R \leftarrow A, B \leftarrow 0, C \leftarrow A
\end{array}
\tag{4.2}
$$

In the above, terminal K(1) is an output of the decoder connected to register T and is a control signal. There are three micro-statements which specify the parallel operation of these micro-operations. When the contents of register T is set to 1, the next clock pulse activates these three transfers.

Although multiple micro-operations can be specified by an execution statement, these micro-operations should not be in conflict. For example, the two direct transfers in the following statements:

Register, A(0–5), B(0–5), R(0–5)

Clock, P   (4.3)

/T*P/   R ← A, R ← B

make the contents of the register R undetermined after the transfers. These parallel operations, though permissible from the syntax, are not logical.

As another example, consider the following statements:

Register, T(0–2), C(0–3)

Decoder, K(0–7) = T

Clock, P   (4.4)

/K(0)*P/ IF (C=0) THEN (T ← 1) ELSE (T ← 2)

The above conditional micro-statement specifies a change of the contents of register T. This change, however, might cause a change of the decoder signal K(0) in the label, which might in turn disturb the completion of the change of the contents of the register T. This chain of events would not happen instantaneously because, as illustrated in Figure 3.2, there exists a delay in the path from the outputs of register T to its inputs. This delay should be long enough to hold the control signal and complete the micro-operation.

4.2 CONTROL SEQUENCES

An execution statement specifies one or more micro-operations as well as the control signal which controls the execution of these micro-operations. To specify a sequence of micro-operations, a sequence of control signals, to be called a *control sequence,* is required.

A control sequence is often generated by a counter. At each state of the counter a control signal is generated, and the sequence of the states of the counter gives a sequence of control signals. Since the state diagram of the counter depicts the sequence of counter states, it may also be used to depict the control sequence. Generation of the control sequence by the counter is now described.

4.2.1 Sequencing by a Ring Counter

A ring counter can be used to generate a control sequence. In statements (3.67b), the ring counter is described by conditional statements. In order to describe a control sequence, the ring counter is now described by the execution statements.

Let register $T(1-4)$ be the ring counter, P be the clock pulse, and POWER (ON) and START(ON) be the two single-position switches. Recall that the single-position switch generates a single-pulse when turned to the ON position. The ring counter is described below.

$$
\begin{array}{ll}
\text{Register,} & T(1{-}4) \\
\text{Switch,} & \text{START(ON)} \\
\text{Clock,} & P \\
/\text{START(ON)}/ & T \leftarrow 10 \\
/T(1)*P/ & T(1{-}2) \leftarrow 01 \\
/T(2)*P/ & T(2{-}3) \leftarrow 01 \\
/T(3)*P/ & T(3{-}4) \leftarrow 01 \\
/T(4)*P/ & T(4,1) \leftarrow 01 \\
& \text{End}
\end{array}
\tag{4.5}
$$

Figure 4.1 shows the control signals that are generated by the ring counter. These control signals are represented by the labels in the above execution statements. When switch START is turned to the ON position, register T is set to octal 10; this initializes the ring counter. When the next clock pulse after bit $T(1)$ is set to 1, the execution statement with label $T(1)*P$ is executed; the execution of this statement resets $T(1)$ to 0 and sets $T(2)$ to 1 (this is equivalent to shifting the register A one bit to the right). Similarly, when the next clock pulse arrives after $T(2)$ is set to 1, the execution statement with the label $T(2)*P$ is executed; execution of this statement resets $T(2)$ to 0 and sets $T(3)$ to 1. This process continues on unless the clock pulse stops. The above End statement which is the last statement indicates the end of the description.

The above statements illustrate the generation of a single control sequence. For a multiple of control sequences, the conditional micro-statement is required. As an example, the ring counter is again used to describe a multiple-sequence counter. The state diagram of

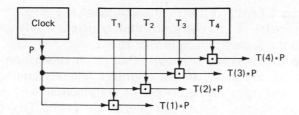

Fig. 4.1 Control signals from the ring counter T

the counter is shown in Figure 4.2. Let register T(0–7) be the ring counter, single-bit registers X, Y, and Z be the control flipflops, P be the clock and START be the starting switch. Let T(0), T(1), . . . ,T(7) represent respectively the states of 0, 1, . . . ,7 in Figure 4.2. The following statements describe the generation of the multiple sequence by the ring counter.

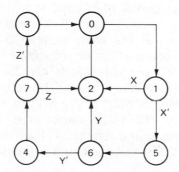

Fig. 4.2 A state diagram describing multiple control sequences

Register,	T(0–7), X,Y,Z	
Switch,	START(ON)	
Clock,	P	
/START(ON)/	T ← 200	
/T(0)∗P/	T(0,1) ← 01	
/T(1)∗P/	IF (X=1) THEN (T(1,2) ← 01) ELSE (T(1,5) ←01)	
/T(2)∗P/	T(2,0) ← 01	(4.6)
/T(3)∗P/	T(3,0) ← 01	
/T(4)∗P/	T(4,7) ← 01	
/T(5)∗P/	T(5,6) ← 01	
/T(6)∗P/	IF (Y=1) THEN (T(6,2) ←01) ELSE (T(6,4) ← 01)	
/T(7)∗P/	IF (Z=1) THEN (T(7,2) ←01) ELSE (T(7,3) ←01)	
	End	

Again, switch START initiates the counter. The above micro-statements set register T partially so that register T changes its state according to the state diagram in Figure 4.2.

The above description shows that each execution statement corresponds to one state of the counter. The sequencing described above is similar to that described in statements (4.5) except that there are conditional micro-statements in (4.6). The conditional micro-statements describe the three states with a branching (i.e., those circles with two outputs in Figure 4.2), while the simple micro-statements describe the other states. At any time, there is only one 1 in register T, but the single 1 does not circulate in the ring counter T any longer; instead, its appearance in register T depends on the states of the control flipflops.

4.2.2 Sequencing by a Control Counter

Generation of a sequence of n control signals by a ring counter requires an n-bit counter. However, if a combination of a counter and a decoder is used for the same number of control signals, the number of bits of the counter can be reduced. For an n-bit counter, a sequence of up to 2^n control signals can be generated. When a counter is used in this manner, it will be referred to as a *control counter* or an *operation counter*.

As an example, let T(0–1) be the counter, K be the outputs of the decoder connected to the register T, P be the clock, and START be the starting switch. The control counter is described below:

Register,	T(0–1)	
Decoder,	K(0–3)=T	
Switch,	START(ON)	
Light,	COMPLETE(ON,OFF)	
Clock,	P	
/START(ON)/	T ← 0	(4.7)
/K(0)∗P/	T ← countup T, COMPLETE ← OFF	
/K(1)∗P/	T ← countup T	
/K(2)∗P/	T ← countup T	
/K(3)∗P/	T ← countup, COMPLETE ← ON	
	End	

The above description is shown in the block diagram in Figure 4.3. When switch START is turned to the ON position, register T is reset to 0 and in turn terminal K(0) of the decoder is activated. When the next clock pulse arrives, control signal K(0)∗P causes the execution

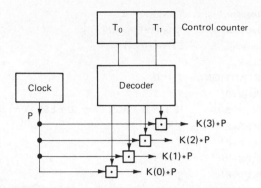

Fig. 4.3 Control signals from the decoder of a control register

of the statement with label K(0)*P. Execution of this statement increments register T one count which in turn activates the decoder terminal K(1). This process continues on unless the clock pulse stops. The sequence of the control signals is K(0),K(1),K(2),K(3),K(0), ... Light COMPLETE is turned on at the end of every counter cycle.

The above description (4.7) may alternatively be described:

Register,	T(0–1)
Decoder,	K(0–3)=T
Switch,	START(ON)
Clock,	P(1–2)
Terminal,	DP(0–3)=P(1)*K(0–3)
/START(ON)/	T ← 0
/P(2)/	T ← countup T
/DP(0)/	
/DP(1)/	
/DP(2)/	
/DP(3)/	

(4.8)

End

In this description, a countup-T micro-operation which occurs at P(2) increments register T. The labels DP(i)'s are actually defined by the terminal statement.

The combination of a counter and a decoder can also be used to generate a multiple of control sequences. The multiple sequence shown by the state diagram in Figure 4.2 is again chosen as an example. Let register T(0–2) be the counter, K be the outputs of the decoder connected to the register T, P be the clock, START be the starting switch, and X, Y, and Z be the control flipflops. The following statements describe the generation of this multiple sequence.

```
Register,        T(0–2),X,Y,Z
Decoder,         K(0–7)=T
Switch,          START(ON)
Clock,           P
/START(ON)/      T ← 0,
/K(0)*P/         T ← 1
/K(1)*P/         IF (X=1) THEN (T ← 2) ELSE (T ← 5)
/K(2)*P/         T ← 0                                    (4.9)
/K(3)*P/         T ← 0
/K(4)*P/         T ← 7
/K(5)*P/         T ← 6
/K(6)*P/         IF (Y=1) THEN (T ← 2) ELSE (T ←4)
/K(7)*P/         IF (Z=1) THEN (T ← 2) ELSE (T ← 3)
                 End
```

In the above description, each execution statement corresponds to one state of the counter. There are three conditional micro-statements which describe the branching shown in the state diagram. At any time, only one of the outputs of the decoder is activated to become the control signal.

4.2.3 Sequencing by a Multiple-phase Clock

The clock pulses in one clock cycle of a multiple-phase clock can be used as a control sequence. As an example, the following clock statement and the labels,

```
Clock,  P(1-4)
/P(1)/
/P(2)/                                                   (4.10)
/P(3)/
/P(4)/
```

declare a four-phase clock and the names of the pulses of these phases $P(1), \ldots, P(4)$. As shown, these pulses are used as labels to indicate the manner of sequencing.

One way to generate multiple control sequences by a multiple-phase clock is to use the combination of a control counter and a decoder. As an example, the description of such a generator is shown below,

Register,	T(0–2)
Decoder,	K(0–7)=T
Switch,	START(ON)
Clock,	P(1–3)
/START(ON)/	T ← 0
/K(0)∗P(1)/	
/K(0)∗P(2)/	
/K(0)∗P(3)/	T ← countup T
/K(1)∗P(1)/	
/K(1)∗P(2)/	
/K(1)∗P(3)/	T ← countup T
. . . . . .	
/K(7)∗P(1)/	
/K(7)∗P(2)/	
/K(7)∗P(3)/	T ← countup T

(4.11)

A block diagram of this generator is shown in Figure 4.4. As shown in the above statements, switch START initializes the sequence by resetting the T register to 0. The first sequence is activated by the decoder output K(0); the second sequence by the output K(1); and so forth. Each sequence consists of the three pulses of the clock cycle. There are eight sequences. During the last clock period of each sequence, the register T is incremented; this activates the next decoder output for the next sequence. The block called the control network in Figure 4.4 is a logic network consisting of 28 logical AND blocks for generating 28 control signals (or labels). Each sequence generated by this description gives a fixed number of control signals.

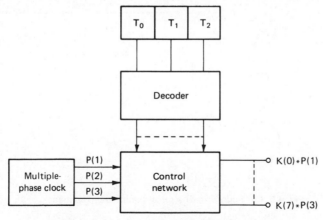

Fig. 4.4 Generation of multiple control sequences

4.3 A SERIAL COMPLEMENT SEQUENCE

With the previous descriptions of the clock, the execution statements, and the control sequence, some examples are now shown to illustrate that a sequence can accomplish a more complex function. The first example is a serial complement sequence.

The configuration for a complement sequence is shown in Figure 4.5. The word to be complemented is stored in register A. When the register is being shifted one bit to the right, the contents in bit $A(1)$ are complemented by the NOT block and then transferred to bit $A(5)$. After the right shift in this manner for five times, each bit of the contents of register A is complemented. Ring counter T is chosen to generate the control sequence, switch START to initialize the ring counter, light FINI to indicate completion of the sequence, and clock P to provide the clock pulse.

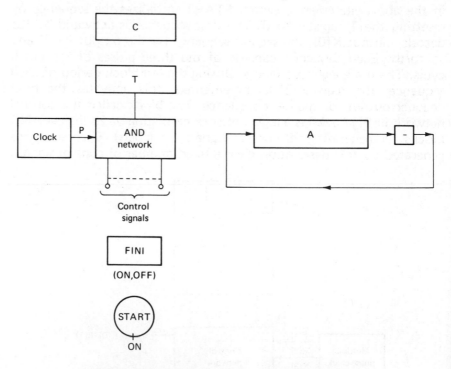

Fig. 4.5 Configuration of a serial complement sequence

4.3.1 By Repeating the Statements

The serial complement sequence is described below,

Register,	A(5–1)	$shift register
	T(1–5)	$control register
Switch,	START(ON)	$start switch
Light,	FINI(ON,OFF)	$completion indicating light
Clock,	P	
/START(ON)/	T ← 20, FINI ← OFF	(4.12)
/T(1)*P/	A ← A(1)'–A(5–2), T (1,2) ← 01	
/T(2)*P/	A ← A(1)'–A (5–2),T (2,3) ← 01	
/T(3)*P/	A ← A(1)'–A(5–2), T (3,4) ← 01	
/T(4)*P/	A ← A(1)'–A(5–2), T (4,5) ← 01	
/T(5)*P/	A ← A(1)'–A(5–2),T (5) ← 0, FINI ←ON	
	End	

Switch START initiates the sequence by setting register T to octal 20 and light FINI to the OFF condition. The labels and the control sequence in the above sequence are almost identical to those described in (4.5). Once initialized, the sequence executes the complement and rightshift micro-statements five times. The sequence stops when register T is cleared during the last execution.

4.3.2 By Using Block and Do Statements

In order to avoid the repeated writing of a group of micro-statements, the block statement and do statement are created. The *block statement* declares the name for a group of micro-statements. Whenever these micro-statements are specified in an execution statement, a *do statement* is used to call them. As an example, the above serial complement sequence is rewritten with the block and do statements and shown below,

Register,	T(1–5), A(5–1)	
Switch,	START(ON)	
Light,	FINI(ON,OFF)	
Clock,	P	
Block,	COMPSHIFT(A ← A(1)'–A(5–2))	
/START(ON)/	T ←20, FINI ← OFF	(4.13)
/T(1)*P/	DO COMPSHIFT, T(1,2) ← 01	
/T(2)*P/	DO COMPSHIFT, T(2,3) ← 01	
/T(3)*P/	DO COMPSHIFT, T(3,4) ← 01	
/T(4)*P/	DO COMPSHIFT, T(4,5) ← 01	
/T(5)*P/	DO COMPSHIFT, T(5) ← 0, FINI ← ON	
	End	

In the above description, the name COMPSHIFT is declared in the block statement to represent the complement and rightshift micro-statements, and a do statement is employed whenever these statements are specified.

4.3.3 By Forming a Loop

The use of block and do statements reduces the repeated writings of a group of micro-statements, but a better approach is to use a loop. Figure 4.6 shows the sequence chart of complementing the contents of register A serially. The beginning of the sequence is indicated by the START switch. The sequence is initialized by setting light FINI to the OFF condition and clearing counter C. The rightshift and complement micro-operations are next performed, and counter C is incremented. Counter C is then tested to determine whether it reaches 5. If it is not, the complement, rightshift, and count micro-operations are repeated; this forms a loop. If it is 5, the loop is broken off. The complementing is completed, and light FINI is turned on. The sequence chart offers a visual description of the sequence. Each rectangular block in the chart represents an execution statement. No label needs to be shown. Once the chart is prepared, the description by the statements can be readily obtained. From the sequence chart in Figure 4.6, we obtain,

Register,	A(5–1),	\$shift register	
	T(1–3),	\$ring register	
	C(0–2),	\$counter	
Switch,	START(ON)	\$start switch	
Light,	FINI(ON,OFF)	\$completion indicator	
Clock,	P		(4.14)
/START(ON)/	$T \leftarrow 4$, FINI $\leftarrow$ OFF, $C \leftarrow 0$		
/T(1)*P/	$A \leftarrow A(1)'$–A(5–2),		
	$C \leftarrow$ countup C, T(1,2) $\leftarrow$ 01		
/T(2)*P/	IF (C=5) THEN (T(2,3) $\leftarrow$ 01) ELSE (T(1,2) $\leftarrow$ 10)		
/T(3)*P/	FINI $\leftarrow$ ON		
	End		

If the number of bits of the register A is increased, the above description remains unchanged except for the subscripts involving the register A and the test condition for breaking off from the loop. This fact is not true for the description (4.12) or (4.13).

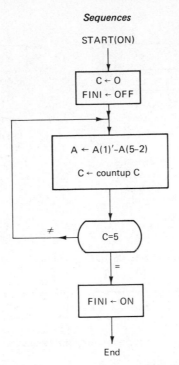

START(ON)

C ← 0
FINI ← OFF

A ← A(1)'–A(5–2)

C ← countup C

C=5

≠

=

FINI ← ON

End

Fig. 4.6 Sequence chart for a serial complement sequence

4.4 A SHIFT SEQUENCE

The basic shift operators, shl and shr, shift the contents of a register one bit to the left or right. If the register is to be shifted either left or right n bit positions, it can be achieved by a shift sequence.

4.4.1 Configuration

The configuration for a shift sequence is shown in Figure 4.7. Shift register A(0–7) receives an 8-bit number from input lines IN1(0–7); this is the number to be shifted. Counter C receives a 3-bit number from input lines IN2(0–2); this number indicates the number of shifts to be performed, and will not be zero. Single-bit register SH receives a one-bit code from input line IN3; this code indicates left (1) or right (0) shift. Ring counter T generates a control sequence and clock P provides the clock pulses. In addition, switch START starts the sequence and light FINI indicates the end of the sequence.

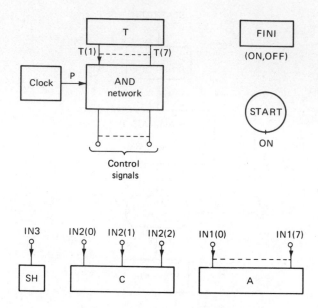

Fig. 4.7 Configuration for a shift sequence

4.4.2 Sequence Chart

The sequence chart for the shift sequence is shown in Figure 4.8. During initialization, light FINI is set to OFF, then the inputs from the input lines IN1, IN 2, and IN 3 are received by registers A, C, and SH. Counter C decrements one count. Register SH is tested; if it is 0, it is a left shift; otherwise, it is a right shift. Counter C is then tested to determine whether it has reached 0. If it has not, counter C decrements another count. Register SH is tested, register A is shifted, and counter C is tested again. This process continues on until C reaches 0; by then, the required number of bits has been shifted, and light FINI is turned on.

4.4.3 Sequence Description

To obtain the description of the organization for a shift sequence, the control signals from the ring counter are assigned to each box of the sequence chart; this gives all the labels. Since each box contains a micro-statement (or micro-statements) or a condition, the execution statement becomes readily available after the micro-statements for the control sequences are set up. The sequence description is now shown below,

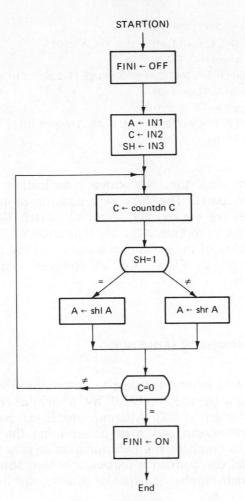

Fig. 4.8 Sequence chart for a shift sequence

Register,	A(0–7),	$shift register
	C(0–2),	$counter
	T(1–7),	$ring counter
	SH	$left or right shift indicator
Terminal,	IN1(0–7),	$input lines for the number
	IN2(0–2),	$input lines for number of shifts
	IN3	$input line for indicating left or right shift
Switch,	START(ON)	$start switch
Light,	FINI(ON,OFF)	$completion indicator
Clock,	P	

(4.15)

```
/START(ON)/    FINI ← OFF, T ← 100₈
/T(1)∗P/       A ← IN1, C ← IN2, SH ← IN3, T(1,2) ← 01
/T(2)∗P/       C ← countdn C, T(2,3) ← 01
/T(3)∗P/       IF (SH=1) THEN (T(3,4) ← 01) ELSE (T(3,5) ← 01)
/T(4)∗P/       A ← shl A, T(4,6) ← 01
/T(5)∗P/       A ← shr A, T(5,6) ← 01
/T(6)∗P/       IF (C=0) THEN (T(6,7) ← 01) ELSE (T(6,2) ← 01)
/T(7)∗P/       FINI ← ON, T(7) ← 0
               End
```

It is apparent now that the above organization description is divided into two parts. The first part consists of the declaration statements which are the register, terminal, switch, light, and clock statements; this part represents the configuration of Figure 4.7. The second part consists of the execution statements; this part represents the sequence chart in Figure 4.8. A complete description must include both parts.

4.5 A SERIAL COMPARISON SEQUENCE

To compare two binary numbers to determine whether they are equal or not can be accomplished by a parallel comparator as described by statement (2.28). Alternatively, it can be done by first performing a subtraction and then determining the difference. A practical way is to compare the two numbers serially by a single-bit comparator. Serial comparison is particularly favorable if one wishes to determine which number is larger or smaller, not merely equal or not equal.

4.5.1 Configuration

A configuration for determining whether two numbers are equal or not is shown in Figure 4.9. The two numbers are in the signed magnitude representation and initially stored in the shift registers A and B. As the numbers in registers A and B are being shifted bit-by-bit to the left, the two bits, one from each register, are being compared by a single-bit comparator. The single-bit comparator is the logical COIN block which gives a 1 or 0 when the two bits are the same or different respectively. If the numbers are not equal, single-bit register NE is set to 1; otherwise, single-bit register EQ is set to 1. Counter C controls the number of single-bit comparisons required. Control register T together with a decoder generates the control sequence. Light FINI, switch START, and clock P are all shown in Figure 4.9.

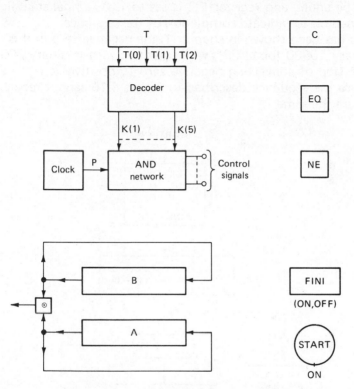

Fig. 4.9 Configuration for a serial comparison sequence

4.5.2 Sequence Chart

The sequence chart for the serial comparison sequence is shown in Figure 4.10. During initialization, registers EQ, NE, C, and T are reset to 0 and light FINI is set to OFF. The first step tests whether the numbers in registers A and B are negative zeros; if either one is, it is set to a positive zero. Then, the A(0) and B(0) bits, which are the sign bits at this first time, are compared. If they are not equal, register NE is set to 1 and the comparison is completed. If they are equal, C is incremented by one and then tested. If C is not equal to 5, registers A and B are both circulated to the left one bit. At this second time, the two most significant bits of the numbers are at A(0) and B(0) and are tested for equality again. If these two bits are not equal, register NE is set to 1; otherwise, the micro-operations of incrementing and then testing C and circulating A and B registers are repeated until either A(0) and B(0) are not equal or counter C reaches a value of 5. When C reaches the value of 5, the two numbers must be equal, and register EQ is set to 1. As a final step, light FINI is turned on to indicate completion of the sequence.

As has been shown in chapter 1, the negative zero in this example is binary 10000 (octal 20), while positive zero is binary 00000. The above step of converting negative zero to positive zero is necessary, because the sequence described in Figure 4.10 cannot recognize that they are the same.

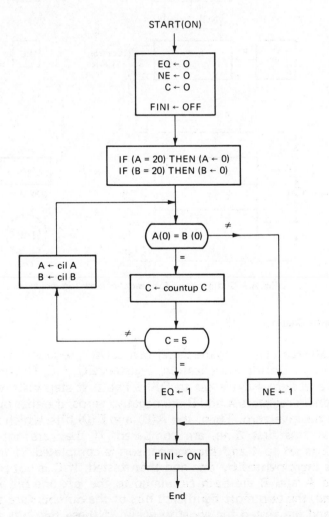

Fig. 4.10 Sequence chart for a serial comparison sequence

4.5.3 Sequence Description

From the configuration and the sequence chart, the description of the serial comparison sequence can be readily obtained. The control sequence is almost identical to that in statements (4.9). The sequence is described below.

Register,	EQ,	$equal indicator
	NE,	$unequal indicator
	A(0–4),	$A(0) is sign bit, A(1) is most sig. bit
	B(0–4),	$B(0) is sign bit, B(1) is most sig. bit
	C(0–2),	$counter
	T(0–2),	$control register
Decoder,	K(0–7)=T	
Switch,	START(ON)	
Light,	FINI(ON,OFF)	
Clock,	P	
/START(ON)/	EQ ← 0, NE ← 0, C ← 0, FINI ← OFF, T ← 0	
/K(0)∗P/	IF (A=20) THEN (A ← 0),	
	IF (B=20) THEN (B ← 0), T ← 1	
/K(1)∗P/	IF (A(0) = B(0)) THEN (T ← 2) ELSE (T ← 5)	
/K(2)∗P/	C ← countup C, T ← 3	
/K(3)∗P/	IF (C=5) THEN (T ← 6) ELSE (T ← 4)	
/K(4)∗P/	A ← cil A, B ← cil B, T ← 1	
/K(5)∗P/	NE ← 1, T ← 7	
/K(6)∗P/	EQ ← 1, T ← 7	
/K(7)∗P/	FINI ← ON	
	End	

(4.16)

In the above description, each execution statement describes one box of the sequence chart. The nine boxes result in the nine execution statements. When the comparison is completed, the two numbers are returned to registers A and B.

The last execution statement will be repeatedly executed as long as there is the clock pulse, because register T will not be advanced. The above comparison sequence can be modified to give a sequence which determines which number is larger if they are not equal.

4.6 A SERIAL ADDITION SEQUENCE

The basic addition operator, add, adds two unsigned numbers to give a sum. It is a parallel operation by means of a parallel adder. The addition is accomplished in one clock period. As has been shown in Figure 3.18, addition by a parallel adder may require as many single-bit full adders as the number of bits of the number. A more practical way is to add serially by addition sequence. It requires only one single-bit full adder at the expense of taking as many clock periods as the number of bits of the numbers.

4.6.1 Configuration

The configuration for a serial addition sequence is shown in Figure 4.11. The two unsigned binary numbers are initially stored in

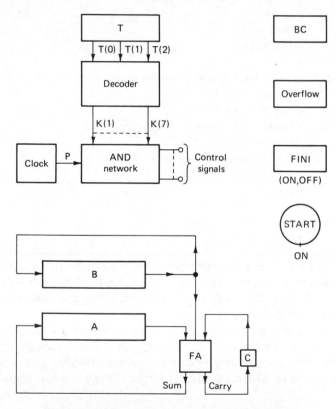

Fig. 4.11 Configuration for a serial addition sequence

the shift registers A and B. As the numbers in registers A and B are being shifted to the right bit by bit, the two bits, one from each register, are being added by the FA block. The FA block is a single-bit full adder which, in conjunction with the carry flipflop C, performs the single-bit addition. The sum is stored in register A by feeding each sum bit from the FA block to the left end of register A, and the original number in register A is lost. If there is a carry during the addition of the most significant bits of the two numbers, overflow occurs. It is indicated by setting register OVERFLOW to 1. Counter BC counts the number of single-bit addition required. Control register T together with a decoder generates the control sequence. In addition, there are light FINI, switch START, and clock P.

4.6.2 Sequence Chart

The sequence chart is shown in Figure 4.12. During initialization, registers C, BC, and OVERFLOW are reset to 0 and light FINI is set

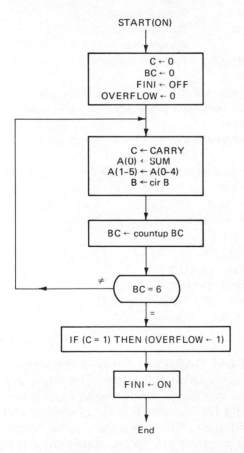

Fig. 4.12 Sequence chart for a serial addition sequence

to OFF. Next begins the loop whose cycling is controlled by counter BC. The single-bit addition and the incrementing and testing of counter BC are repeated until BC reaches a value of 6. Then, overflow is sensed and, if it occurs, indicated. Finally, light FINI is turned on.

4.6.3 Sequence Description

From the configuration in Figure 4.11 and the sequence chart in Figure 4.12, the serial addition sequence is described by the following statements:

Register,	A(0–5),	$shift register
	B(0–5),	$shift register
	T(0–2),	$control register
	BC(0–2),	$bit counter
	C,	$carry register
	OVERFLOW,	$overflow indicator
Decoder,	K(1–5)=T,	
Terminal,	SUM=A(5)⊕B(5)⊕C,	$sum output of full adder
	CARRY=A(5)∗B(5)+B(5)∗C+C∗A(5)	$carry output of full adder
Switch,	START(ON)	
Light,	FINI (ON,OFF)	
Clock,	P	(4.17)
/START(ON)/	T ← 1, BC ← 0, C ← 0, OVERFLOW ← 0, FINI ← OFF	
/K(1)∗P/	C ← CARRY,	
	A(0) ← SUM,	
	A(1–5) ← A(0–4),	
	B ← cir B,	
	T ← 2	
/K(2)∗P/	BC ← countup BC, T ← 3	
/K(3)∗P/	IF (BC=6)– THEN (T ← 4) ELSE (T ← 1)	
/K(4)∗P/	IF (C=1) THEN (OVERFLOW ← 1), T ← 5	
/K(5)∗P/	FINI ← ON, T ← 0	
	End	

In the above, SUM and CARRY defined in the terminal statement are the outputs of a single-bit full adder. The labels are assigned in the order of binary numbers. While register A is being replaced bit-by-bit by the SUM bit, register B is circulating its contents and is not lost after the addition. The sequence "stops," because decoder output K(0) neither controls any micro-statement nor advances the control counter T. If the adder is replaced by a single-bit full subtracter together with a proper change in setting the OVERFLOW register, one obtains a serial subtraction sequence for unsigned binary numbers.

4.7 A SIMPLE DIGITAL COMPUTER

The previous descriptions (4.14) through (4.17) show several examples of sequences. In a digital computer, there are many sequences, often one for each instruction of the instruction set. In order to illustrate organization and sequencing of multiple sequences, a simple digital computer is now described.

4.7.1 Configuration

This computer has a random access memory, six registers, three switches, one decoder, one parallel add-subtracter, and a clock. The configuration is shown in the block diagram of Figure 4.13.

This computer is organized from a memory unit, a control unit, and an arithmetic unit. The memory unit has a capacity of 4096 words and requires a 12-bit address. The word length is 12 bits. The 12-bit register C is the address register and the 18-bit register R is the buffer register of the memory.

The control unit consists of the 6-bit control register F to which a decoder is attached, the 12-bit program register D, the single-bit register G, the clock, and switches POWER, START, and STOP. Register D stores the next instruction address. Register F together with the decoder generates command signals K(0–16) for the eleven sequences. The single-phase clock generates a sequence of clock signals P. When register G is 1, the computer is in the go state; when 0, it is in the wait state. When turned one, switch POWER initializes, switch START starts, and switch STOP stops computer operation.

The arithmetic unit consists of the 18-bit register A, the previously mentioned register R, and an 18-bit parallel adder-subtracter. Register A serves as an accumulator where arithmetic and shift operations occur. The parallel adder-subtracter adds the number in register R to or subtracts the number in register R from the number in register A. This addition and subtraction treat the numbers as if they were unsigned binary numbers. Overflow is not indicated.

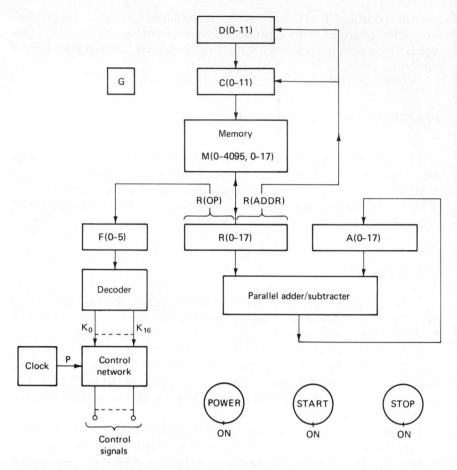

Fig. 4.13 Configuration of a simple, stored-program computer

The configuration of this computer is now described by the following statements:

$$
\begin{aligned}
\text{Register,} \quad & R(0\text{--}17), \\
& A(0\text{--}17), \\
& C(0\text{--}11), \\
& D(0\text{--}11), \\
& F(0\text{--}5), \\
& G
\end{aligned}
\tag{4.18}
$$

$$
\begin{aligned}
\text{Subregister,} \quad & R(OP)=R(0\text{--}5), \\
& R(ADDR)=R(6\text{--}17) \\
\text{Memory,} \quad & M(C)=M(0\text{--}4095,0\text{--}17) \\
\text{Decoder,} \quad & K(0\text{--}16)=F
\end{aligned}
$$

Switch,	POWER(ON),
	START(ON),
	STOP(ON)
Clock,	P
Terminal,	ADD=K(0),
	SUB=K(1),
	JOM=K(2),
	STO=K(3),
	JMP=K(4),
	SHR=K(5),
	CIL=K(6),
	CLA=K(7),
	STP=K(8),
	FETCH=K(9),
	WAIT=K(10)

In the above description, subregisters R(OP) and R(ADDR) are declared to denote respectively the op-code part and the address part of register R. Some of the terminals from the decoder are given symbolic names by the terminal statement to signify the sequences which the command signals at these terminals command.

4.7.2 Formats and Instruction Set

There are two formats for the words in the memory: instruction format and number format. As an instruction, the word consists of an op-code part and an address part. The op-code part is the leftmost 6 bits and the address part the rightmost 12 bits. As a number, the word consists of a sign bit (the leftmost bit) and 17 number bits. The numbers are in the signed two's complement representation (see section 1.2.1). The instruction and number formats are shown in Figure 4.14.

There are nine instructions: ADD, SUB, JOM, STO, JMP, SHR, CIL, CLA, and STP. These instructions and their op-codes are shown in Table 4.1 where m denotes a memory address in the address part of the instruction; this address can be either an instruction address or an operand address. Instruction SHR shifts the word in the accumulator one bit to the right, instruction CIL shifts the word in the accumulator circularly one bit to the left, and instruction STP stops the computer operation; these instructions require no address m. Instruction ADD adds the number in the memory location at address m to the number in the accumulator, and similarly instruction SUB subtracts the number from the number in the

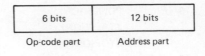

Op-code part   Address part

(a) Instruction format

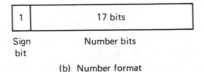

Sign   Number bits
bit
(b) Number format

Fig. 4.14 Word formats

accumulator; these addresses are operand addresses. Instruction JMP takes the next instruction from the memory location at address m and instruction JOM takes the next instruction from the memory location at address m if the number in the accumulator is negative; these addresses are instruction addresses. Instruction CLA clears the accumulator and then adds the number in the memory location at address m to the accumulator, and instruction STO stores the number in the accumulator into the memory location at address m; these addresses are again operand addresses.

Table 4.1 The Instruction Set

Instruction name	Symbolic code	Op-code
addition	ADD m	00
subtraction	SUB m	01
jump on minus	JOM m	02
store	STO m	03
jump	JMP m	04
shift right	SHR	05
circular leftshift	CIL	06
clear add	CLA m	07
stop	STP	10

Note: m denotes a memory address.

4.7.3 Sequence Chart

The sequential operation of this computer is described by the sequence chart in Figure 4.15. The operation consists of the start-stop sequence, the wait sequence, the fetch sequence, and the execution sequences.

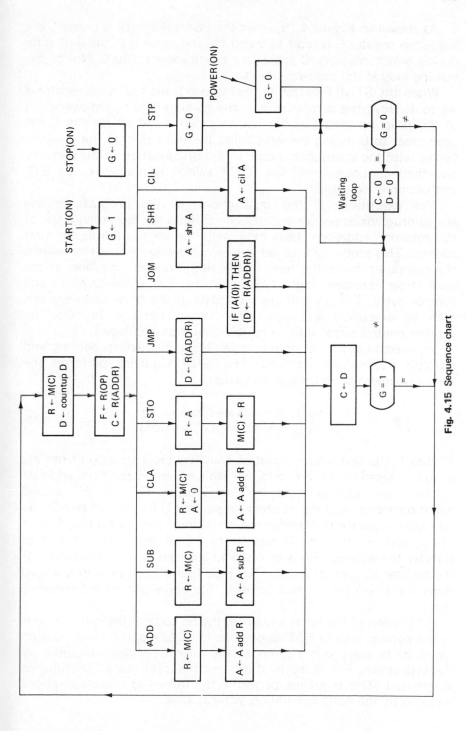

Fig. 4.15 Sequence chart

As shown in Figure 4.15, when the POWER switch is pressed, the start-stop register G is reset to 0 and the computer is in the wait state during which registers C and D are continually set to 0. Notice the waiting loop in the sequence chart.

When the START switch is next pressed, the start-stop register is set to 1. Now, the computer is in the go state and begins execution of the program stored in the memory. Since address register C has been reset to 0 during the wait state, the execution of the program begins with the instruction stored in the first location of the memory and then continues until the STOP switch is pressed or an STP instruction is executed.

The execution of the instructions of the program in the stored-program computer sequentially follows the ascending order of the memory addresses, beginning with the instruction at the first address. This sequence is called the *normal sequence.* In other words, the computer takes the next instruction from the location at the next larger memory address. Each instruction is executed in one control cycle. The *control cycle* consists of the *fetch sequence* and then an *execution sequence.* One control cycle is followed by another control cycle until computer operation is stopped.

In executing the fetch sequence, both instruction address and operand address are involved. The fetch sequence performs the following micro-operations in two steps,

$$\text{Step 1, } R \leftarrow M(C) \text{ and } D \leftarrow \text{countup } D$$
$$\text{Step 2, } F \leftarrow R(OP) \text{ and } C \leftarrow R(ADDR)$$

(4.19)

In step 1, the first micro-operation transfers the instruction from the memory location at the address (this is an instruction address) specified by address register C to register R, and the second micro-operation increments program counter D by one. In step 2, the two micro-operations transfer the op-code of the instruction now in the op-code part of the R register to the control register F and to transfer the address (this is an operand address) in the address part of the register to address register C. These four micro-operations in two steps are shown by the two boxes in the upper part of the sequence chart.

At the end of the fetch sequence, the op-code of the instruction is in the control register F. This op-code initiates a particular execution sequence to carry out a series of the micro-operations required by the instruction. For example, if the op-code is 00, the ADD sequence is initiated. This sequence performs the following micro-operations required by the ADD instruction in three steps,

Step 1, R ← M(C),

Step 2, A ← A add R   (4.20)

Step 3, C ← D

The first micro-operation fetches the operand from the memory and stores it in register R. The second micro-operation adds the number in register R to the number in register A by means of the parallel adder. The third micro-operation transfers the next instruction address in register D to address register C. These three steps are shown in the sequence chart. At the completion of the ADD sequence, register G is interrogated. If it contains a 1, the computer continues with the fetch sequence.

If the op-code is 01, the SUB sequence is initiated. The sequence is identical to the ADD sequence except a subtraction by the parallel subtracter is performed and is also shown in the sequence chart. If the op-code is 04, the JMP sequence is initiated. This sequence performs the following micro-operations in two steps,

Step 1, D ← R(ADDR),

Step 2, C ← D   (4.21)

The first micro-operation transfers the instruction address in the address part of register R to the D register, and the second micro-operation transfers this instruction address from the D register to the C register. The two steps of this sequence are shown in the sequence chart. If the op-code is 02, the JOM sequence is initiated. This sequence is identical to the JMP sequence except that micro-operation, D ← R(ADDR), is executed if the number in the A register is negative. The steps for this and other execution sequences are all shown in the sequence chart. There are nine execution sequences: ADD, SUB, CLA, STO, JMP, JOM, SHR, CIL, and STP which implement respectively the nine instructions. Each of these sequences takes two or three steps except the STP sequence which clears register G and then enters the waiting loop.

4.7.4 Statement Description

With the addition of control signals generated by the decoder and the clock, the sequences in the sequence chart can be described by the following statements,

Comment, here begins the computer sequences.

Comment, here begins the start-stop sequence.   (4.22)

/POWER(ON)/   G ← 0, F ← 12_8

/START(ON)/ $G \leftarrow 1$

/STOP(ON)/ $G \leftarrow 0$

Comment, here begins the wait sequence.

/WAIT*P/   IF (G=0) THEN (C $\leftarrow$ 0, D $\leftarrow$ 0) ELSE (F $\leftarrow$ 11_8)

Comment, here begins the fetch sequence.

/FETCH*P/   R $\leftarrow$ M(C), D $\leftarrow$ countup D, F $\leftarrow$ 15_8

/K(13)*P/   F $\leftarrow$ R(OP), C $\leftarrow$ R(ADDR)

Comment, here begins the execution sequences.

Comment, here begins the stop sequence.

/STP*P/   G $\leftarrow$ 0, F $\leftarrow$ 12_8

Comment, here begins the add sequence.

/ADD*P/   R $\leftarrow$ M(C), F $\leftarrow$ 14_8

/K(12)*P/   A $\leftarrow$ A add R, F $\leftarrow$ 13_8

Comment, here begins the sub sequence.

/SUB*P/   R $\leftarrow$ M(C), F $\leftarrow$ 17_8

/K(15)*P/   A $\leftarrow$ A sub R, F $\leftarrow$ 13_8

Comment, here begins the jump sequence.

/JMP*P/   D $\leftarrow$ R(ADDR), F $\leftarrow$ 13_8

Comment, here begins the jump on minus sequence.

/JOM*P/   IF (A(0)) THEN (D $\leftarrow$ R(ADDR)), F $\leftarrow$ 13_8

Comment, here begins the store sequence.

/STO*P/   R $\leftarrow$ A, F $\leftarrow$ 20_8

/K(16)*P/   M(C) $\leftarrow$ R, F $\leftarrow$ 13_8

Comment, here begins the shift-right one-bit sequence.

/SHR*P/   A $\leftarrow$ shr A, F $\leftarrow$ 13_8

Comment, here begins the circulate-left one-bit sequence.

/CIL*P/   A $\leftarrow$ cil A, F $\leftarrow$ 13_8

Comment, here begins the clear add sequence.

/CLA*P/   R $\leftarrow$ M(C), A $\leftarrow$ 0, F $\leftarrow$ 16_8

/K(14)*P/   A $\leftarrow$ A add R, F $\leftarrow$ 13_8

/K(11)*P/   C $\leftarrow$ D, IF (G) THEN (F $\leftarrow$ 11_8) ELSE (F $\leftarrow$ 12_8)

                   End

The above description consists of 12 groups with each group being headed by a comment statement. These 12 groups describe the start-stop sequence, the wait sequence, the fetch sequence, and the nine execution sequences. Except the start-stop sequence, the first execution statement of each of these groups is indicated in the label by command signals such as WAIT and ADD; these command signals have been defined in terminal statements (4.18). The operators in the above description (add, sub, shr, cil, and countup) are those defined in Tables 3.2 and 3.3 in chapter 3.

If the STOP switch is pressed while the computer is executing an instruction, the computer does not stop immediately but proceeds until execution of the current instruction is completed. Upon being started again by pressing the START switch, the computer begins again by fetching the instruction in the first location of the memory. These operations and sequencing can be noticed from the above description as well as from the sequence chart.

4.8 PROCEDURAL DESCRIPTIONS

If the order of the statements in descriptions (4.15) through (4.17) for the three sequences is changed (except the last End statement), the description is still valid (though it may become less readable). This order-independent property of the description by statements is called nonprocedural. On the other hand, if a description is *procedural,* the order of the statements of a sequence represents the order of the sequential operations of the sequence. In this case, parallel operations are still permissible, because there can be more than one micro-statement in one execution statement.

It is sometimes desirable to describe a sequence in a procedural manner, particularly when one is not concerned about the generation of the control signals. There are the following differences between the procedural and nonprocedural descriptions.

a. Declaration statements for generating control signals are not needed.
b. The normal order of the statements in the description for a sequence is the order of the sequential operations of the sequence.
c. A goto micro-statement is created for changing the order from the normal order.
d. Symbolic labels are required only for those statements that are used in conjunction with the goto micro-statements. The names of the symbolic labels can be arbitrarily chosen.
e. A semicolon is employed to indicate the end of an execution statement. It should be noted that in a procedural description an execution statement may not have a label.

4.8.1 A Shift Sequence

As an example of a procedural description, description (4.15) for the shift sequence is rewritten and shown below.

Register,	A(0–7),	
	C(0–2),	
	SH	
Terminal,	IN1(0–7),	
	IN2(0–2),	
	IN3,	
Switch,	START(ON),	
Light,	FINI(ON,OFF),	(4.23)
	IF (START(ON)) THEN (FINI←OFF) ELSE (GOTO T8);	
	A ← IN1, C ← IN2, SH ← IN3;	
/T2/	C ← countdn C;	
	IF (SH≠1) THEN (GOTO T5);	
	A ← shl A, GOTO T6;	
/T5/	A ← shr A;	
/T6/	IF (C≠0) THEN (GOTO T2);	
	FINI←ON;	
/T8/	End	

In comparing descriptions (4.15) and (4.23), register T and clock P in the former disappear. Similarly, micro-statements in setting a constant to register T also disappear. In description (4.23), a semicolon appears at the end of each execution statement. Notice that the order of executing the statements in these two descriptions is actually the same, though there is need for only four labels in description (4.23). Symbolic labels T2, T5, and T6 are required because they are called by their respective micro-statements. The statements in description (4.23) are executed in the following order. Setting light FINI to the OFF condition is first executed. Inputs IN1, IN2, and IN3 are next transferred to registers A, C, and SH respectively. This is followed by decrementing C by one, then by testing register SH for 1, and so forth. Thus, to rewrite the nonprocedural description (4.15) into a procedural one is a simple task.

4.8.2 A Simple Digital Computer

As another example of procedural description, the simple digital computer described by statements (4.18) and (4.22) is now described by the following procedural description:

Register,	R(0–17),	
	A(0–17),	
	C(0–11),	(4.24)
	D(0–11),	
	G	

Subregister,   R(OP)=R(0-5),

                R(ADDR)=R(6-17)

Memory,   M(C)=M(0-4095,0-17)

Switch,   POWER(ON),

                START(ON),

                STOP(ON);

Comment, here begins the computer sequences.

Comment, here begins the start-stop sequence.

          IF (POWER(ON)) THEN (G←0) ELSE (GOTO FINI);

          IF (START(ON)) THEN (G←1) ELSE (GOTO FINI);

          IF (STOP(ON)) THEN (G←0, GOTO FINI);

Comment, here begins the wait sequence.

/WAIT/   IF (G=0) THEN (C←0, D ←0), GOTO SHARE;

Comment, here begins the fetch sequence.

/FETCH/   R ←M(C), D←countup D;

          F←R(OP), C←R(ADDR);

          IF (F=0) THEN (GOTO ADD),

          IF (F=1) THEN (GOTO SUB),

          IF (F=2) THEN (GOTO JOM),

          IF (F=3) THEN (GOTO STO).

          IF (F=4) THEN (GOTO JMP),

          IF (F=5) THEN (GOTO SHR),

          IF (F=6) THEN (GOTO CIL),

          IF (F=7) THEN (GOTO CLA),

          IF (F=8) THEN (GOTO STP),

          IF (F=9) THEN (GOTO FETCH),

          IF (F=10) THEN (GOTO WAIT);

Comment, here begin the execution sequences.

Comment, here begins the stop sequence.

/STP/   G←0, GOTO WAIT;

Comment, here begins the add sequence.

/ADD/   R←M(C);

          A←A add R, GOTO SHARE;

Comment, here begins the sub sequence.

/SUB/   R←M(C);

          A←A sub R, GOTO SHARE;

Comment, here begins the jump sequence.

/JMP/   D←R(ADDR), GOTO SHARE;

Comment, here begins the jump on minus sequence.

/JOM/   IF (A(C)) THEN (D←R(ADDR)), GOTO SHARE;

Comment, here begins the store sequence.

/STO/   R←A;

          M(C)←R, GOTO SHARE;

Comment, here begins the shift-right one-bit sequence.

/SHR/   A←shr A, GOTO SHARE;

Comment, here begins the circulate-left one-bit sequence.

/CIL/   A←cil A, GOTO SHARE;

Comment, here begins the clear add sequence.

/CLA/   R←M(C), A←0;

           A←A add R;

/SHARE/   C←D, IF (G) THEN (GOTO FETCH) ELSE (GOTO WAIT);

/FINI/   End

In the above description, the operation of the three switches, POWER, START, and STOP, is sequentialized; thus, the procedural description produces some differences from the nonprocedural description. Furthermore, the decoding of the op-code is described by an execution statement which consists of eleven conditional micro-statements.

PROBLEMS

4.1   If the control sequence in description (4.14) is to be generated by a control register instead of a ring counter, what changes are to be made in the description? What changes are to be made if a multiple-phase clock is used?

4.2   What changes are to be made in the description (4.14) if register A is replaced by register B(1–3,5–7,9–12)?

4.3   Describe a control sequence which generates the states of the state diagram in Figure 3.16.

4.4   If the 3-bit number from input lines IN2(0–2) in description (4.15) can be zero, what changes should be made in the sequence chart and in the description(4.15)?

4.5   Given register A(0–29), describe a shift sequence which is similar to the sequence (4.15) but shifts register A to the left or right two bits at a time. Input lines IN2(0–2) now indicate the number of two-bit shifts.

4.6   Describe a sequence which counts the number of 1's in the 25-bit register and stores the answer in counter C. Register A receives the 25 bits serially from an input line.

4.7   Given a binary word stored in register A(0–35), describe a sequence which serially generates an odd parity check and stores it in a single-bit register. Require a sequence chart and sequence description.

4.8 Given two 5-bit binary numbers in the signed magnitude representation, describe a serial comparison sequence which determines whether they are equal and, if they are not, which is larger?

4.9 Repeat problem 4.7 when the two binary numbers are in signed 2's complement representation.

4.10 What changes are to be made in the serial addition sequence (4.17) so that the two binary numbers can be added
(a) at two bits at a time,
(b) at three bits at a time
What kinds of adders are required for the above two cases?

4.11 What changes are to be made in the serial addition sequence (4.17) if the binary numbers are in the signed 2's complement representation?

4.12 Repeat problem 4.11 if the numbers are in the signed magnitude representation.

4.13 Repeat problem 4.11 if the numbers are in the signed 1's complement representation.

4.14 A memory MEM(0–127,0–11) is given together with buffer register $X(0–11)$, address register $M(6–0)$, and two single-bit registers READ and WRITE for the read and write operations. The memory stores instructions each of which has two fields: MEM(,0–4) and MEM(,5–11). The former field represents an operation code and the latter field a memory address. Describe a fetch sequence which takes an instruction from the memory, then stores the operation code field in operation register F and the address field in address register M, and finally reads another word from the memory.

4.15 Repeat problem 4.14 except with the following changes:
(a) the memory is replaced by MEM(0–127,0–5),
(b) the buffer register is replaced by X(0–5),
(c) each instruction still has 12 bits. (This means that two memory read operations are required to take an instruction out of the memory.)

4.16 Rewrite description (4.16) for the serial comparison sequence into a procedural description.

4.17 Rewrite description (4.17) for the serial add sequence into a procedural description.

4.18 Given the following statements

Clock,	P
Register,	A, B, C, D
Terminal,	EXE
/P/	A ← B
/EXE∗P/	C ← D

When clock pulse P occurs, the first execution statement is executed, but the execution of the second execution statement depends on the value of terminal EXE being 1 or 0. Rewrite these two execution statements for use in a procedural description.

5

Simulation of

Computer

Organizations

In order to become familiar with functional organization and sequential operation of a digital computer, simulation on an available digital computer is very instructive. This chapter first discusses the choice of simulation languages and then illustrates simulations of computer elements, micro-operations, sequences, and a simple, stored-program computer. Simulations by using the Computer Design Language Simulator are also illustrated.

5.1 SIMULATION LANGUAGES

To simulate on a digital computer, one has to select a simulation language. There are a number of considerations when one selects a simulation language for simulating a computer organization and sequential operations. First, the language should have a simulator available for simulation. It should be nonambiguous, concise, precise, and highly expressive in binary representation and binary manipulation. It should have means of expressing parallel operations, timing signals, control commands, and serial and parallel transfers. Last but not least, the language should be close to natural language so that it can serve well the important functions of communication and documentation.

There are two choices, the use of an available algorithmic programming language and the use of a language specially developed for simulation of digital computer organization. In this chapter, one language from each of these two types of languages is chosen and simulations by using both languages are illustrated.

5.1.1 Use of an Algorithmic Programming Language

The use of an available algorithmic programming language is a practical choice, because the compiler (now used as a simulator) is also available. The most common of these languages are Fortran (10,18), MAD (9,17), Algol (6), and PL/1 (34). In this chapter, Fortran is chosen as one simulation language as it is the most widely used algorithmic programming language. The particular dialect of Fortran used here is the Fortran IV language (10). For this version, the word length of a Fortran constant or variable is 36 bits (unless otherwise specified such as a double precision word). As will be shown, Fortran allows five types of constants and variables. However, only two types (integer and logical) are useful because simulations described in this chapter do not deal with floating-point numbers, but with integers (actually bits) and logical quantities.

There are three Fortran logical operators, .NOT., .AND., and .OR. which operate on a logical expression and give a truth value of .TRUE. or .FALSE.. For the above-mentioned version 13, there are three special logical operators, AND, OR, and COMPL, which operate on all the 36 bits of the 7090/7094 word. When any one of these three operators is used, the result gives a real number. In order to make the equivalent of a real number to an integer, an EQUIVALENCE statement is required as will be shown. These three special operators are quite useful and will be used often in this chapter.

5.1.2 Use of a Computer Simulation Language

The available algorithmic programming languages such as Fortran, MAD, and Algol are designed primarily for computational purposes. There are difficulties in describing computer elements, micro-operations, timing and control signals, sequences, and parallel operations. Therefore, simulation by such an algorithmic language is often not precise or not descriptive.

A computer simulation language is a specially designed language for describing the functional organization and sequential operations of a digital computer. As a result, the difficulties encountered in using an available algorithmic programming language are removed. A number of such computer simulation languages that have been proposed or developed differ from one another in the degree of closeness and preciseness to the physical implementation. Most of these simulation languages have no simulator.

In this chapter, the Computer Design Language (CDL) (14) is selected as another simulation language. As will be shown, the CDL is a subset of the notations for describing or specifying the computer organization and operations in the previous chapters. In addition, the CDL simulator has been available since the summer of 1967.

5.2 SIMULATION OF COMPUTER ELEMENTS

Computer elements were described in Chapter 2. To simulate them by Fortran programming, the registers, memories, switches, and lights are described by DIMENSION or INTEGER statements. The logic network is described by arithmetic statements with logical expressions. The delay element is incorporated by properly sequencing the statements.

5.2.1 Registers

Registers are described by DIMENSION or INTEGER statements. Consider registers B and P,

$$\text{Register,} \quad B(1-5), \quad P(3-0) \tag{5.1}$$

The description of these registers by Fortran statements is,

$$\begin{array}{l} \text{COMMENT } B(1-5), \ P(3-0) \\ \text{INTEGER } B, P \end{array} \tag{5.2}$$

where one memory word of 36 bits each is reserved for registers B and P. The subscripts for identifying each bit of the register in statement (5.1) are not available in statement (5.2). The least significant 5 bits of integer variable B and the least significant 4 bits of integer variable P represent registers B and P, respectively. The use of only 5 bits of integer B for register B and 4 bits of integer P for register P is noted by the COMMENT statement; this use of COMMENT statement reminds the programmer that only a part of

36 bits represents the register. To describe a register with more than 36 bits, two or more memory words are needed.

In the remainder of this chapter, the least significant bits of an integer are employed to simulate the register unless otherwise specified.

To describe a subregister or a casregister, masks and Fortran logical operators are also needed. Consider subregister R(OP),

$$
\begin{array}{ll}
\text{Register,} & \text{R(0–17)} \\
\text{Subregister,} & \text{R(OP)=R(0–5)}
\end{array}
\tag{5.3}
$$

which is the op-code part of register R, not a new register. The description of this subregister by Fortran statements is,

```
INTEGER  R, ROP
EQUIVALENCE  (ROP,REAL)                    (5.4)
DATA  MASKOP/0770000/
REAL=AND(MASKOP,R)
ROP=ROP/4096
```

where the least significant 18 bits of integer R represent register R. Mask MASKOP is defined by the DATA statement. Integer ROP represents the subregister R(OP). MASKOP and the Fortran logical operator AND extract the op-code part of register R. The result of using the special operator gives a real number REAL. The above EQUIVALENCE statement makes real number REAL equivalent to integer ROP. And division of ROP by 4096 shifts the op-code part to the correct 12-bit positions. Notice that ROP is a new integer, but not a part of integer R as it should be.

Consider the following casregister AQ,

$$
\begin{array}{ll}
\text{Register,} & \text{A(0–5), Q(0–5)} \\
\text{Casregister,} & \text{AQ(0–10)=A–Q(1–5)}
\end{array}
\tag{5.5}
$$

which consists of register A and the least significant 5 bits of register Q. Thus, casregister AQ is not a new register. The description of this casregister by Fortran statements is,

```
INTEGER  A, Q, AQ
DATA  MASK/037/
EQUIVALENCE  (J,REAL)                      (5.6)
REAL=AND(Q,MASK)
AQ=A*32+J
```

where the least significant 6 bits of integers A and Q are regarded as registers A and Q, respectively. Subregister Q(1–5) is obtained by mask MASK and the special Fortran logical AND operation. The EQUIVALENCE statement is required again because of the use of the special Fortran logical operator which gives the result a real number. Multiplication of integer A by 32 shifts integer A 5 bits to the left. Cascading of registers A and Q(1–5) is conveniently obtained by addition. Notice that integer AQ is a new integer, not a cascade of original integers as it should be.

5.2.2 Memories

Memories are also described by DIMENSION or INTEGER statements. Consider memory M with buffer register B and address register C as described below,

$$\text{Register,} \quad B(0-5), C(0-5)$$
$$\text{Memory,} \quad M(C)=M(0-63,0-5) \tag{5.7}$$

The description of this memory by Fortran statements is,

$$\text{COMMENT} \quad M(C)=M(0-63,0-5)$$
$$\text{DIMENSION } M(64) \tag{5.8}$$
$$\text{INTEGER B, C}$$

Since the variable name of the memory begins with letter M, a DIMENSION statement suffices. Notice that the memory address specified by the subscript of the DIMENSION statement begins with 1 through 64, while the actual address of the memory begins with 0 through 63.

5.2.3 Switches and Lights

Switches and lights are simulated by using INTEGER statements. Consider switches START, POWER, and SWQ, and lights ALARM, LTSIGN, and LTQ,

$$\text{Switch,} \quad \text{START(ON), POWER(ON,OFF), SWQ(0–5)(ON)}$$
$$\text{Light,} \quad \text{ALARM(ON), LTSIGN(ON,OFF), LTQ(0–5)(ON,OFF)} \tag{5.9}$$

The description of these switches and lights by Fortran statements is,

```
INTEGER START, POWER, SWQ(6)
INTEGER ALARM, LTSIGN, LTQ(6),ON,OFF                    (5.10)
DATA ON,OFF/2HON,3HOFF/
```

The names of the switches and lights are declared as integers. Each switch or light is assigned one memory word. The switch positions and light conditions are regarded as alphanumerical constants and their names are defined by the DATA statement.

Switches with more than two positions and lights with more than two conditions may be similarly handled. Consider switch MODE and light COLOR,

```
Switch,   MODE(DM,AEM,IM,PM)
                                                        (5.11)
Light,    COLOR(RED,BLUE,GREEN,OFF)
```

The description of the above switch and light by Fortran statements is,

```
INTEGER MODE, DM, AEM, IM, PM
INTEGER COLOR, RED, BLUE, GREEN, OFF
                                                        (5.12)
DATA DM,AEM,IM,PM/2HDM,3HAEM,2HIM,2HPM/
DATA COLOR,RED,BLUE,GREEN,OFF/5HCOLOR,3HRED,4HBLUE,5HGREEN,3HOFF/
```

5.2.4 Logic Networks

As presented in Chapter 2, a logic network is described by a terminal statement. Consider the parallel complementer described by statements (2.19) and (2.20). There are three inputs A(0–2) and three outputs B(0–2). Each output gives the complement of the respective input. The description of this complementer by Fortran statements is,

```
INTEGER  A,  B
EQUIVALENCE (J1,B1), (J2,B2), (J3,B3)
DATA  M1,M2,M3/04,02,01/
B1=AND((A+4),M1)                                        (5.13)
B2=AND((A+2),M2)
B3=AND((A+1),M3)
B=J1+J2+J3
```

The least significant 3 bits of integers A and B represent respectively register A and the outputs. Bits A(0), A(1), and A(2) are complemented by adding 4, 2, and 1, respectively. They are extracted by masks M1, M2, and M3 and the special Fortran logical AND operation and are then assembled by addition to give the outputs. Again, the use of the EQUIVALENCE statement is due to the use of the Fortran logical operator AND.

As also mentioned in Chapter 2, a decoder may be described by a decoder statement. Consider the following decoder,

$$\text{Register,} \quad N(0\text{--}2)$$
$$\text{Decoder,} \quad K(0\text{--}5)=N \tag{5.14}$$

This decoder may be described by a Fortran Computed GO TO statement as follows:

$$N1=N+1$$
$$\text{GO TO } (1,2,3,4,5,6), N1 \tag{5.15}$$

where numbers 1, . . ., 6 are Fortran statement numbers. Fortran statement number begins with 1, while the subscript for terminal K begins with 0. The arithmetic statement for N1 is provided to offset this discrepancy.

A decoder may also be simulated by an Assigned GO TO statement or by a combination of a DO statement and Logical IF statements. Examples of such decoder simulations will be shown.

5.3 SIMULATION OF MICRO-OPERATIONS

As stated in Chapter 3, a micro-operation is an elementary, functional operation physically built into the digital computer. A micro-operation is described by a micro-statement. A micro-statement can be a simple micro-statement or a conditional micro-statement. A simple micro-statement can be translated into a Fortran arithmetic statement. A conditional micro-statement is translated into one or more Fortran IF statements. The descriptions of various micro-operations by Fortran statements are presented below.

5.3.1 Set-constant Micro-operations

A set-constant micro-operation sets a register to a particular constant, a switch to a particular position, or a light to a particular light condition. For example, the following micro-statements describe set-constant micro-operations:

$$
\begin{aligned}
&\text{Register,} && A(0\text{--}17),\ F(1\text{--}4),\ C(6\text{--}1) \\
&\text{Switch,} && \text{CLEAR(ON)} \\
&\text{Light,} && \text{FINI(ON,OFF)} \\
&A \leftarrow 0 \\
&F \leftarrow 11 \\
&C \leftarrow 77 \\
&\text{CLEAR} \leftarrow \text{ON} \\
&\text{FINI} \leftarrow \text{OFF}
\end{aligned}
\tag{5.16}
$$

where numbers 11 and 77 are octal. The description of these simple micro-statements by Fortran statements is,

```
INTEGER  A, F, C
INTEGER  CLEAR,  FINI,ON,OFF
DATA  ON,OFF/2HON,3HOFF/
A=0
F=9
C=63
CLEAR=ON
FINI=OFF
```
(5.17)

The least significant bits of integers A,F, and C represent registers A,F, and C. Note that octal numbers 11 and 77 are converted respectively into decimal numbers 9 and 63 for use in the Fortran statements. The names of the switch and light which are regarded as alphanumerical constants are defined by the DATA statement.

5.3.2 Simple Transfer Micro-operations

A simple transfer micro-operation transfers the contents of a register, a subregister, or a casregister to another register, subregister, or casregister. For example, the following statements describe a simple transfer micro-operation from register D to register C,

$$
\begin{aligned}
&\text{Register,} && C(0\text{--}5),\ D(0\text{--}5) \\
&&& C \leftarrow D
\end{aligned}
\tag{5.18}
$$

The description of this transfer micro-operation by Fortran statements is,

> INTEGER   C, D
>
> C=D

(5.19)

Consider the following simple transfer micro-operations from a subregister to register F and from a casregister to register G,

> Register,   F(0–5), R(0–17), A(0–5), Q(0–5), G(0–10)
>
> F ← R(0–5)
>
> G ← A–Q(1–5)

(5.20)

The descriptions of these micro-operations by Fortran statements are,

> INTEGER   F, R, A, Q, G
>
> EQUIVALENCE (J,REALJ), (K,REALK)
>
> DATA   MASK1, MASK2/0770000,037/
>
> REALK=AND(R,MASK1)
>
> F=K/4096
>
> REALJ=AND(Q,MASK2)
>
> G=A*32+J

(5.21)

The least significant bits of integers F,R,A,Q, and G represent the registers. The expressions in the above arithmetic statements are similar to those in statements (5.4) and (5.6).

For memory transfers, consider the following memory transfer micro-operation

> B←M(C)

(5.22)

for the memory described by statement (5.7). The description by Fortran statements is,

> DIMENSION   M(64)
>
> INTEGER   B, C
>
> C=1
>
> B=M(C)

(5.23)

Here, the address represented by integer C is chosen 1, but it can be any value except 0.

5.3.3 Unary Micro-operations

A unary micro-operation is one which employs a unary operator. Basic unary operators have been shown in Table 3.2 in Chapter 3. Consider the following unary micro-operations,

```
Register, A(0–5), B(0–5), C(0–5), D(0–5), E(0–5)
A ← A'
B ← countup B
C ← countdn C                                    (5.24)
D ← shl D
E ← shr E
```

The descriptions of these micro-operations by Fortran statements are,

```
INTEGER  A, B, C, D, E
EQUIVALENCE  (J,REALJ), (A,REALA), (D,REALD), (E,REALE)
DATA  MASK/077/
REALJ=COMPL(A)
REALA=AND(J,MASK)
A=REALA                                          (5.25)
B=B+1
B=MOD(B,64)
C=C–1
C=MOD(C,64)
REALD=AND((D*2),MASK)
REALE=AND((E/2),MASK)
```

The least significant bits of integers A, B, C, D, and E represent the registers. The complement micro-operation is first operated on by the Fortran special logical COMPL operation and then extracted by mask MASK and the Fortran special logical AND operation. The up-count and down-count micro-operations are merely addition and subtraction of one, respectively. Function MOD is a Fortran built-in function which makes the counting to be modular 64. The left-shift and right-shift micro-operations are obtained respectively by multiplication and division of 2 and then by extraction of the proper bits.

5.3.4 Binary Micro-operations

A binary micro-operation is one which employs a binary operator. Basic binary operators have been shown in Table 3.3 in Chapter 3.

Consider the following binary micro-operations,

```
Register,  A(0-2), B(0-2), C(0-2)
Register, X(1-9), Y(1-9), Z(1-9)
A←A+C
B←B*C                                                    (5.26)
X←X add Z
Y←Y sub Z
```

The descriptions of these binary micro-operations by Fortran statements are,

```
INTEGER   A, B, C, X, Y, Z
EQUIVALENCE (A,AREAL), (B,BREAL), (X,XREAL), (Y,YREAL)
DATA   MASK/0777/
AREAL=OR(A,C)                                            (5.27)
BREAL=AND(B,C)
XREAL=AND((X+Z),MASK)
YREAL=AND((Y-Z),MASK)
```

The Fortran special logical operators OR and AND represent operators + and * almost perfectly. Since operators add and sub respectively add and subtract unsigned binary numbers, Fortran arithmetical operators + and − represent operators add and sub well except when an overflow occurs. Since operators add and sub do not accommodate the overflow, the overflow is removed in the above Fortran statements by MASK and the special logical AND operation.

5.3.5 Use of Fortran Subprograms

The basic operator (as well as the special operator) can be specified in Fortran by using Function subprogram or Subroutine subprogram. When the micro-operation results in a single value (i.e., one integer), the operator is specified by a Function subprogram; if it results in more than one value, the operator should be specified by a Subroutine subprogram.

Consider the following unary micro-operation,

```
Register,  A(0-8)
A←cil A                                                  (5.28)
```

This micro-operation circularly shifts the 9 bits in register A one bit to the left. The description in Fortran statements is,

```
INTEGER  A,CIL
A=CIL(A)
- - - - - - -
- - - - - - -
INTEGER FUNCTION CIL(I)
INTEGER 0400, 0777
DATA 0400,0777/0400,0777/
EQUIVALENCE (J,RJ), (K,RK)
RJ=AND(I,0400)
RK=AND((I*2),0777)
IF (J.NE.0) K=K+1
CIL=K
RETURN
END
```

In the above, the least significant 9 bits of integer A represent register A. Function CIL is defined as a Fortran integer function with parameter I. The left-shifting is carried out by multiplication of 2, extraction by masking, and conditional addition of 1 for the circulated bit. Since the result from using any of the three special Fortran logical operators is a real number, the EQUIVALENCE statement specifies equivalence of real numbers RJ and RK respectively with integers J and K. Note that CIL must be declared as an integer in the manner shown above.

5.3.6 Conditional Micro-operations

Conditional micro-operations are described by conditional micro-statements. In a conditional micro-statement, the logical expression is tested to determine whether it is true (represented by 1); if it is true, the associated one or more micro-statements are executed. Consider the following conditional micro-operations,

```
Register,  B(0-5), C(0-5), D(0-5)
Register,  X(1-8), Y(1-8), Z(1-8)
IF (B(0)=0) THEN (X ←0)
IF (B(4)=1) THEN (Y ←0) ELSE (Z ←0)
IF (C≠77) THEN (D←0)
```
(5.30)

Notice the two types of conditional micro-statements: IF-THEN and IF-THEN-ELSE.

The descriptions of these conditional micro-operations by Fortran statements are,

        INTEGER B, C, D, X, Y, Z, E, F
        EQUIVALENCE (E,EREAL), (F,FREAL)
        DATA M1,M2/040,02/
        EREAL=AND(B,M1)
        FREAL=AND(B,M2)   (5.31)
        IF (E.EQ.0) X=0
        IF (F.EQ.2) Y=0
        IF (F.NE.2) Z=0
        IF (C.NE.63) D=0

A Fortran logical-IF statement is sufficient to represent the above conditional micro-statement of the IF-THEN type. But two Fortran statements are required to represent the above conditional micro-statement of the IF-THEN-ELSE type. The two test conditions of equal and unequal (= and $\neq$) are readily represented by Fortran relational operators .EQ. and .NE. which are valid for both single-bit and multiple-bit tests.

5.3.7 An Example

Consider the following register, switches, lights, and switch logic,

        Register, X(0–5)
        Switch,   SWXM(OFF), SWX(0–5) (ON)
        Light, LTX(0–5) (ON, OFF)   (5.32)
        /SWXM(ON)/ X←0,LTX(0–5)←OFF
        /SWX(0–5) (ON)/ X(0–5)←1, LTX(0–5)←ON

The above statements show that there is a light LTX to indicate each bit of register X. A single switch SWXM resets all bits of register X to 0 and all lights LTX to OFF condition. But one switch is provided to set one bit of register X to 1 and the associated light LTX to the ON condition.

When the above statements are described by Fortran statements, we have,

        INTEGER X, SWXM, SWX(6), LTX(6), ON, OFF
        EQUIVALENCE (X,XREAL)   (5.33)
        DATA ON, OFF/2HON,3HOFF/, 040/040/

```
      5 READ (5,100) X, SWXM, SWX, LTX
    100 FORMAT (02, 13A3)
        IF (SWXM.NE.OFF) GO TO 15
        X=0
        DO 10 I=1, 6
        LTX(I) =OFF
     10 CONTINUE
     15 DO 20 I=1, 6
        IF (SWX(I) .NE.ON) GO TO 20
        J=040/2**(I-1)
        XREAL=OR(X,J)
        LTX(I)=ON
     20 CONTINUE
        WRITE (6,200) X, SWXM, SWX, LTX
    200 FORMAT  (1H0,10X,11HREGISTER X=,I1,2X,5HSWXM=,A3,3X,
      1       4HSWX=,6(A3,2X),4HLTX=,6(A3,2X))
        GO TO 5
        END
  $DATA
    44OFFON OFFON OFFON OFFON OFFON OFFON OFF
```

In the above, the initial contents of register X and the initial conditions of lights and switches are set by the READ statement and are printed out by the WRITE statement. Each conditional micro-statement is represented by five or more Fortran statements including a DO statement. The DO statement gives a simpler description for handling the row of switches and the row of lights. Notice that the above arithmetic statement with the special Fortran Logical OR operation sets the individual bits of register X to 1.

5.4 SIMULATION OF SEQUENCES

Fortran is a procedural language; this means that the order of the statements of a Fortran program determines the order of execution of the statements unless execution encounters certain control statements such as GO TO statement and Computed GO TO statement. In order that the statement can be referred by such control statements, a statement number may be given to a statement. The statement number resembles the label of an execution statement described in the previous chapters; thus, the labels in a CDL description are represented numerically in a Fortran simulation.

5.4.1 Sequencing by Using GO TO Statements

The use of GO TO statements to describe sequencing is illustrated by the following example.

INTEGER statement
DATA statement
FORMAT statement
5 READ statement
IF (START. EQ.ON) GO TO 10
GO TO 5
10 statement,
IF (logical expression) GO TO 20
statement   (5.34)
statement
20 IF (logical expression) GO TO 30
statement
statement
30 IF (logical expression) GO TO 40
statement
40 statement
GO TO 5
END

In the above, the GO TO statements are used conditionally and unconditionally to alter the sequencing. Parallel operations described by micro-statements in one execution statement are represented serially by using more than one Fortran statement. The Fortran description is similar to the procedural description in Chapter 3, though the latter permits description of parallel operations.

5.4.2 Simulation of Sequencing by a Ring Counter

As described in Chapter 4, a control sequence can be generated by means of a ring counter, and an example of generating a multiple-control sequence by a ring counter was shown. The state diagram of the ring counter, which represents the multiple-control sequence, was shown in Fig. 4.5.

Fortran GO TO statements may be used to describe the sequencing specified by the state diagram of Fig. 4.5. Let the numbers in the state diagram be the statement numbers except that number 0 be changed to statement number 8 (because Fortran statement number begins with 1). Similar to the description in statements (4.9), we now have,

```
         INTEGER  X, Y, Z
         INTEGER START,ON,OFF
         DATA  ON,OFF/2HON,3HOFF/
     10 READ  (5,20)  X, Y, Z, START
         IF (START.NE.ON) GO TO 10
      1 IF (X.EQ.0) GO TO 5
      2 GO TO 8
      3 GO TO 8
      4 GO TO 7
      5 GO TO 6
      6 IF (Y.EQ.1) GO TO 2
         GO TO 4
      7 IF (Z.EQ.1) GO TO 2
         GO TO 3
      8 GO TO 1
     20 FORMAT (3I1, A3)
         END
```

(5.35)

The above READ statement reads in the values of X,Y,Z, and START. This program should not be run without further modification, because it will execute a closed loop.

5.4.3 Simulation of Sequencing by a Control Counter

As also described in Chapter 4, a control sequence can be generated by a combination of a control counter and a decoder. As an example, consider the control sequence described by statements (4.10). The description of the control sequence by Fortran statements is,

```
         INTEGER START, COMPLE,ON,OFF
         DATA ON,OFF/2HON,3HOFF/
     20 READ (5,15) START
     15 FORMAT (A3)
         IF (START.NE.ON)  GO TO 20
         N=1
     10 GO TO (1, 2, 3, 4), N
      1 COMPLE=OFF
         N=N+1
         GO TO 10
      2 N=N+1
         GO TO 10
```

(5.36)

```
      3 N=N+1
        GO TO 10
      4 COMPLE=ON
        N=1
        GO TO 10
        END
```

Notice that integer N represents the counter and the Computed GO TO statement represents the decoder.

As another example, consider the multiple-control sequence whose state diagram was shown in Fig. 4.5. In this case, a control register is used instead of a control counter. Again let the numbers in the state diagram be the statement numbers except that number 0 be changed to statement number 8. The Fortran description is shown below.

```
        INTEGER  START,X,Y,Z,ON,OFF
        DATA ON,OFF/2HON,3HOFF/
     20 READ (5,25) START
     25 FORMAT (A3)
        IF (START.NE.ON)  GO TO 20
     30 ASSIGN 1 TO N
    100 GO TO N, (1,2,3,4,5,6,7,8)
      1 IF (X.EQ.1)  GO TO 12
        ASSIGN 5 TO N
        GO TO 100
     12 ASSIGN 2 TO N
        GO TO 100
      2 ASSIGN 8 TO N                        (5.37)
        GO TO 100
      3 ASSIGN 8 TO N
        GO TO 100
      4 ASSIGN 7 TO N
        GO TO 100
      5 ASSIGN 6 TO N
        GO TO 100
      6 IF (Y.EQ.1)  GO TO 14
        ASSIGN 4 TO N
        GO TO 100
     14 ASSIGN 3 TO N
        GO TO 100
      7 IF (Z.EQ.1)  GO TO 16
        ASSIGN 3 TO N
        GO TO 100
```

```
16 ASSIGN 2 TO N
   GO TO 100
   END
```

In the above description, integer N represents the control register. The ASSIGN statement sets the value of N and the ASSIGN GO TO statements act like the decoder. This description requires more Fortran statements than that in statements (5.35) where GO TO statements are used.

5.4.4 Simulation of a Shift Sequence

As an example of simulating a sequence, the shift sequence described by statements (4.18) is now described by the Fortran program shown below.

```
   INTEGER A,C,SH,START,ON,OFF,0377,FINI
   EQUIVALENCE (A,AREAL)
   DATA ON,OFF/2HON,3HOFF/, 0377/0377/
10 READ (5,20) START
20 FORMAT (A3)
   IF (START.NE.ON) GO TO 10
30 FINI=OFF
 1 READ (5,40) A, C, SH
40 FORMAT (3O3)
 2 C=C-1
 3 IF (SH.EQ.1) GO TO 4                              (5.38)
   GO TO 5
 4 AREAL=AND(2*A,0377)
   GO TO 6
 5 A=A/2
 6 IF (C.EQ.0) GO TO 7
   GO TO 2
 7 FINI=ON
   WRITE (6,50)  A
50 FORMAT (O3)
   STOP
   END
```

In the above program, the clock and the ring counter are not represented, but the sequencing is essentially the same. This program bears a close similarity with the procedural description for the same sequence in statements (4.6).

5.4.5 Simulation of a Control Sequence*

A control sequence which consists of a two-phase clock, add-control signals, and timing signals will be described in Chapter 8. Statements (8.1) describe the two-phase clock, CP1 and CP2. Statements (8.2) describe the add-control signals, T(0–3) and TD. Statements (8.7) describe the timing signals DP(0–15). These statements are now shown together below.

```
Switch,       CLEAR(ON)
Comment, two-phase clock
Clock,        CP
Register,     RUN2
Terminal,     CP1=CP*RUN2,
              CP2=ΔCP1
Comment, add-control signals
Register,     AC(1–0)
Decoder,      N(0–3)=AC
Terminal,     T(0–3)=N(0–3)*CP1,
              TD=N(0)*CP2
Comment, timing signals                          (5.39)
Register,     D(3–0),
Decoder,      B(0–15)=D,
Terminal,     DP(0–15)=B(0–15)*T(0)
Comment, here begin execution statements
/CLEAR(ON)/   RUN2 ← 1, AC ← 0, D ← 0
/TD/          D ← countup D
/DP(5)/       AC ← countup AC
/DP(15)/      RUN2 ← 0
/T(1)/        AC ← countup AC
/T(2)/        AC ← countup AC
/T(3)/        AC ← countup AC
              End
```

In the above, eight execution statements are provided in order to combine the clock and timing signals to function as a control sequence. Statements (5.39) generate the following control sequence:

$$DP(0),\ldots,DP(5),T(1),T(2),T(3),DP(6),\ldots,DP(15) \qquad (5.40)$$

The interruption of the timing signals DP(i)'s is due to the incrementing AC micro-operation specified by the above third micro-statement. The three signals T(i)'s form a subcontrol sequence

---

*This section may be deferred until Chapter 8 is presented.

for the three-step addition subsequence, as having been explained previously.

The two-phase clock may be simulated by the following Fortran statements:

```
      INTEGER RUN2, CP(2)
      IF (CP(1).EQ.1.AND.RUN2.EQ.0) GO TO 1000
      CP(2)=1-CP(1)
 1000 STOP
```
(5.41)

Notice that clock CP(1) alternates with CP(2). When RUN2 becomes 0 and CP(1) is 1, simulation is terminated. The add-control signals may be simulated by the following Fortran statements:

```
      INTEGER AC,N(4), T(4),TD
      DO 50 K=1, 4
      IF (AC.EQ.(K-1))   N(K)=1
      IF (AC.NE. (K-1))  N(K)=0
      IF (N(K).EQ.1.AND.CP(1).EQ.1)  T(K)=1
   50 IF (N(K).EQ.0.OR. CP(1).EQ.0)  T(K)=0
      IF (N(1).EQ.1.AND.CP(2).EQ.1)  TD=1
      IF (N(1).EQ.0.OR. CP(2).EQ.0)  TD=0
```
(5.42)

Note that the values of the subscripts of integers N and T are 1,2,3, and 4, each of which is, respectively, one larger than the values of the subscripts of terminals N and T in statements (5.39). The first four Logical IF statements generate the four T(i) signals and the last two Logical IF statements generate signal TD. The timing signals may be simulated by the following Fortran statements:

```
      INTEGER D, B(16), DP(16)
      DO 60 K=1, 16
      IF (D.EQ.(K-1))   B(K)=1
      IF (D.NE.(K-1))   B(K)=0
      IF (T(1).EQ.1.AND.B(K).EQ.1)  DP(K)=1
   60 IF (T(1).EQ.0.OR. B(K).EQ.0)  DP(K)=0
```
(5.43)

Statements (5.42) and (5.43) show two examples of simulating a decoder by a combination of a DO statement and Logical IF statements. The execution statements in statements (5.39) may be readily simulated by GO TO statements and Logical IF statements. A Fortran program which simulates the control sequence in statements (5.39) is shown in Fig. 5.1. This program combines Fortran statements (5.41) through (5.43). PRINT statements are

```
C*****SIMULATION OF A CONTROL SEQUENCE
      INTEGER RUN2,CP(2),AC,N(4),T(4),TD,D,B(16),DP(16)
      INTEGER CLEAR,ON,OFF
      DATA ON,OFF/2HON,3HOFF/
C*****SIMULATE CLEAR SWITCH
    5 READ (5,20) CLEAR
   20 FORMAT (A5)
      WRITE (6,100)
      IF (CLEAR.NE.ON) GO TO 5
   30 RUN2=1
      AC=0
      D=0
      CP(1)=1
C*****SIMULATE TWO-PHASE CLOCK
   40 IF (CP(1).EQ.1.AND.RUN2.EQ.0) GO TO 1000
      CP(2)=1-CP(1)
C*****SIMULATE ADD-CONTROL SIGNALS
      DO 50 K=1, 4
      IF (AC  .EQ. (K-1))              N(K)=1
      IF (AC  .NE. (K-1))              N(K)=0
      IF (N(K).EQ.1.AND.CP(1).EQ.1)    T(K)=1
   50 IF (N(K).EQ.0.OR. CP(1).EQ.0)    T(K)=0
      IF (N(1).EQ.1.AND.CP(2).EQ.1)    TD  =1
      IF (N(1).EQ.0.OR. CP(2).EQ.0)    TD  =0
C*****SIMULATE TIMING SIGNALS
      DO 60 K=1,16
      IF (D  .EQ. (K-1))              B(K)=1
      IF (D  .NE. (K-1))              B(K)=0
      IF (T(1).EQ.1.AND.B(K).EQ.1)    DP(K)=1
   60 IF (T(1).EQ.0.OR. B(K).EQ.0)    DP(K)=0
C*****SIMULATE EXECUTION STATEMENTS
      IF (TD.EQ.0) GO TO 11
      D=D+1
   11 IF (DP(6).EQ.0)  GO TO 12
      AC=AC+1
      IF (AC.EQ.4) AC=0
   12 IF (DP(16).EQ.0) GO TO 13
      RUN2=0
   13 IF (T(2).EQ.0) GO TO 14
      AC=AC+1
      IF (AC.EQ.4) AC=0
   14 IF (T(3).EQ.0) GO TO 15
      AC=AC+1
      IF (AC.EQ.4) AC=0
   15 IF (T(4).EQ.0) GO TO 16
      AC=AC+1
      IF (AC.EQ.4) AC=0
C*****PRINT OUTPUT
   16 WRITE (6,200) CP(1),CP(2),RUN2,AC,N,TD,T,D,B,DP
  100 FORMAT (1H1//43H0    CP(1) CP(2) RUN2 AC N(1-4) TD  T(1-4)  D,
     *6X,24HB(1-16)           DP(1-16))
  200 FORMAT (1H ,5X,I1,5X,I1,5X,I1,3X,I1,2X,4I1,3X,I1,2X,4I1,2X,I2,
     *1X,16I1,1X,16I1)
      CP(1)=CP(2)
      GO TO 40
 1000 STOP
      END
$DATA
ON
      DATA M1,M2,M3/077777,040000000,0777777/
      DATA ON,OFF/ 2HON,3HOFF/
```

Fig. 5.1 Listing of Fortran Simulation of a Control Sequence

provided in order to print out the contents of all integers after each clock. Notice that clock CP(1) takes the value of CP(2) near the end of the program.

5.5 SIMULATION OF A DIGITAL COMPUTER

In order to illustrate simulation of a digital computer by Fortran programming, the simple digital computer described in Chapter 4 is chosen to serve as an example. The subsequent Fortran program simulates the organization and operations of the computer described in statements (4.21) and (4.25) in Chapter 4.

5.5.1 Simulation of the Configuration

The memory, the registers, the START switch, and the clock of the computer are described by the following declaration statements:

$$
\begin{array}{ll}
\text{DIMENSION M(4096)} & \\
\text{INTEGER P,R,A,C,D,F,G} & (5.44) \\
\text{INTEGER START, ON, OFF} &
\end{array}
$$

The STOP and POWER switches are not directly simulated. The decoder is simulated by the following two statements:

$$
\begin{array}{l}
\text{I=F+1} \\
\text{GO TO (17,1,2,3,4,5,6,7,8,9,10,11,12,13,14,15,16), I}
\end{array} \qquad (5.45)
$$

where statement numbers 1,2,. . .,16 correspond respectively to subscripts 1,2,. . .,16 in terminal K(i) except that subscript 0 corresponds to statement number 17.

Masks M1=07777, M2=0400000, and M3=0777777 extract respectively the address part of the word, the sign bit of the word, and the 18-bit word of the simple computer from the 36-bit word of the 7090/7094 Computer. In addition, ON and OFF are defined as alphanumeric constants. These are described by the two DATA statements,

$$
\begin{array}{l}
\text{DATA M1,M2,M3/07777,0400000,0777777/} \\
\text{DATA ON,OFF/ 2HON,3HOFF/}
\end{array} \qquad (5.46)
$$

In the subsequent Fortran program, the special Fortran logical operator AND is again used. As mentioned previously, the result of using this operator gives a real number. In order to make integers A,C,D, and J (a temporary storage location) respectively equivalent to real numbers AREAL, CREAL, DREAL, and JREAL, the following EQUIVALENCE statement is included.

$$\text{EQUIVALENCE (A,AREAL), (C,CREAL), (D,DREAL), (J,JREAL)} \qquad (5.47)$$

5.5.2 Loading, Initializing, and Outputting

In a simulation program, loading the test program, initializing the simulation, and printing the output are usually required. Here, the test program is loaded by the statements,

```
     READ (5,1000) N
     READ (5,1002)  (M(I),I=1,N)
     READ (5,1002)  (M(I),I=65,66)                      (5.48)
1000 FORMAT (16)
1002 FORMAT (06)
```

where variable N in the first READ statement represents the number of instructions to be loaded. The second READ statement loads the 11 instructions and the third READ statement loads the two data words. The simulation is initialized (to replace the POWER switch) by the statements,

$$
\begin{aligned}
P &= 0\\
G &= 0 \qquad (5.49)\\
F &= 10
\end{aligned}
$$

The above setting integer F to 10 leads to the WAIT sequence. The print output is specified by the statements,

```
     WRITE (6,1004)
 100 WRITE (6,1006) P,R,A,C,D,F,G
                                                         (5.50)
1004 FORMAT (1H1,10X,1HP,6X,1HR,8X,1HA,7X,1HC,6X,1HD,5X,1HF,3X,1HG)
1006 FORMAT (1H,8X,I3,3X,06,3X,06,3X,04,3X,04,3X,02,3X,I1)
```

where the first WRITE statement prints out a heading and the second WRITE statement prints out the contents of integers P,R,A,C,D,F, and G.

5.5.3 Fetch Sequence

The fetch sequence is described by the following Fortran statements:

```
    9 R=M(C+1)
      D=D+1
      F=13
      GO TO 100                                        (5.51)
   13 F=R/4096
      CREAL=AND(R,M1)
      GO TO 100
```

The four micro-operations of the fetch sequence in statements (5.45) are described by the above first, second, fifth, and sixth Fortran statements. The address for array M is C+1 (instead of C) because the subscript of array M begins from 1 while the actual address begins from 0. The above third statement sets integer F to 13 and the fourth GO TO statement leads to a print output and to the decoding of integer F. Division of integer R by 4096 shifts R 12 bits to the right; this extracts the op-code part of R. The address part of R is extracted by mask M1; note that variable CREAL (instead of C) is used. The last GO TO statement performs the same function as the fourth GO TO statement.

5.5.4 Execution Sequences

The ADD sequence is described by the following Fortran statements:

```
   17 R=M(C+1)
      F=12
      GO TO 100
   12 A=A+R
      IF (A.LT.0) A=0-A
      AREAL=AND(A,M3)
      F=11                                             (5.52)
      GO TO 100
   11 C=D
      F=10
      IF (G.EQ.1) F=9
      GO TO 100
```

The three mico-operations of the ADD sequence in statements (5.46) are described by the above first, fourth, and ninth statements. Since the operator add in the above fourth statement adds unsigned binary numbers, Fortran operator + is equivalent to operator add except when the sum is negative or when the sum overflows. When the sum from the fourth statement is negative, the sum should be in the signed 2's complement representation instead of the signed magnitude representation as Fortran gives. The above fifth statement produces the sum in the signed 2's complement representation by subtracting the result from 0. When the sum overflows, operator add ignores it, while Fortran operator + keeps the overflow because it adds Fortran integer in 36 bits. The above sixth statement is provided to extract the 18 bits of the word. If integer G is 0, integer F is set to 10 and the next sequence is the WAIT sequence; otherwise, integer F is set to 9 and the next sequence is the fetch sequence.

The WAIT sequence and the start operation are described by the following Fortran statements:

```
   10  IF (G.EQ.0) GO TO 104
       F=9
       GO TO 100
  104  C=0
       D=0
  106  READ (5,1008) START                    (5.53)
 1008  FORMAT (A3)
       IF (START.EQ.ON) GO TO 108
       GO TO 106
  108  G=1
       GO TO 100
```

The above first five Fortran statements constitute the WAIT sequence, and the remaining six statements simulate the start operation. If integer G is 1, integer F is set to 9 and the next sequence is the fetch sequence. If integer G is 0, the simulation enters a waiting loop during which integers C and D are first reset to 0 and then an input card (this simulates the START switch) is read to find out the position of the START switch. If the position is ON, integer G is set to 1 and the next sequence is the fetch sequence; otherwise, execution continues to read the input cards as long as there are such input cards in the card reader.

The descriptions of the eight other sequences of the simple computer by FORTRAN statements are similar to those explained above.

5.5.5 Fortran Program

A listing of the complete Fortran program is shown in Fig. 5.2 where the 15 data cards at the end of the listing are for the four READ statements. Among the 15 data cards is the test program shown in Table 5.1. This program which employs all the nine instructions of the instruction set tests the sequential operations of the computer. It consists of 11 instructions and 5 data words. It is shown in the instruction chart in Fig. 5.3 where each box represents one memory word. Notice the loop for circularly left-shifting the number in the accumulator. Numbers 010001_8 and 001001_8 are initially stored in the locations at addresses 100_8 and 101_8, respectively. After execution of the test program is completed, the locations at addresses 102_8 through 104_8 contain, respectively, numbers 011002_8, 440100_8, and 427076_8, and the accumulator contains number 213437_8.

5.6 SIMULATION BY USING THE CDL SIMULATOR

Computer organization is commonly described by block diagrams with English narrative. Such a description usually gives one a general idea, but it lacks preciseness and depth for thorough understanding. Because of this serious limitation, logic designer resorts to logic diagrams or boolean equations. Though the logic diagram or the boolean equation can give a precise description, the description is highly nondescriptive and indeed difficult for one to comprehend how the computer functions. In either of the above approaches, the description of sequential operation of a digital computer is not comprehensible. A third choice is the use of an algorithmic programming language. This previously described approach gives a sequential description, but it is highly nondescriptive of computer elements and micro-operations. It is cumbersome, if not inadequate, in describing timing and command signals. It cannot describe parallel operations. For these and other reasons, a higher order language specially developed for describing computer organization is highly desirable.

5.6.1 Computer Design Language

A number of such higher order languages have been reported during recent years (4–5,11–14,20–24,31–32). One of these

languages, called the Computer Design Language or simply CDL (14),
has been developed to describe functional organization and
sequential operations of a digital computer. This language is highly

```
C*****SIMULATION OF A SIMPLE DIGITAL COMPUTER
      DIMENSION M(4096)
      INTEGER P,R,A,C,D,F,G
      INTEGER START,ON,OFF
      DATA M1,M2,M3/07777,0400000,0777777/
      DATA ON,OFF/2HON,3HOFF/
      EQUIVALENCE (A,AREAL),(C,CREAL),(D,DREAL),(J,JREAL)
C*****LOAD TEST PROGRAM*****
      READ (5,1000) N
      READ (5,1002) (M(I),I=1,N)
      READ (5,1002) (M(I),I=65,66)
 1000 FORMAT (I6)
 1002 FORMAT (O6)
C*****INITIALIZATION*****
      P=0
      G=0
      F=10
C*****PRINT OUTPUT*****
      WRITE (6,1004)
  100 WRITE (6,1006) P,R,A,C,D,F,G
 1004 FORMAT(1H1,10X,1HP,6X,1HR,8X,1HA,7X,1HC,6X,1HD,5X,1HF,3X,1HG)
 1006 FORMAT(1H ,8X,I3,3X,O6,3X,O6,3X,O4,3X,O4,3X,O2,3X,I1)
      P=P+1
      I=F+1
      GO TO (17,1,2,3,4,5,6,7,8,9,10,11,12,13,14,15,16),I
C*****ADD SEQUENCE *****
   17 R=M(C+1)
      F=12
      GO TO 100
C*****K(12)*P
   12 A=A+R
      IF (A.LT.0) A=0-A
      AREAL=AND(A,M3)
      F=11
      GO TO 100
C*****SUB SEQUENCE*****
    1 R=M(C+1)
      F=15
      GO TO 100
C*****K(15)*P
   15 A=A-R
      IF (A.LT.0) A=0-A
      AREAL=AND(A,M3)
      F=11
      GO TO 100
C*****JOM SEQUENCE*****
    2 IF (AND(A,M2).NE.0.) GO TO 4
      GO TO 102
C*****JMP SEQUENCE*****
    4 DREAL=AND(R,M1)
  102 F=11
      GO TO 100
C*****STO SEQUENCE*****
    3 R=A
      F=16
      GO TO 100
C*****K(16)*P
   16 M(C+1)=R
      F=11
      GO TO 100
C*****SHR SEQUENCE*****
    5 A=A/2
      F=11
      GO TO 100
```

Fig. 5.2 Listing of Fortran Simulation of a Simple Digital Computer

```
C*****CIL SEQUENCE*****
   6 JREAL=AND(A,M2)
     AREAL=AND((A*2),M3)
     IF (J.NE.0) A=A+R
     F=11
     GO TO 100
C*****CLA SEQUENCE*****
   7 R=M(C+1)
     A=0
     F=14
     GO TO 100
C*****K(14)*P
  14 A=A+R
     IF (A.LT.0) A=0-A+R
     AREAL=AND(A,M3)
     F=11
     GO TO 100
C*****STP SEQUENCE*****
   8 G=0
     F=10
     GO TO 100
C*****FETCH SEQUENCE*****
   9 R=M(C+1)
     D=D+1
     F=13
     GO TO 100
C*****K(13)*P
  13 F=R/4096
     CREAL=AND(R,M1)
     GO TO 100
C*****WAIT SEQUENCE*****
  10 IF (G.EQ.0) GO TO 104
     F=9
     GO TO 100
 104 C=0
     D=0
C*****START OPERATION*****
 106 READ (5,1008) START
1008 FORMAT (A3)
     IF (START.EQ.ON) GO TO 108
     GO TO 106
 108 G=1
     GO TO 100
C*****K(11)*P
  11 C=D
     F=10
     IF (G.EQ.1) F=9
     GO TO 100
     END
$DATA
        11
070100
000101
030102
060000
020006
040003
030103
010102
030104
050000



100000
010001
001001
ON
```

Fig. 5.2 (continued)

Table 5.1 A test program

Memory Address	Memory Word	Symbolic Program
0000	070100	CLA 0100
0001	000101	ADD 0101
0002	030102	STO 0102
0003	060000	CIL 0000
0004	020006	JOM 0006
0005	040003	JMP 0003
0006	030103	STO 0103
0007	010102	SUB 0102
0010	030104	STO 0104
0011	050000	SHR 0000
0012	100000	STP 0000
0100	010001	
0101	001001	
0102	011002*	
0103	440100*	
0104	427076*	

*These numbers occur after the test program is executed.

descriptive in identifying computer elements such as registers, decoders, switches, lights, memories, and terminals. It is precise and concise in describing elements, functions, and operations. It is highly expressive at the bit level, word level, and bit-array level. It can express timing signals and control commands. It can describe serial and parallel transfers and parallel operations. No background in electronics is required to understand and use this language.

The CDL is indeed the set of notations that has been used to describe computer elements, micro-operations, sequences, and stored-program computers in the previous chapters. It has been tested by describing the functional organizations and sequential operations of several commercial digital computers (24,27,35). A simulator which accepts description of computer organization in the CDL has been developed.

5.6.2 CDL Simulator

Version 1 of the CDL simulator has been available since the

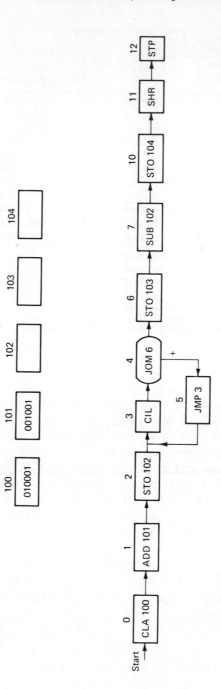

Fig. 5.3 Instruction chart of the test program

summer of 1967; this version allows a limited set of the Computer Design Language (28). Version 2 has been available since February, 1968; this version implements most of the features of the language (33). Version 2 was further improved to become version 3. Version 3 has been available since the fall of 1968. (All three versions were written in Fortran IV with several routines in assembly language MAP for the IBM 7090 family of computers.)

The CDL simulator consists of two parts, a translator program and a simulator program. The translator program accepts a description in the CDL punched on a deck of cards, translates it into a program called "Polish String," and establishes various tables and a storage array. The simulator program consists of five parts: Loader, Output routine, Switch routine, Simulate routine, and Reset routine. The Loader accepts test data from punched cards and stores them into the simulated memories and registers of the CDL described computer. The Output routine handles the printout of the contents of the chosen registers, memory words, and positions of the switches during the simulation. The Switch routine simulates the operation of manual switches. The Simulate routine executes the Polish String in an interpretive mode. The Reset routine reinitializes the simulator program for a next simulation run.

Execution of the Polish String by the Simulate routine is carried out in a control loop, called *Label Cycle.* During a Label Cycle, the following processing is performed:

a. If a manual switch operation has occurred, the micro-statements of the execution statement with the switch as the label are executed.
b. Labels of all execution statements are evaluated. Those labels which are activated are noted. Activated labels are those whose logical values are 1.
c. The micro-statements of those execution statements with the activated labels are executed. To simulate parallel nature of these micro-statements, the expressions of the micro-statements are first all evaluated before any of the values from the evaluations is stored into the specified register or memory word.
d. Condition for simulation termination is checked. If the condition is fulfilled, the run is terminated; otherwise, it proceeds to the next Label Cycle.

5.6.3 Card Formats

The simulation deck consists of three types of punched cards: system control cards, CDL statement cards, and simulation control cards. The system control cards are the means by which the user communicates with the operating system of a computer installation. Since system control cards vary with different computer installations, they will not be further discussed. The CDL statement cards constitute the description of a sequence or a computer organization to be simulated. The simulation control cards are the means by which the user communicates with the CDL Simulator. The formats for the latter two types of cards are described below.

There are four types of CDL statement cards: comment, declaration, execution, and end. The formats of these statements are shown in Table 5.2. These rules for formats are quite close to those that have been used in the descriptions by the CDL statements in the previous chapters. However, there are some important differences as enumerated below.

Table 5.2 Formats of CDL statement cards

Card Type	Format
Comment	Any card with letter C in column 1 is a comment card.
Declaration	(a) Declaration statement must use columns 2–72. The name of the declaration statement appears first and declared items follow. They are separated by commas. Blanks may be used freely.
	(b) If letter 1 is punched in column 1, the card is a continuation card. The name of declaration statement is not repeated on a continuation card.
Execution	(a) Execution statement must use columns 2–72. The label appears first and micro-statements then follow. Blanks may be used freely. Micro-statements are separated by comma.
	(b) The label is indicated by a pair of enclosing slashes.
	(c) A continuation card requires no special punch except that the label is not repeated and the card is placed immediately thereafter.
End	A card with word END appears anywhere in columns 2–72 but with no other punches.

a. Light statement is not provided in the CDL simulator. (Normally, use Register statement instead.)

b. Subscripts as well as constants are all octal and should not exceed 12 octal digitals except where the cascade symbol "-" is used. (In these cases, any constant must be represented by 0 or 1 or a cascade of 0's and 1's.)

c. Declaration statements must be placed before their use in execution statements.

d. All variable names must be unique and consist of 1 to 6 alphanumeric characters of which the first must be alphabetic.

e. These names (IF,THEN,ELSE,DO,CALL,RETURN,END) are the reserved names and may not be used as variable names by the user.

f. Operators ←, =, ≠, ⊕, and countup are respectively replaced by =, .EQ., .NE., .ERA., and .COUNT..

g. Operators ⊙, countdn, shl,shr, cil, and cir previously shown in Tables 3.2 and 3.3 are not provided in the CDL simulator.

There are eight types of simulation control cards: heading, load, output, switch, simulate, reset, data, and call-simulator-program. The formats of these control cards are shown in Table 5.3 The heading card indicates that the subsequent cards are the CDL statement cards. The call-simulator-program card calls the simulator program.

Table 5.3 Formats of simulation control cards*

Card Type	Format
Heading	*MAIN in columns 1–5
Call-simulator-program	$SIMULATE in columns 1–9
Load	*LOAD in columns 1–5
Output	*OUTPUT in columns 1–5 LABEL or CLOCK in columns 11–15 (n)=in columns 16–20 "list"
Switch	*SWITCH in columns 1–7 L, in columns 11–12 NAME=POSITION in columns 13–
Simulate	*SIM in columns 1–4 n,r in columns 11–
Reset	*RESET in columns 1–6 "options" in columns 11–
Data	Items of the following formats, (a) REG = d (b) M(L) = d (c) $M(L_1 - L_m) = d_1, \ldots, d_m$ (d) $M(L_1-) = d_1, \ldots, d_m$ are entered in columns 2–80. These items are separated by commas. Blanks may be inserted anywhere. Load data only into declared full registers and memory words. Data must be octal.

*See text for explanations of symbols and quotations.

This card should immediately follow the END card. The loader card indicates that the subsequent cards are data cards to be loaded into the specified registers and memories. The data card has four formats for loading the data into the declared registers and memory words.

(Full register and memory words must be used.) In Table 5.3, REG is the name of the register and M(L) is the memory word at octal address L of memory M. Letters d, d_1, and the like are octal numbers to be loaded into registers or memory words. In format (c), $L_1 - L_m$ denotes the memory addresses beginning from address L_1 up to address L_m. In format (d), $L_1 -$ denotes memory address beginning from address L_1 until the address to be determined by the number of octal numbers d's. Data must be octal numbers whose preceding zeros may be deleted. Each data card must have both the data and the names of registers and memories into which the data are to be loaded. An example of the load card together with the data cards is,

```
*LOAD
R=0, AC=20, SEP=32, M(0–3)=1,2,3,4, M(77)=345,
M(10-)=70, 71,72,73,74,75,76
```

The output card specifies the names of the registers, memory words, and switches whose contents are to be printed out. Either word LABEL or word CLOCK(n) is chosen to indicate that the output be printed at every Label Cycle or every nth clock. Quotation list means a list of the names of registers, switches, and memory words whose contents are to be printed. The list can be continued on the next card or cards as long as column 1 remains blank. An example of the output cards is shown below,

```
*OUTPUT        CLOCK(10)=RR,START,M(0),M(777),
AC,MQ,M(10),OVER
```

The switch card imitates the operation of a manual switch. One card is required for specifying the position of one switch. In Table 5.3, L specifies the Lth Label Cycle immediately before which the switch operation occurs. NAME denotes the name of the switch and POSITION denotes the position of the switch.

The simulate card starts the simulation and specifies terminating conditions denoted by "n" and "r". Terminating condition "n" denotes the maximum number of Label Cycles allowed for the simulation. Terminating condition "r" denotes the allowed maximum number of consecutive Label Cycles during which the same group of labels is activated repeatedly. Specification of this latter condition is desirable because it terminates any possible closed loop that meets this terminating condition; this closed loop may occur due to an error. The reset card reinitializes the simulator program and thus permits the next simulation run. Quotation option means the selection of one or more of these words: OUTPUT, SWITCH,

CLOCK, CYCLE. If OUTPUT or SWITCH is selected, the previous output or switch card becomes invalid and another output or switch card is expected, following the reset card. Similarly, if CLOCK is selected, the clock-cycle counter is reset for the next run. If CYCLE is selected, the clock-cycle and label-cycle counters are both reset. An example of the reset card is shown below.

        *RESET   CYCLE, OUTPUT

An output card and possibly a load card and data cards follow this reset card.

5.6.4 Examples of Simulation

Four examples of simulation of using CDL simulator are shown below. The listings of these four examples are shown in Figs. 5.4 through 5.7. In these listings, the system control cards are not shown, but the CDL statements which constitute the simulation description proper as well as the simulation control cards are shown.

The first example is the serial complement sequence described in statements (4.17) in Chapter 4. The listing in Fig. 5.4 and statements (4.17) are almost identical except that light FINI and operator countup in statements (4.17) are replaced, respectively, by operator .COUNT. and register FINI. There are 14 simulation control cards at the end of the listing. The first control card calls the simulator program. The second through sixth control cards are those for the first simulation run. The second card specifies that the contents of registers A, T, C, and FINI be printed out at every clock cycle. The third control card simulates the ON position of the START switch. The fourth card loads the number on the fifth data card into register A. The sixth card specifies that simulation run be terminated at the end of 30 Label Cycles or when three consecutive Label Cycles with a group of repeatedly activated labels occur. The seventh through tenth control cards are those for the second simulation run, and the eleventh through fourteenth control cards for the third simulation run. The seventh and eleventh RESET cards reinitialize the simulator program. The eight and ninth cards load octal number 13 into register A for the second run, and the twelfth and thirteenth cards for the third run. Since the simulate card starts the simulation, it is required for each simulation run; this explains the need of the tenth and fourteenth cards.

The second example is the shift sequence described in statements (4.18). In addition to the replacement of light FINI by register FINI,

```
*MAIN
C
C      COMMENT    *****A SERIAL COMPLEMENT SEQUENCE
C
       REGISTER,      A(5-1),
                      T(1-3),
       1              C(0-2),
       1              FINI
       SWITCH,        START(ON)
       CLOCK,         P
       /START(ON)/    T=4,
                      FINI=0,
                      C=0
       /T(1)*P/       A(5-1)=A(1)'-A(5-2),
                      C=C.COUNT,
                      T(1,2)=1
       /T(2)*P/       IF (C.EQ.5) THEN (T(2,3)=1) ELSE (T(1,2)=2)
       /T(3)*P/       FINI=1
                      END
       $SIMULATE
       *OUTPUT     CLOCK(1)=A,T,C,FINI
       *SWITCH     1,START=ON
       *LOAD
             A=26
       *SIM        30,3
       *RESET      CYCLE
       *LOAD
             A=13
       *SIM        30,3
       *RESET      CYCLE
       *LOAD
             A=05
       *SIM        30,3
```

Fig. 5.4 Listing of CDL simulation of a serial complement sequence

input terminals IN1, IN2, and IN3 are replaced by registers because the load control card cannot load input terminals. Furthermore, the basic operators shl, shr, and countdn are not provided in the CDL simulator. The shl and shr micro-statements are replaced by two transfer micro-statements. The countdn micro-operation is replaced by a countup micro-operation by first taking the 1's complement of the number of the count and then testing counter C for 7. The three steps for this counting up operation are,

Step 1, C=C
Step 2, C=C.COUNT.
Step3,   IF (C.EQ.7) THEN . . . .

There are eleven simulation control cards at the end of the listing in Fig. 5.5. These control cards specify two simulation runs.

The third example is the simple stored-program computer described by statements (4.21) and (4.25). The listing is shown in

Fig. 5.6 which is almost identical to statements (4.21) and (4.25) except that subscripts in the listing are all octal and that the micro-operations with basic operators shr and cil are replaced by transfer micro-operations. Notice that proper use of comment cards significantly enhances readability. There are nine simulation control cards. The load control card loads the test program in Table 5.1 into the memory at the specified locations.

The fourth example is the control sequence described in statements (5.39). The listing is shown in Fig. 5.7. A two-phase clock is used instead of delays. Terminals T(0–3) and DP(0–15) are now individually defined. At the end of the listing, there are four simulation control cards which call the simulator program, specify the print output, simulate switch operation, and set terminating conditions.

PROBLEMS*

5.1 Describe the following registers by Fortran statements.
  Register,   A(10–2), Q(1–3,P,4–6)
  Subregister, A(M)=A(1–3), Q(N)=(4–6)
  Casregister, AQ(1–12)=A(10–2)–Q(1–3)

5.2 Describe the following comparator by Fortran statements,
  Register,   A(0–2), B(0–2)
  Terminal,   C(0–2)=A(0–2)$\odot$B(0–2)

5.3 Describe the following switches by Fortran statements,
  Switch, SWQ(0–5) (ON)
       BICON(1–2,0–7) (ON)

5.4 Describe the following transfer micro-operations by Fortran statements,
  (a) Register, A(0–5), R(0–5)
    A(1–5) ← R(0–4)
  (b) Register, A(0–5), R(0–2)
    A(0,2,5) ← R(1,0,2)
  (c) Register, A(0–2), R(0–5)
    A ← R(3,1,4)

---

*The solutions from Problems 5.15 through 5.23 may give the student a simulator which simulates the Bitran Six Computer. These problems may be given as a term project, but they should not be assigned until the appropriate chapters are presented.

```
*MAIN
C
COMMENT      ****A SHIFT SEQUENCE
C
 REGISTER,       A(0-7),
1                C(0-2),
1                T(1-7),
1                SH,
1                FINI
 REGISTER,       IN1(0-7),
1                IN2(0-2),
1                IN3
 SWITCH,         START(ON)
 CLOCK,          P
 /START(ON)/     FINI=0,
                 T=100
 /T(1)*P/        A=IN1,
                 C=IN2,
                 SH=IN3,
                 T(1,2)=1
 /T(2)*P/        C=C',
                 T(2,3)=1
 /T(3)*P/        C=C.COUNT.,
                 IF (SH.EQ.1) THEN (T(3,4)=1) ELSE (T(3,5)=1)
 /T(4)*P/        A=A(1-7)-0,
                 T(4,6)=1
 /T(5)*P/        A=0-A(0-6),
                 T(5,6)=1
 /T(6)*P/        IF (C.EQ.7) THEN (T(6,7)=1) ELSE (T(6,3)=1)
 /T(7)*P/        FINI=1,
                 T(7)=0
                 END
$SIMULATE
*OUTPUT     CLOCK(1)=A,C,T,SH,FINI
*SWITCH     1,START=ON
*LOAD
     IN1=231, IN2=5, IN3=1
*SIM        60,3
*RESET      CYCLE
*SWITCH     1,START=ON
*LOAD
     IN1=312, IN2=6, IN3=0
*SIM        70,3
```

Fig. 5.5 Listing of CDL simulation of a shift sequence

5.5 Describe the following conditional micro-statement by Fortran statements,
        Register, A, B, R(0-1)
        IF (A=0) THEN (IF (B=0) THEN (R← 0) ELSE (R← 1))
                ELSE (IF (B=0) THEN (R← 1) ELSE (R← 2))

5.6 Describe the following micro-operations by Fortran statements,
        Register,   A(1-10), B(1-10)
                    A ← 3 cil A
                    B ← 5 shr B

5.7   Describe in Fortran statements the 5-bit parallel adder by statements
      (3.71) and shown in Fig. 3.18 of Chapter 3.

```
*MAIN
C
COMMENT      **** SIMULATION OF A SIMPLE DIGITAL COMPUTER
C
 REGISTER,       R(0-21),
1                A(0-21),
1                C(0-13),
1                D(0-13),
1                F(0-5),
1                G
 SUBREGISTER,    R(OP)=R(0-5),
1                R(ADDR)=R(6-21)
 MEMORY,         M(C)=M(0-7777,0-21)
 DECODER,        K(0-20)=F
 SWITCH,         POWER(ON),
1                START(ON),
1                STOP(ON)
 TERMINAL,       ADD=K(0),
1                SUB=K(1),
1                JOM=K(2),
1                STO=K(3),
1                JMP=K(4),
1                SHR=K(5),
1                CIL=K(6),
1                CLA=K(7),
1                STP=K(10),
1                FETCH=K(11),
1                WAIT=K(12)
 CLOCK,          P
C
COMMENT, MANUAL START SEQUENCE BEGINS HERE.
 /POWER(ON)/     G=0,
                 P=12
 /START(ON)/     G=1
 /STOP(ON)/      G=0
C
COMMENT, WAIT SEQUENCE BEGINS HERE.
 /WAIT*P/        IF (G.EQ.0) THEN (C=0, D=0) ELSE (F=11)
C
COMMENT, HERE BEGINS THE FETCH SEQUENCE.
 /FETCH*P/       R=M(C),
                 D=D.COUNT.,
                 F=15
 /K(15)*P/       F=R(OP),
                 C=R(ADDR)
C
COMMENT, HERE BEGIN THE EXECUTION SEQUENCES.
C
COMMENT, HERE BEGINS THE STOP SEQUENCE.
 /STP*P/         G=0,
                 F=12
C
COMMENT, HERE BEGINS THE ADD SEQUENCE.
 /ADD*P/         R=M(C),
                 F=14
 /K(14)*P/       A=A.ADD.R,
                 F=13
```

Fig. 5.6 Listing of CDL simulation of a simple digital computer

```
C
COMMENT, HERE BEGINS THE SUB SEQUENCE.
 /SUB*P/          R=M(C),
                  F=17
 /K(17)*P/        A=A.SUB.R,
                  F=13
C
COMMENT, HERE BEGINS THE JUMP SEQUENCE.
 /JMP*P/          D=R(ADDR),
                  F=13
C
COMMENT, HERE BEGINS THE JUNP ON MINUS SEQUENCE.
 /JOM*P/          IF (A(0)) THEN (D=R(ADDR)),
                  F=13
C
COMMENT, HERE BEGINS THE STORE SEQUECNE.
 /STO*P/          R=A,
                  F=20
 /K(20)*P/        M(C)=R,
                  F=13
C
COMMENT, HERE BEGINS THE SHIFT-RIGHT ONE-BIT SEQUENCE.
 /SHR*P/          A=0-A(0-20),
                  F=13
C
COMMENT, HERE BEGINS THE CIRCULAR-LEFT ONE-BIT SEQUENCE.
 /CIL*P/          A=A(1-21)-A(0),
                  F=13
C
COMMENT, HERE BEGINS THE CLEAR ADD SEQUENCE.
 /CLA*P/          R=M(C),
                  A=0,
                  F=16
 /K(16)*P/        A=A.ADD.R,
                  F=13
 /K(13)*P/        C=D,
                  IF (G) THEN (F=11) ELSE (F=12)
                  END
$SIMULATE
*OUTPUT   CLOCK(1)=R,A,C,D,F,G,M(100),M(101),M(102),M(103),M(104)
*SWITCH   1,POWER=ON
*SWITCH   1,START=ON
*LOAD
    M(0-)=070100,000101,030102,060000,020006,040003,030103,
    M(7-)=010102,030104,050000,100000,
    M(100-)=010001,001001,0,0,0
*SIM      400,3
```

Fig. 5.6 (continued)

5.8 Write a Fortran Function subprogram for expression, k cir A, where cir is an operator shown in Table 3.3 and A is register A(1-10).

5.9 Simulate the serial comparison sequence described in statements (4.19) by a Fortran program, and compare its procedural description from Prob. 4.15.

5.10 Simulate the serial addition sequence described in statements (4.20) by a Fortran program, and compare its procedural description from Prob. 4.16.

```
*MAIN
C
COMMENT      **** SIMULATION OF GENERATION OF CLOCK PULSES
C                 AND TIMING SIGNALS
C
 SWITCH,          CLEAR(ON)
C
COMMENT, TWO PHASE CLOCK
 CLOCK,           CP(1)
C
 REGISTER,        RUN2
 TERMINAL,        CP0=CP(0)*RUN2,
1                 CP1=CP(1)*RUN2
C
COMMENT, ADD-CONTROL CLOCK
 REGISTER,        AC(1-0)
 DECODER,         N(0-3)=AC
 TERMINAL,        T0=N(0)*CP0,
1                 T1=N(1)*CP0,
1                 T2=N(2)*CP0,
1                 T3=N(3)*CP0,
1                 TD=N(0)*CP1
C
COMMENT, TIMING SIGNALS
 REGISTER,        D(3-0)
 DECODER,         B(0-17)=D
 TERMINAL,        DP 0=B( 0)*T0,
1                 DP 1=B( 1)*T0,
1                 DP 2=B( 2)*T0,
1                 DP 3=B( 3)*T0,
1                 DP 4=B( 4)*T0,
1                 DP 5=B( 5)*T0,
1                 DP 6=B( 6)*T0,
1                 DP10=B(10)*T0,
1                 DP11=B(11)*T0,
1                 DP12=B(12)*T0,
1                 DP13=B(13)*T0,
1                 DP14=B(14)*T0,
1                 DP15=B(15)*T0,
1                 DP16=B(16)*T0,
1                 DP17=B(17)*T0
C
COMMENT, HERE BEGINS EXECUTION STATEMENTS
 /CLEAR(ON)/      RUN2=1,
                  AC=0,
                  D=0
 /DP 5/           AC=AC.COUNT.
 /DP17/           RUN2=0
 /T1/             AC=AC.COUNT.
 /T2/             AC=AC.COUNT.
 /T3/             AC=AC.COUNT.
 /TD/             D=D.COUNT.
                  END
$SIMULATE
*OUTPUT    CLOCK(1)=RUN2, AC, D
*SWITCH    1,CLEAR=ON
*SIM       50,25
```

Fig. 5.7 Listing of CDL simulation of generation of clock pulses

5.11 If the binary numbers in the simple, stored-program computer are represented by the signed magnitudes, revise the ADD and SUB sequences in descriptions (4.22) and (4.26) accordingly. Overflow and negative zero should be properly accommodated.

5.12 If op-code 11 is assigned to represent multiplication, add multiplication sequence MPY to the stored-program computer with the revised ADD and SUB sequence described in Problem 5.11.

5.13 If op-code 12 is assigned to represent division, add division sequence DIV to the stored-program computer with the revised ADD and SUB sequences described in Problem 5.11. Division overflow check should be included.

5.14 Simulate by a Fortran program the stored-program computer with the revised ADD and SUB sequences as well as the MPY and DIV sequences as described in Problems 5.11 through 5.13.

5.15 Write a Fortran program to simulate the fetch sequence described by the following configuration and execution statements for the following two cases:
(a) simulate the labels described by statements (5.39),
(b) do not simulate the labels described by statements (5.39) but simulate the procedural version of the fetch sequence.

Register,	M(6–0),	
	X(0–5),	
	P(6–1),	
	I(5–0),	
	D(3–0),	
	AE,	
	IE,	
	RUN1,	
	EL,	
	OV,	
	LZ,	
	SI,	
Subregister,	M(P)=M(6–1)	(5.54)
Memory,	MEM(M)=MEM(0–127,0–5)	
Switch,	ERRORSTOP(NOBP,AVBP,BP)	
	MR(ON,OFF),	
	JS(ON,OFF),	
	MODE(DM,AEM,IM,PM)	
Terminal,	READ	
	DIE=K(0)+K(1)+K(2)+K(3)+K(12)+K(13)+K(14)+K(15),	
	DMR=MODE(DM)*MR(ON),	
	AEMR=MODE(AEM)*MR(ON),	
	IMR=MODE(IM)*MR(ON)	

Comment, fetch sequence begins here

/AE'∗DP(0)/	M←0
/Δ(AE'∗DP(0))/	M(P)←P
/AE'∗DP(1)/	READ←1
	X←0
/Δ(AE'∗DP(1))/	X←MEM(M)
/AE'∗DP(2)/	I←0,
	IE←0
/AE'∗DP(3)/	I←X
/AE'∗DP(4)/	IF (DIE=1) THEN (IE←1)
	IF (DIE∗ERRORSTOP(NOBP)=1) THEN (RUN1←1)
/AE'∗DP(5)/	IF (AEMR'∗IMR'=1) THEN (P←countup P)
/AE'∗DP(10)/	M(0)←1
/AE'∗DP(11)/	READ←1
	X←0
/Δ(AE'∗DP(11))/	X←MEM(M)
/AE'∗DP(15)/	M←0
/Δ(AE'∗DP(15))/	M(5–0)←X,
	M(6)←I(0)

Comment, fetch sequence ends here

/DP(14)/	OV←0,
	LZ←0,
	SI←0,
/DP(15)/	EL←0,
	IF (AEMR=0) THEN (AE←AE')
/TD/	IF (DMR=0) THEN (D←countup D)

5.16 Write a Fortran program to describe the four jump sequences described in statements (13.1) through (13.4).

5.17 Write a Fortran program to describe the two store sequences described in statements (13.5) and (13.6).

5.18 Write a Fortran program to describe the two shift sequences described in statements (13.7) and (13.8).

5.19 Write a Fortran program to describe the four sequences described in statements (13.9) through (13.12).

5.20 Given the following configuration, write a Fortran program to simulate the ADD sequence described in statements (10.16).

Comment, configuration of add sequence begins here

Register,	X(0–5),
	A(0–5),
	SI,
	OV,

LZ,

RUN1,

AV,

Subregister,	$A(M)=A(1-5)$,
	$X(M)=X(1-5)$,
Memory,	$MEM(0-127,0-5)$,
Switch,	$ERRORSTOP(NOBP,AVBP,BP)$,
	$MODE(DM,AEM,IM,PM)$,
	$MR(ON,OFF)$,
Light,	$LTAV$,
Terminal,	$DMR=MODE(DM)*MR(ON)$,
	$AEMR=MODE(AEM)*MR(ON)$, (5.55)
	$T(0-3)=N(0-3)*CP1$,
Terminal,	$C(4)=A(5)*X(5)$,
	$C(3)=G3$,
	$C(2)=A(3)*X(3)$,
	$C(1)=G1+G3*P3$,
	$C(0)=P1*G1+P1*P3*G3$
	$G3=X(4)*X(5)*A(5)'+X(5)*A(4)'*A(5)'+X(4)*A(4)'$
	$G1=X(2)*X(3)*A(3)'+X(3)*A(2)'*A(3)'+X(2)*A(2)'$
	$G0=A(1)*X(1)$
	$P3=A(2)*A(3)$
	$P1=A(1)$

5.21 Write a Fortran program to simulate the RAU sequence described in statements (10.22).

5.22 Write a Fortran program to simulate the MPY sequence described in statements (11.2).

5.23 Write a Fortran program to simulate the DIV sequence described in statements (11.3).

6

A

Stored

Program

Computer

The previous chapters introduce computer elements, micro-operations, and sequences. With the understanding of these functional units, the organization of a digital computer can now be described. In order to be realistic, it is preferred to choose a digital computer that has actually been built. And this digital computer should be a relatively simple but nontrivial, stored program computer so that a complete description is not cumbersome. A digital computer which met these requirements was chosen from the commercially available computers. This digital computer was designed and built specially for the educational purpose. The organization of this digital computer is now described (15).

In this chapter, the concept of the stored program computer is first presented. The configurations, the formats, and the instruction set of the chosen digital computer are then described. Symbolic programming of this digital computer is presented in the next chapter. Various sequences which implement this digital computer will be described in the succeeding chapters.

6.1 STORED PROGRAM CONCEPT

Consider computation of this simple problem by a digital computer:

$$Z = (W + X) - Y$$

where   W = +30

X = +10

Y = +25

Let register A be the accumulator where addition and subtraction are performed and the numbers for variables W,X, etc., be stored in the memory as shown in Fig. 5.1. The steps for computing the above problem are:

Step 1. Load W to Accumulator
Step 2. Add X to Accumulator
Step 3. Subtract Y from the Accumulator
Step 4. Store Accumulator to Z
Step 5. Stop computing

The first step takes the number (i.e., +30) located by W (i.e., an address) in the memory and transfers it to the accumulator. The second step takes the number (i.e., +10) located by X in the memory, adds it to the contents of the accumulator and leaves the sum (i.e., +40) in the accumulator. Similarly, during the third step, the number (i.e., +25) located by Y is taken from the memory and is then subtracted from the contents of the accumulator; the difference (i.e., +15) is left in the accumulator. During the fourth step, the number in the accumulator is stored at the memory location Z. As the last step, the computer is instructed to stop computing. The contents of the accumulator and the memory at the end of each of these steps are shown in Fig. 6.1.

6.1.1 Symbolic Programming

If, instead of a simple problem, the problem is of some complexity, the steps for computation can be many. Experience indicated that some abbreviation in describing the steps is necessary. Let the step to load W to accumulator be abbreviated to LDA W where L, D, and A are taken from the letters underlined in the above step 1. Similarly, by taking the underlined letters in the other steps, we have abbreviated the above steps into:

Step 1. LDA X
Step 2. ADD Y
Step 3. SUB W
Step 4. STA Z
Step 5. STP

Each of the above steps is called an *instruction*, and the sequence of these instructions is called a *program*. The order of the instructions in the program is important because it denotes the order that the instructions are executed.

Each of the above instructions except the last one consists of two parts, an operation code (or op-code) and an address. This is called the *instruction format*. The operation code such as LDA and ADD specifies the operation to be done on the data word and the address such as X and Y specifies the location of the data word in the memory. Since an address is not needed when the computer is instructed to stop computing, the last instruction has only the operation code part. The operation codes and the addresses of these instructions are all symbolic (i.e., they are not numbers); these instructions are called symbolic instructions and the program is called a *symbolic program*. The task of preparing a symbolic program is called *symbolic programming*. Symbolic programming is often called *assembly language programming*.

There needs to be another format to specify how the numbers for the variables are represented; this is called the *number format.* The number format in the above example is simply that each memory word represents a signed integer as shown in the block representing the memory in Fig. 6.1.

6.1.2 Execution of the Program

If the above symbolic program is to be computed by a stored-program computer, the program and data must first be loaded into the memory before the computation actually begins. Fig. 6.2(a) shows the manner in which the program and data of the above symbolic program are stored in the memory. When the computer starts to compute, it goes to the first location of the memory and reads out the instruction, LDA W; it then transfers the address W to the memory address register so that the number +30 can be read out. The micro-operations necessary for these operations are carried out

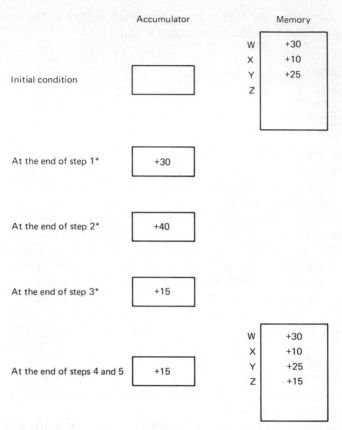

Fig. 6.1 Changes in the accumulator and the memory during the computation of a simple problem

in a sequence called the *fetch sequence* (or acquisition sequence). After the fetch sequence is completed, the number +30 is read out and the operation denoted by the operation code LDA is performed. This first instruction loads the number +30 into the accumulator; the micro-operations necessary for this instruction are carried out in a sequence called the load sequence. When the load sequence is completed, the computer performs another fetch sequence except that, at this time, the second instruction, ADD X, is fetched and made ready for execution. This second instruction is carried out by the add sequence. When the add sequence is completed, another fetch sequence is performed and then followed by a subtract sequence. This process continues on until the computer is instructed to stop by the last instruction. The fetch sequence is also known as *instruction cycle* or *I cycle*.

*No change in the memory during this step.

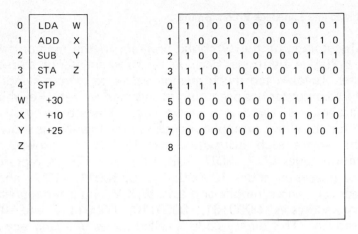

0	LDA	W
1	ADD	X
2	SUB	Y
3	STA	Z
4	STP	
W	+30	
X	+10	
Y	+25	
Z		

0	1 0 0 0 0 0 0 0 0 1 0 1
1	1 0 0 1 0 0 0 0 0 1 1 0
2	1 0 0 1 1 0 0 0 0 1 1 1
3	1 1 0 0 0 0 0 0 1 0 0 0
4	1 1 1 1 1
5	0 0 0 0 0 0 0 1 1 1 1 0
6	0 0 0 0 0 0 0 0 1 0 1 0
7	0 0 0 0 0 0 0 1 1 0 0 1
8	

(a) Storing the symbolic code   (b) Storing the binary code

Fig. 6.2 Storing a program in the memory

Execution of the instructions of the above program is carried out by the load sequence, the add sequence, the subtract sequence, the store sequence, and the stop sequence; these sequences are called *execution sequences*. The execution sequences are different for different instructions, but the fetch sequence is the same for all the instructions. The execution of a program, after beginning by a fetch sequence, is carried out by alternate execution of the fetch sequence and an execution sequence as indicated in Fig. 6.3; this is the manner in which a program in a stored program computer is executed. The execution sequence is also known as *execution cycle* or *E cycle*.

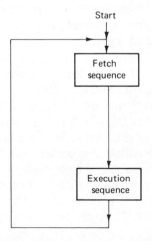

Fig. 6.3 Alternate operation of the fetch and execution sequences

6.1.3 Machine Language Programming

The storage of the symbolic program in the memory shown in Fig. 6.2(a) is fictitious, because the program is not stored in this manner. It takes too much memory space to store a symbolic code (and no computer has been built in this manner yet). For this reason, the program is stored in a *binary code*. The storage of the binary code for the above symbolic program in the memory is shown in Fig. 6.2(b), where each instruction has 12 bits. As shown, symbolic operation codes LDA, ADD, SUB, STA, and STP are represented by binary operation codes 100000, 10010, 10011, 11000, and 11111, respectively, and symbolic addresses W,X,Y, and Z are represented by binary addresses 0000101, 0000110, 0000111, and 0001000, respectively. This binary code is called a *machine language program* and the task of preparing a machine language program is called *machine language programming*.

When the electronic stored-program computer was first developed, the program was prepared in the machine language. Machine language programming was fraught with errors. It was not long before symbolic programming was introduced. If a program is written symbolically, it needs another program called an assembler (or assembly program) which "assembles" the symbolic program into a machine language program. The computer then executes the machine language program and gives the result. It goes without saying that the assembler is written in the machine language.

6.1.4 Why Stored Program Computers?

A machine which stores both the program and the data in an internal memory is called a *stored program computer.* The idea of storing the instructions of a program in the same way as the data was credited to Burks, von Neumann, and Goldstine (1,2,7). As a result, the internal memory of a stored program computer should be accessible at any location, because either an instruction or a data word can then be read from or stored in any memory location. A stored program computer usually has a suitable set of instructions to program many classes of problems. For this reason, a stored program computer is more often called a *general purpose digital computer*.

A stored program computer is extremely flexible. By changing the program stored in the machine, a different class of problems is solved or a different set of data is processed by the same machine without "rewiring the machine." And the program can be changed automatically when the execution of one program is completed. Since the stored program computer can assess its own instructions, it can therefore change these instructions; this makes possible, for example, the change of a method of solution depending upon the intermediate result during the computation. The internal memory can, within the limit of its capacity, accommodate a long program with little data or a short program with considerable data. Because of the above described flexibility together with the very high operating speed due to today's computer technology, most of the modern digital computers are stored program computers.

6.2 CONFIGURATIONS

The organization of a digital computer may conceptually be divided into five functional units: internal memory, arithmetic unit, control unit, input devices, and output devices. The block diagram of such an organization is shown in Fig. 6.4. The memory is the random access memory where the program and data are stored. The arithmetic unit whose major element is the accumulator is where arithmetic and other functional operations on the data are performed. The input devices and output devices receive and deliver the incoming and outgoing information, respectively. The control unit issues command and control signals whereby various sequences of micro-operations are carried out. The organization shown in Fig. 6.4 is analogous to a man sitting at a desk and doing computation.

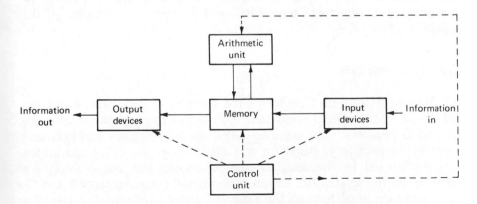

Fig. 6.4 Five functional units of a digital computer organization

The baskets for receiving problem sheets and for delivering computed results correspond to the input and output devices. The calculator on his desk is comparable to the arithmetic unit. His pencil and paper serve as the memory. And the man himself performs the control function.

Configurations for each of the five functional units of the stored program computer are now described.

6.2.1 Memory

The random access memory of this computer is a magnetic core memory with a cycle time of 15 microseconds. The memory, named MEM, has a capacity of 128 words; each word has 6 bits. The memory address register is named M and the buffer register (or exchange register here) is named X. Two subregisters X(M) and M(P) are declared. To initiate a read or a write operation of the memory, terminals READ and WRITE are provided. The memory configuration is described by the statements

Register,	M(6–0),	$memory address register	
	X(0–5)	$memory buffer register	
Subregister,	X(M)=X(1–5),	$magnitude part of X register	
	M(P)=M(6–1)	$program address part of M register	(6.1)
Memory,	MEM(M)=MEM(0–127,0–5)	$memory proper	
Terminal,	READ	$initiate memory read	
	WRITE	$initiate memory write	

Note that the subscripts for registers M and X are in a different order. These registers, terminals, and memory are shown in the diagram of Fig. 6.5.

6.2.2 Arithmetic Unit

The arithmetic unit performs the arithmetic and other functions of the computer. Two important registers in the arithmetic unit are A and Q registers; they are also called the accumulator and quotient register, respectively. Addition and subtraction and other operations are performed in the accumulator. Multiplication and division are performed in register AQ which is combined from registers A and Q. The addition is performed by a parallel adder with group carries; the parallel adder will be described later when the add sequence is

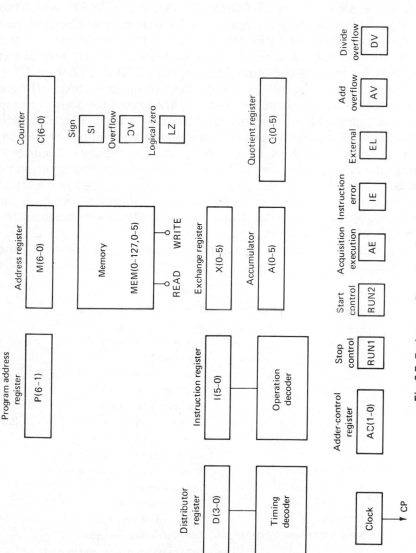

Fig. 6.5 Register configuration of the computer

described. There are three flipflops OV,SI, and LZ which indicate, respectively, overflow, sign, and logic zero during the add sequence. There are flipflop AV and light LTAV to indicate addition overflow and flipflop DV and light LTDV to indicate divide overflow. In addition, there is switch ERRORSTOP (NOBP,AVBP,BP) which has three positions: NOBP (no bypass), AVBP (add overflow bypass), and BP (bypass). When the ERRORSTOP switch is at NOBP position and when an addition overflow, a divide overflow, or an instruction overflow (to be discussed later) occurs, light LTAV, LTDV, or LTIE is turned on, respectively, and the computer stops. If the ERRORSTOP switch is at BP position, the computer does not stop but the light which indicates the error is turned on. If switch ERRORSTOP is at AVBP position, the computer does not stop when there is an add overflow error. There are two registers: Counter C and adder-control register AC; they control sequencing in some execution sequences. These registers may be considered as a part of the control unit. It should be noted that flipflop OV indicates the overflow from the parallel adder, while flipflop AV indicates the overflow from an addition.

The configuration of the arithmetic unit is described by the statements

Register,	A(0–5),	$accumulator
	Q(0–5),	$multiplier-quotient register
	C(6–0),	$counter
	AC(1–0),	$adder-control register
	SI,	$sign indicator
	OV,	$overflow indicator
	LZ,	$logic zero indicator
	AV,	$add overflow indicator
	DV	$division overflow indicator (6.2)
Subregister,	A(M)=A(1–5),	$magnitude part of A register
	Q(M)=Q(1–5),	$magnitude part of Q register
	AQ(M)=AQ(1–10)	$magnitude part of AQ casregister
Casregister,	AQ(0–10)=A–Q(M)	$AQ casregister
Light,	LTAV(ON,OFF),	$add overflow light
	LTDV(ON,OFF)	$division overflow light
Switch	ERRORSTOP(NOBP,AVBP,BP)	$three positions: no bypass, add overflow bypass, and bypass

These registers are shown in the diagram of Fig. 6.5, while these lights and switch are shown in the diagram of Fig. 6.6.

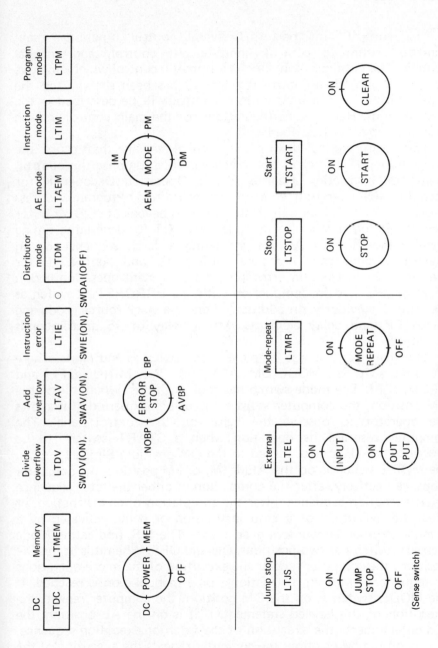

Fig. 6.6 Manual control switches and indicating lights on the control panel

6.2.3 Control Unit

The control unit performs several control functions: main control, arithmetic control, input-output control, and manual control. The configuration for the arithmetic control which employs counter C and adder-control register AC has been shown, and the configuration for the input-output control will be described in the next sections. Here, the configurations for the main control and the manual control are described.

The main control issues the control signals that cause the instructions to be fetched and executed. To accomplish this control, there are Instruction Register I and Operation Decoder K for decoding the operation code of an instruction, Program Address Register P for sequencing the instructions to be executed, Distributor Register D together with Timing Decoder DT for generating timing signals, and flipflop AE for indicating a fetch sequence or an execution sequence. There are flipflop IE and light LTIE for indicating an instruction error (i.e., a nonexistent operation code); they are operated in conjunction with the ERRORSTOP switch as mentioned previously. In addition, there is a clock source producing pulses CP, and delay elements with a delay of 15 microseconds employed.

The main control also employs some switches and lights. There are three switches: MODE(DM, AEM, IM, PM), MR(ON,OFF) and JS(ON,OFF). The mode switch has four positions. When it is on the DM position, the computer stops after each clock period; this allows the operator to observe the lights on the control panel. The computer resumes its operation when a START switch (to be described later) is next turned to the ON position. Similarly, when the MODE switch is on the AEM, IM, or PM position, the computer stops, respectively, after the completion of either the fetch sequence or an execution sequence, after the completion of an instruction, or after the execution of a stop instruction or being activated by a manual stop or encountering an error. The MR (indicating Mode Repeat) switch has two positions, ON and OFF. When it is at the ON position, the computer repeats the execution of the micro-operations or sequences, until an instructional or a manual stop is reached. If the MODE switch is on the DM position, the computer repeats the execution of the labeled statement. If it is on the AE position, the computer repeats the execution of the fetch or execution sequence. If it is on the IM position, the computer repeats the execution of the instruction. The computer ignores the signal if the MODE switch is on the PM position. The JS (indicating Jump Stop) switch (which is a so-called sense switch) has two positions, ON and OFF. When the JS switch is at the ON position, the computer stops before the execution of a jump when odd jump instructions (jump and jump instructions are to be described later) are being executed. The computer resumes its operation when a START switch is next turned to the ON position. The lights employed for the main control are those to indicate the instruction error, the four modes of the MODE switch, and the positions of the MR and JS switches.

The configuration for the main control is described below:

Register,	I(5–0),	$instruction register	
	P(6–1),	$program address register	
	D(3–0),	$distributor register	
	AE,	$acquisition-execution indicator	
	IE,	$instruction error indicator	
Clock,	CP,		
Decoder,	K(0–31)=I(5–1),	$operation decoder	
	DT(0–15)=D,	$timing decoder	
Switch,	MODE(DM,AEM,IM,PM),	$4-position mode switch	(6.3)
	MR(ON,OFF),	$mode repeat switch	
	JS(ON,OFF),	$sense switch	
Delay,	Δ=15,		
Light,	LTIE(ON,OFF),	$instruction error indicator	
	LTDM(ON,OFF),	$DM mode indicator	
	LTAEM(ON,OFF),	$AEM mode indicator	
	LTIM(ON,OFF),	$IM mode indicator	
	LTPM(ON,OFF),	$PM mode indicator	
	LTMR(ON,OFF),	$mode repeat indicator	
	LTJS(ON,OFF),	$jump stop indicator	

The registers, decoders, and clock are shown in Fig. 6.5 while these switches and lights are shown in Fig. 6.6.

The manual control performs the functions of starting and stopping computer operation, clearing the registers, and loading the program and data into the memory. The configuration to accomplish the start-stop and master-clear control functions is

Register,	RUN1,	$stop flipflop	
	RUN2,	$start flipflop	
Switch,	POWER(DC,MEM,OFF),	$turn power on or off	
	START(ON),	$initiate computer start manually	
	STOP(ON),	$initiate computer stop manually	(6.4)
	CLEAR(ON),	$master clear	
	RCS(ON),	$start computer remotely	
	BIS(ON),	$start computer from bi-octal converter	

Light,	LTSTART(ON,OFF)	$start indicator
	LTSTOP(ON,OFF)	$stop indicator
	LTDC(ON,OFF)	$display DC position of switch POWER
	LTMEM(ON,OFF)	$display MEM position of switch POWER

Switch POWER controls the power to the computer. Register RUN1 controls the stop and register RUN2 controls the start of the computer operation. Switch CLEAR clears all the registers, switch RCS starts the operation remotely, and switch BIS starts the operation from the bi-octal converter which is an input device available to the computer. The registers are shown in Fig. 6.5, while the lights and switches (except switches RCS and BIS) are shown in Fig. 6.6.

6.2.4 Input Devices

Switches are provided to insert the data directly into most of the registers. These switches are described by the statement:

Switch,	SWA(0-5)(ON),	$each sets one bit of register A to 1	
	SWAM(OFF),	$clear register A	
	SWQ(0-5)(ON),	$each sets one bit of register Q to 1	
	SWQM(OFF),	$clear register Q	
	SWX(0-5)(ON),	$each sets one bit of register X to 1	
	SWXM(OFF),	$clear register X	
	SWM(0-6)(ON),	$each sets one bit of register M to 1	
	SWMM(OFF),	$clear register M	
	SWI(0-5)(ON),	$each sets one bit of register I to 1	
	SWIM(OFF),	$clear register I	
	SWP(0-6)(ON),	$each sets one bit of register P to 1	
	SWPM(OFF),	$clear register P	
	SWD(0-3)(ON),	$each sets one bit of register D to 1	(6.5)
	SWDM(OFF),	$clear register D	
	SWC(0-6)(OFF),	$each resets one bit of register C to D	
	SWCM(ON),	$set all bits to 1	
	SWAC(1-0)(ON),	$each sets one bit of register AC to 1	
	SWACM(OFF),	$clear register AC	
	SWAE(ON),	$sets register AE to 1	
	SWAEM(OFF),	$clear register AEM	
	SWLZ(ON),	$sets register LZ to 1	
	SWLZM(OFF),	$clear register LZ	
	SWOV(ON),	$sets register OV to 1	
	SWOVM(OFF),	$clear register OV	

SWSI(ON),	$sets register SI to 1
SWSIM(OFF),	$clear register SI
SWDV(ON),	$sets register DV to 1
SWAV(ON),	$sets register AV to 1
SWIE(ON),	$sets register IE to 1
SWDAI(OFF),	$clear registers DV, AV, and IE

As described above, a row of single-position switches is provided for registers A,Q,X,M,I,P,D, and AC to set each bit of the register to 1; however, only a single-position switch is provided for each register to reset the entire register to 0. In the case of register C, a row of single-position switches is provided to reset each bit of the register to 0, but a single-position switch is used to set every bit of the register to 1. A single-position switch is provided for single-bit registers AE,LZ,OV,SI,DV,AV, and IE to set to 1 and another single-position switch for each of these registers to reset to 0.

Data can be inserted into the memory manually through the switches or by program control (i.e., by an instruction in a program). The configuration to accomplish this storing is described by the statements:

Register,	EL,	$I/O data transfer indicator	
Light,	LTEL(ON,OFF),	$indicate I/O data transfer when ON	
Switch,	INPUT(ON),	$enable to accept input manually	(6.6)
Terminal	E(0–5),	$six external data lines	
	INPLEASE,	$control line to an input device	
	DATAIN,	$control line from an input device	

There are six external lines named E from which the data from an input device are transferred to register X and then to the memory. Under program controlled transfer from an input device, terminals INPLEASE and DATAIN are provided. A signal on terminal INPLEASE issued by the computer notifies the input device to deliver a data word to the X register, while a signal on terminal DATAIN issued by the input device indicates to the computer that the data word has been delivered to the X register. This transfer is indicated by register EL and light LTEL. For manual loading, switch INPUT as well as the previously mentioned switches CLEAR, SWM, SWX, and START are used. This transfer is indicated by light LETL.

6.2.5 Output Devices

The output devices for this computer are lights which display the contents of registers and the conditions of switches. These lights are described by the statement:

Light,	LTA(0–5)(ON,OFF),	$a row of lights displaying register A	
	LTQ(0–5)(ON,OFF),	$a row of lights displaying register Q	
	LTX(0–5)(ON,OFF),	$a row of lights displaying register X	
	LTM(0–6)(ON,OFF),	$a row of lights displaying register M	
	LTI(0–5)(ON,OFF),	$a row of lights displaying register I	
	LTP(1–6)(ON,OFF),	$a row of lights displaying register P	
	LTD(0–3)(ON,OFF),	$a row of lights displaying register D	
	LTC(6–0)(ON,OFF),	$a row of lights displaying register C	(6.7)
	LTAC(1–0)(ON,OFF),	$a row of lights displaying register AC	
	LTAE(ON,OFF),	$display register AE	
	LTLZ(ON,OFF),	$display register LZ	
	LTOV(ON,OFF),	$display register OV	
	LTSI(ON,OFF),	$display register SI	
	LTDV(ON,OFF),	$display register DV	
	LTAV(ON,OFF),	$display register AV	
	LTIE(ON,OFF),	$display register IE	

It is interesting to mention that for those registers each flipflop has both a switch and a light associated with it, the switch and the light are implemented by a so-called light switch. The light switch has a translucent button which illuminates when the light is turned on by the switch. These light switches are indicated in the diagram of Fig. 6.7.

Any data word in the memory can be displayed in the X register manually or transferred to an output device by program control. The configuration to accomplish this display or transfer is described by the statements:

Switch,	OUTPUT(ON),	$enable to accept output manually	
Terminal,	OUTPLEASE,	$control line to an output device	(6.8)
	DATAOUT,	$control line from an output device	

The output lines from the X register are the data lines connected to an output device. Under program controlled transfer to an output device, terminals OUTPLEASE and DATAOUT are used. A signal on terminal OUTPLEASE issued by the computer notifies the output device that the data is ready in the X register, while a signal on terminal DATAOUT issued by the output device indicates to the computer that the data has been accepted. This transfer is also indicated by register EL and light LTEL. For manual display, switch OUTPUT as well as the previously mentioned switches CLEAR, SWM, and START are used. This transfer is also indicated by light LTEL.

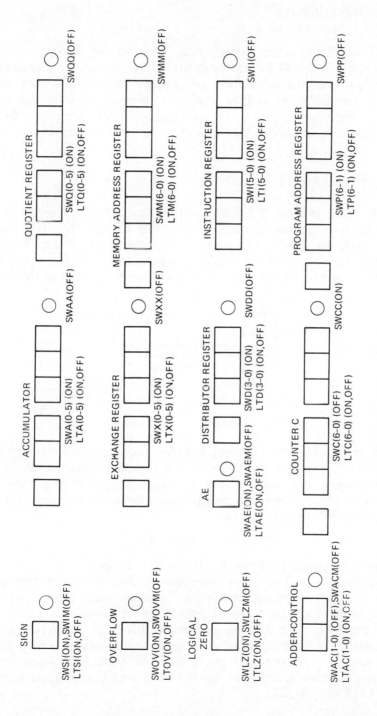

Fig. 6.7 Light switches and clear switches on the panel

6.3 WORD FORMATS

A word in a computer is an ordered set of digits which is processed as a unit in the computer. Word format is the arrangement of the bits of the word for a particular meaning. The word formats for a computer should be carefully selected, as they significantly affect the organization of the computer. In this computer, there are two formats, a number format and an instruction format.

6.3.1 Number Format

A word is treated by the arithmetic unit as a number and the format is called the *number format.* The number format is shown in Fig. 6.8. As shown, the number is a six-bit word (i.e., a memory word). It is a signed, fractional, binary number. It is a signed binary number as one of the bits of the word is designated as the sign bit.

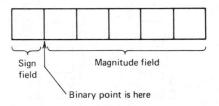

Sign field

Magnitude field

Binary point is here

Fig. 6.8 The number format

And it is a fractional binary number because the remaining bits of the word are designated as a fractional magnitude. With these designations, it is implied that an imaginary point, called the binary point, exists between the sign bit and the most significant bit of the fraction as illustrated below,

$$X_0 . X_1 X_2 X_3 X_4 X_5$$

where X_i represents a bit. X_0 is the sign bit and $X_1 . . . . . X_5$ are the magnitude bits. The point between X_0 and X_1 is the binary point whose existence is assumed when addition, subtraction, multiplication, or division is performed by the arithmetic unit.

When bit X_0 is 0, it represents a positive sign; when bit X_0 is 1, it represents a negative sign. All the signed binary numbers that are allowed in the computer are shown in Table 6.1. As shown, the largest number is 0.11111 (or +31/32) and the smallest number is 1.11111 (or −31/32).

Table 6.1 The signed binary numbers of the computer

Signed binary number	Decimal number
0.11111	+31/32
0.11110	+30/32
------------	----------
0.00001	+1/32
0.00000	0
1.00001	–1/32
------------	---------
1.11110	–30/32
1.11111	–31/32

One number which is possible but not shown in Table 6.1 is 1.00000. This number has a negative sign and zero magnitude; it is a "negative zero." The true zero or "positive zero" is 0.00000. Since only one zero is allowed, negative zero is considered illegal. Negative zero should not be inserted into the X register or into the memory; otherwise, the computed result may be erroneous.

6.3.2 Instruction Format

A word is treated by the control unit as an instruction, and the format is called the *instruction format*. The instruction of this computer consists of two parts (or two fields), the operation-code part and the address part. The instruction format is shown in Fig. 6.9. Each instruction consists of 12 bits or two words, 5 bits for the operation code and 7 bits for the address. Since there is only one address in the format, it is known as *single address format*.

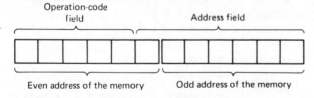

Fig. 6.9 The instruction format

There are two kinds of addresses: Operand address and instruction address. Since the memory has 128 six-bit words, it requires a seven-bit address to locate a number in the memory, and this 7-bit address is called an *operand address*. Since each instruction requires 12 bits, the memory can hold only 64 instructions and a 6-bit address is sufficient to address an instruction. This 6-bit address is called an *instruction address*. The address in the address field of an instruction can be either an operand address or an instruction address depending on the operation code; this will be further described. The two memory words which form an instruction must be two consecutive words. For simplicity, it is required that the instruction begin with a memory location with an even address. In other words, the address for the operation code field of an instruction must be an even address and that for the address field, an odd address; this is shown in Fig. 6.8.

It is possible to have a single word length for both the number and instruction. If the memory word were 12 bits, then each word stores either an instruction or a number. However, the memory becomes more expensive for the same number of words. The choice of one word length for the number and another word length for the instruction in this computer is for the sake of economy.

As an example, consider the program in Fig. 6.2(b) which is stored in a memory with a word length of 12 bits. In the case where the memory word length is 6 bits, the stored program is shown in Fig. 6.10. The 5-bit operation codes for LDA, ADD, SUB, STA, and

Memory address		Remark
0000000	1 0 0 0 0 0	
0000001	0 0 1 0 1 0	This is operand address W now 10
0000010	1 0 0 1 0 0	
0000011	0 0 1 0 1 1	This is operand address X now 11
0000100	1 0 0 1 1 0	
0000101	0 0 1 1 0 0	This is operand address Y now 12
0000110	1 1 0 0 0 0	
0000111	0 0 1 1 0 1	This is operand address Z now 13
0001000	1 1 1 1 1 0	
0001001	0 0 0 0 0 0	
0001010	0 1 1 1 1 0	
0001011	0 0 1 0 1 0	
0001100	0 1 1 0 0 1	
0001101		

Fig. 6.10 Storing a binary program in a memory (The instruction and the number have different word lengths)

STP remain unchanged, but the binary addresses for W,X,Y, and Z are changed; these operand addresses are now 0001010 (10), 0001011 (11), 0001100 (12), and 0001101 (13), respectively. The first instruction is stored in the memory at addresses 000000 and 000001, and the address for this instruction is 000000. Similarly, the instruction addresses for the other four instructions are 0000010, 0000100, 0000110, and 0001000; they are always even.

6.4 THE INSTRUCTION SET

The instruction set consists of 30 instructions: five load and store instructions, six arithmetic instructions, four input-output instructions, eight jump instructions, four shift instructions, and three miscellaneous instructions. The names, op-codes, and descriptions of these instructions are shown in Table 6.2. Notice that the symbolic codes are derived from certain letters of the instruction names, and the instructions are described by the statements. These instructions will be described precisely in the later chapters.

The instruction format in Fig. 6.9 applies only to the first fifteen instructions in Table 6.2; the other instructions have formats which are slightly different. There are actually six instruction formats in all; these formats are shown in Fig. 6.11. As shown, the major differences of these formats lie in the 5-bit or 6-bit op-codes and in the 6-bit or 7-bit addresses. Because of practical considerations, it is quite common for a commercially available stored program computer to have multiple instruction formats.

6.4.1 Load and Store Instructions

As shown in Table 6.2, there are three load instructions: LDA, LDN, and LDC. They follow the format in Fig. 6.11(a). *Instruction LDA* clears the accumulator and adds the number in the memory location at address m to the accumulator where m is a 7-bit operand address. *Instruction LDN* is identical to LDA except a subtraction instead of an addition is performed. *Instruction LDC* transfers the contents of the memory location at address m to the memory location at address (m+1).

5 bits	7 bits
op-code	operand address m

(a) For load, store, arithmetic, and input-output instructions

6 bits	6 bits
op-code	instruction address n

(b) For jump instructions

6 bits	6 bits
op-code	shift count k

(c) For shift instructions

5 bits	7 bits
op-code	load count j

(d) For load C register instruction

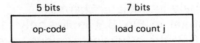

5 bits	
op-code	

Not used

(e) For change accumulator sign instruction

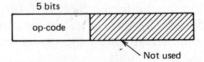

5 bits		6 bits
op-code		instruction address n

Not used

(f) For stop instruction

Fig. 6.11 Instruction formats of the computer (m and j represent 7-bit fields, and n and k 6-bit fields)

Table 6.2 Description of the instruction set

Instruction name	Symbolic code*	Op-code	Description in statements[+]
LoaD A	LDA m	10000	Step 1, A ← O 2, M ← m 3, X ← MEM(M) 4, A ← A add X
LoaD A Negative	LDN m	10001	Step 1, A ← O 2, M ← m 3, X ← MEM(M) 4, A ← A sub X
LoaD Consecutive	LDC m	11100	Step 1, M ← m 2, X ← MEM(M) 3, M ← countup M 4, MEM(M) ← X
STore A	STA m	11000	Step 1, X ← A 2, M ← m 3, MEM(M) ← X
STore Q	STQ m	11001	Step 1, X ← Q 2, M ← m 3, MEM(M) ← X
ADD	ADD m	10010	Step 1, X ← MEM(m) 2, A ← A add X 3, IF (ovfl) THEN (LTAV ← ON,RUN1 ←1)
SUBtract	SUB m	10011	Step 1, X ← MEM(m) 2, A ← A sub X
Replace Absolute Unity	RAU m	10100	Step 1, X ← MEM(m) 2, A ← 1 3, A ← A add X 4, X ← A 5, MEM(M) ← X
Replace Subtract Unity	RSU m	10101	Step 1, X ← MEM(m) 2, A ← 1 3, A ← A sub X 4, IF (ovfl) THEN (LTAV ← ON,RUN1 ←1) 5, X ← A 6, MEM(M) ← X
MultiPlY	MPY m	10110	Step 1, Q ← 0 2, X ← MEM(m) 3, determine product sign 4, Q(M) ← X(M) 5, X ← A 6, A ← 0 7, AQ(M) ← X mpy Q

Table 6.2 (continued)

Instruction name	Symbolic code*	Op-code	Description in statements+
DIVide	DIV m	10111	Step 1, X ← MEM(m) 2, test for divide ovfl 3, IF (no div-ovfl) THEN (Q ← AQ(M) div X)
MaNual Input	MNI m	01000	Step 1, RUN1 ← 1 2, wait for data; when come, RUN2 ← 1 3, MEM(M) ← X 4, C ← countdn C 5, M ← countup M 6, IF (C ≠ 0) THEN (go to step 1) 7, complete
MaNual Output	MNO m	01001	Step 1, X ← MEM(M) 2, RUN1 ← 1 3, wait for data to be accepted; when ac- cepted, RUN2 ← 1 4, C ← countdn C 5, M ← countup M 6, IF (C ≠ 0) THEN (go to step 1) 7, complete
EXternal Input	EXI m	01010	Step 1, initiate to load E(0–5) into X 2, RUN1 ← 1 3, wait for data; when come, RUN2 ← 1 4, MEM(M) ← X 5, C ← countdn C 6, M ← countup M 7, IF (C ≠ 0) THEN (go to step 1) 8, complete
EXternal Output	EXO m	01011	Step 1, X ← MEM(M) 2, initiate to unload X to E(0–5) 3, RUN1 ← 1 4, wait for data to be accepted; when accepted, RUN2 ← 1 5, C ← countdn C 6, M ← countup M 7, IF (C ≠ 0) THEN (go to step 1) 8, complete

Table 6.2 (continued)

Instruction name	Symbolic code*	Op-code	Description in statements[+]
UNconditional Jump Even	UNE n	001010	M(P) ← n
UNconditional Jump Odd	UNO n	001011	IF (JS(ON)) THEN (RUN1 ← 1), IF (JS(OFF) + START(ON)) THEN (M(P) ← n)
Negative Accumulator Jump Even	NAE n	001100	IF (A(0)) THEN (M(P) ← n)
Negative Accumulator Jump Odd	NAO n	001101	IF (JS(ON) * A(0)) THEN (M(P) ← n)
Non-Zero Jump Even	NZE n	001110	IF (A(M) ≠ 0) THEN (M(P) ← n)
Non-Zero Jump Odd	NZO n	001111	IF (JS(ON) * (A(M) ≠ 0)) THEN (RUN1 ← 1), IF (JS(OFF) * (A(M) ≠ 0)) + START(ON)) THEN (M(P) ← n)
SuBroutine Jump Even	SBE n	001000	Step 1, M ← 0000001 2, X ← P 3, MEM(M) ← X 4, M(P) ← n
SuBroutine Jump Odd	SBO n	001001	IF (JS(ON)) THEN (RUN1 ← 1), IF (JS(OFF) + START(ON)) THEN (step 1, M ← 0000001, 2, X ← P, 3, MEM(M) ← X, 4, M(P) ← n)
Shift AQ Right Even	SRE k	110100	AQ(M) ← k shr AQ(M)
Shift AQ Right Odd	SRO k	110101	Step 1, Q ← 0 2, AQ(M) ← k shr AQ(M)
Shift AQ Left Even	SLE k	110110	AQ(M) ← k shl AQ(M)
Shift AQ Left Odd	SLO k	110111	Step 1, A(0) ← A(0) 2, AQ(M) ← k shl AQ(M)
Load CounT Register	LCT j	11101	C ← j

Table 6.2 (continued)

Instruction name	Symbolic code*	Op-code	Description in statements[+]
Change Accumulator Sign	CAS	11110	$A(0) \leftarrow A(0)'$
SToP	STP n	11111	Step 1, RUN1 ← 1
			2, IF (START(ON))
			THEN (M(P) ← n)

*m and j represent 7-bit fields, while n and k represent 6-bit fields.

+operators mpy and div are explained in the text. ovfl denotes that overflow occurs.

There are two store instructions: STA and STQ. They also follow the format in Fig. 6.11(a). *Instruction STA* stores the contents of the accumulator in the memory location at address m and *instruction STQ* stores the contents of register Q instead.

The statement descriptions in Table 6.2 give the descriptions to carry out these instructions in steps.

6.4.2 Arithmetic Instructions

There are six arithmetic instructions: ADD, SUB, RAU, RSU, MPY, and DIV. They follow the format in Fig. 6.11(a). *Instruction ADD* adds the number in the memory location at address m to the accumulator. *Instruction SUB* subtracts that at address m from the accumulator. *Instruction RAU* adds a least significant bit to the contents of the memory location at address m. The addition treats the contents as a 6-bit unsigned binary integer. In using this instruction, m should be an odd address and the contents of the memory location at address (m−1) should be 0. In this case, the overflow, if it occurs, is then stored at the least significant bit position of the memory location at address (m−1). *Instruction RSU* subtracts a least significant bit from the contents of the memory location at address m. Both RAU and RSU instructions are used for address modification. If overflow occurs during the execution of an ADD or RSU instruction, light AV will be turned on and the computer stops.

Instruction MPY multiplies the number in the accumulator by the number in the memory location at address m, and leaves a 10-bit product plus sign bit at the AQ register. Operator MPY in Table 6.2 denotes this multiplication. To accomplish the multiplication, a prior LDA instruction to load the multiplicand into the accumulator is required.

Instruction DIV divides the 10-bit dividend plus sign in the AQ register by the divisor in the memory location at address m, and produces a quotient in register Q and a reminder in the accumulator. Again, operator DIV in Table 6.2 denotes this division. LDA and LDQ instructions are required prior to the division to load the dividend into the AQ register. The division requires that the dividend be less than the divisor so that the quotient is fractional. This condition is tested before the division actually begins. If this condition is not met, the divide overflow condition occurs. Light DV is turned on and the computer stops.

6.4.3 Input-output Instructions

There are two manual input-output instructions, MNI and MNO, and two program controlled input-output instructions, EXI and EXO. They follow the format in Fig. 6.11(a). *Instruction MNI* stores the data words inserted manually into the X register to the consecutive memory locations at the addresses beginning with address m. *Instruction MNO* transfers the data words in the consecutive memory locations at the addresses beginning with address m to the X register for visual output. In either of the two instructions, the number of data words to be transferred is determined by the contents of register C which has to be loaded with a desired number by instruction LCT.

Instruction EXI stores data words taken from an input device in the memory locations at the addresses beginning with address m. *Instruction EXO* transfers the data words from the consecutive memory locations at the addresses beginning with address m to an output device. In either of these two instructions, the number of data words to be transferred is determined by the contents of register C which has to be loaded with a desired number by instruction LCT.

In the statement descriptions of these instructions in Table 6.2, the computer stops when flipflop RUN1 is set to 1, and resumes its operation when flipflop RUN2 is set to 1. The steps in executing these instructions will be more precisely described in the later chapters.

6.4.4 Jump Instructions

In this computer, the normal sequence of instruction executions means the sequence which follows the ascending order of memory addresses. Jump refers to a break from the normal sequence. Jump instructions are those which cause a break from the normal sequence. There are eight instructions which follow the format in Figure 6.11(b). Each instruction has a 6-bit op-code and a 6-bit instruction address. This instruction address is one-half of a 7-bit memory address to which the program should jump. For example, to jump to memory address 28 (octal 34), the instruction address in the jump instruction should be 14 (octal 16).

Instructions UNE and UNO are unconditional transfer instructions. *Instruction UNE* takes the next instruction in the memory location at the 6-bit address n. Address n will be transferred to M(6–1) part of the register M while M(0) is made 0. *Instruction UNO* stops the computer operation if JS switch is at the ON position and executes an UNE instruction when switch START is turned on. If the JS switch is at the OFF position, this instruction again executes an UNE instruction. Instructions SBE and SBO are also unconditional transfer instructions. *Instruction SBE* first stores the contents of register P in the memory location at address 00000001 and then takes the next instruction in the memory location at address n. *Instruction SBO* stops the computer operation if JS switch is ON and executes a SBO instruction when switch START is turned on. If the JS switch is OFF, this instruction again executes an SBO instruction.

Instructions NAE and NAO are conditional jump instructions. If A(0) is 1 (i.e., the number in the accumulator is negative), *instruction NAE* takes the next instruction in the memory location at address n; otherwise, it follows the normal sequence. If the JS switch is ON, *instruction NAO* takes the next instruction in the memory location at address n if A(0) is 1; otherwise, instruction NAE is executed. *Instructions NZE and NZO* are also conditional jump instructions. They are similar to instructions NAE and NAO, respectively, except that the condition is the number in the accumulator not equal to zero.

6.4.5 Shift Instructions

There are four shift instructions: SRE, SRO, SLE, and SLO. They follow the format in Fig. 6.11(c). *Instruction SRE* shifts the contents of register AQ(M) k bit positions to the right. *Instruction SRO* first clears register Q and then shifts the contents of register AQ(M) k bit positions to the right. *Instruction SLE* shifts the contents of register AQ(M) k bit positions to the left. *Instruction SLO* also shifts the contents of register AQ(M) k bit positions to the left; in addition, it transfers sign bit Q(0) to sign bit A(0).

6.4.6 LCT, CAS, and STP Instructions

Instruction LCT, load count register, follows the format in Fig. 6.11(d). It transfers load count j to register C. *Instruction CAS,* change accumulator sign, complements sign bit A(0). It follows the format in Fig. 6.11(e). *Instruction STP,* stop, follows the format in Fig. 6.11(f). It stops the computer by setting flipflop RUN1 to 1. When switch START is next turned ON, it takes the next instruction in the memory location at address n.

6.5 COMPUTER CHARACTERISTICS

The computer is a commercially available, stored program computer. It was designed and built especially for educational purposes. The characteristics are summarized in Table 6.3. It has a

Table 6.3 The characteristics of the computer

1. *Application*	educational and general purpose
2. *Word structure*	
number base	2
number representation	signed magnitude
number format	fractional
word length	6 bits
number of instruction set	30
instruction length	two words per instr.
3. *Arithmetic unit*	
addition	1.75 milliseconds
subtraction	1.75 milliseconds
multiplication	3.15 milliseconds
division	4.70 milliseconds
4. *Memory unit*	
storage elements	magnetic cores
number of words	128
number of bits per word	6
memory cycle time	15 microseconds
5. *Control unit*	
control	stored program
timing	synchronous
clock period	50 microseconds
operation	parallel transfers
instruction type	single address
6. *Input-output devices*	
input devices	switches
output devices	lights

ferrite core memory of 128 six-bit words with a cycle time of 15 micro-seconds. It is a binary, fractional computer. The numbers are six bits, including a sign bit in length, and are in the signed magnitude representation. There are 30 instructions. Each instruction requires two consecutive memory words.

The computer operates synchronously with a clock period of 50 microseconds (or a rate of 20,000 pulses per second). The internal transfers which are all in parallel contribute a simpler description of the organization. Most of the registers are displayed by lights, and switches are provided as input devices. Single and multiple position switches are also provided for control purposes. These switches enable the operator to start/stop the computer operation, to input/output the data, and to exert program and error control.

Of particular importance is the MODE switch which allows the operator to observe the contents of the registers after each clock pulse, after the execution of each sequence, after the execution of each instruction, or after the execution of the entire program.

PROBLEMS

6.1 Similar to the example given in this chapter, write a program to compute,

$$Z = (W + X)Y - U/V$$

where $U = 2$

     $V = 1$

     $W = 3$

     $X = 4$

     $Y = 5$

The op-codes for multiplication and divide are 10110 and 10111, respectively. Show the storage of the binary code in the memory, if the memory has a word length of

(a) 12 bits, and

(b) 6 bits.

6.2 If the memory has a word length of 24 bits, an address of 15 bits, and a capacity of 32,768 words, describe

(a) the memory configuration,

(b) the configuration for the arithmetic unit, and

(c) the configuration for the main control

by referencing the descriptions of the computer in this chapter.

6.3 From the memory given in problem 6.2, if six bits of the 24-bit word are allocated for operation codes, how many instruction formats are required for the 30 instructions in Table 6.2?

6.4 Write a program which must use one or more jump instructions. Store the program in the memory and discuss the relation of the 6-bit instruction addresses of the jump instructions to the 7-bit memory addresses.

7

Computer

Programming

This chapter shows the use of the instructions in writing programs and introduces some programming techniques. A complete program usually consists of two parts, instructions and data. The program must first be placed in the memory; this operation is called loading. The data may be loaded initially or during the execution of the program or both; this depends on how the data are introduced into the program. The addresses of the memory locations where the instructions are stored are called *instruction addresses* and those where operands are stored are called *operand addresses.* Recall that two consecutive memory locations are required to store one instruction. Since the address for the first location must be even, the memory addresses for the instructions are always even.

A number of programs are presented in this chapter. The first program is shown in both symbolic and binary codes. Since symbolic code is easier to write and easier to comprehend, only symbolic codes are shown in the succeeding programs. Additional examples of programs may be found elsewhere (19).

7.1 BINARY POINT AND SCALING

It has been previously mentioned that the binary numbers represented in this computer are fractional. This means that the binary point of the number in register A is located between bits A(0) and A(1), that in register X is located between bits X(0) and X(1). These locations of binary points that make the numbers fractional are called *normal locations.*

If one prepares a program in which there are numbers not normally located (i.e., the numbers are not fractional), the numbers have to be scaled and the locations of the binary points of the numbers have to be kept track of. The rules in scaling and tracking the binary point for addition, subtraction, multiplication, and division are described below.

7.1.1 Addition and Subtraction

When a signed binary number is added to (or subtracted from) another signed binary number, the augend (or minuend) is in the accumulator and the addend (or subtrahend) is in the X register; this situation previously indicated in Table 6.2 is now illustrated in Figures 7.1(a), 7.2(a), and 7.3(a). The sum after the addition (or the difference after the subtraction) is in the accumulator and the augend (or minuend) is lost; this is illustrated in Figures 7.1(b), 7.2(b), and 7.3(b). If the numbers are signed fractional numbers, the sum (or difference) remains normally located; this is the example shown in Figure 7.1. If the numbers are signed integers or signed

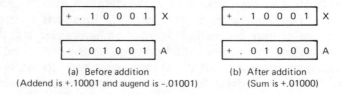

(a) Before addition
(Addend is +.10001 and augend is -.01001)

(b) After addition
(Sum is +.01000)

Fig. 7.1 Location of the binary points before and after addition (or subtraction) for signed fractional numbers

mixed numbers, the sum (or difference) is no longer normally located. For the example in Figure 7.2 where the augend and addend (or minuend and subtrahend) are both signed integers, the sum (or difference) is again an integer. For the example in Figure 7.3 where the augend and addend (or minuend and subtrahend) are both signed mixed numbers, the binary points of the two numbers must be first aligned before addition (or subtraction); this is shown in Figure 7.3(b). The sum (or difference) in this example is again a mixed number as shown in Figure 7.3(c). The moving of the binary point of a number for adapting to calculation is called *scaling*.

7.1.2 Multiplication

When a signed binary multiplicand is to be multiplied by a signed

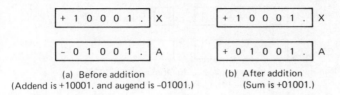

(a) Before addition
(Addend is +10001. and augend is –01001.)

(b) After addition
(Sum is +01001.)

Fig. 7.2 Location of the binary points before and after addition (or subtraction) for signed integers

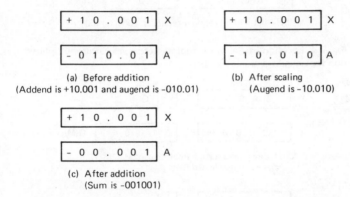

(a) Before addition
(Addend is +10.001 and augend is –010.01)

(b) After scaling
(Augend is –10.010)

(c) After addition
(Sum is –001001)

Fig. 7.3 Location of the binary points before and after addition (or subtraction) for signed mixed numbers

binary multiplier, the multiplicand and the multiplier are initially in the X and Q registers, respectively, and the accumulator is initially cleared; this situation indicated previously in Table 6.2 is now illustrated in Figures 7.4(a), 7.5(a), and 7.6(a). After the multiplication, the 10-bit product plus sign is in the AQ casregister, the multiplicand remains in the X register, and the multiplier is lost; this is illustrated in Figures 7.4(b), 7.5(b), and 7.6(b). If the numbers are signed fractional numbers, the product is normally located; this is the example shown in Figure 7.4. If the numbers are signed integers or signed mixed numbers, the binary point of the product is no longer normally located. The binary point of the product is determined by the rule that *the fractional bits of the product are equal to the sum of the fractional bits of the multiplicand and the multiplier.* For the example in Figure 7.5 where the multiplicand and the multiplier are both signed integers, this rule locates the binary point of the product at the right of bit Q(5) and the product is again an integer. For the example in Figure 7.6, where the multiplicand and multiplier are both signed mixed numbers, this rule locates the binary point of the product between bits A(4) and A(5) and the product in this example is again a mixed number.

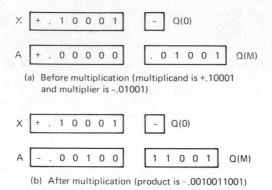

Fig. 7.4 Location of the binary points before and after multiplication for signed fractional numbers

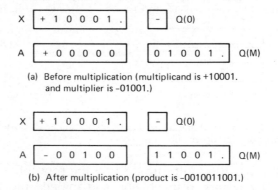

Fig. 7.5 Location of the binary points before and after multiplication for signed integers

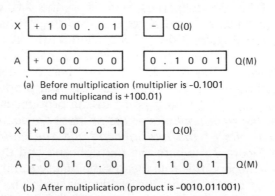

Fig. 7.6 Location of the binary points before and after multiplication for signed mixed numbers

7.1.3 Division

When a signed binary dividend is to be divided by a signed binary divisor, the 10-bit dividend plus sign is initially in the AQ casregister and the divisor in the X register; this situation indicated previously in Table 6.2 is now illustrated by Figures 7.7(a), 7.8(a), and 7.9(a). After the division, the quotient is in the Q register and the remainder in the accumulator; this is illustrated in Figures 7.7(b), 7.8(b) and 7.9(b). If the numbers are signed fractional numbers, the quotient is normally located; this is the example shown in Figure 7.7. If the numbers are signed integers or signed mixed numbers, the binary point of the quotient is no longer normally located. The binary point of the quotient is determined by the rule that *the fractional bits of the quotient are equal to the difference obtained by subtracting the number of fractional bits of the divisor from the number of fractional bits of the dividend.* For the example of Figure 7.8 where the dividend and the divisor are both integers, this rule locates the binary point of the quotient at the right of Q(5) and the quotient is again an integer. For the example of Figure 7.9 where the dividend and the divisor are both signed mixed numbers, this rule locates the binary point of the quotient between bits Q(2) and Q(3) and the quotient in this example is again a mixed number.

The tracking of the binary point in programming is annoying. This is the problem of scaling. If the numbers are not properly scaled during the computation, the results are erroneous.

7.1.4 Examples for Programming Division

If dividend X and divisor Y are both normally located and if their magnitudes are both of 5 bits, the magnitude of dividend X must be expanded into a magnitude of 10 bits by adding 5 zeros. Let X and Y be, respectively, $-.10001$ and $+.10101$. Division of X by Y requires the following instructions,

$$
\begin{array}{lll}
\text{m0} & \text{LDA} & \text{m3} \\
\text{m1} & \text{SRO} & \text{00} \\
\text{m2} & \text{DIV} & \text{m4} \\
\text{m3} & \text{--.10001} \\
\text{m4} & \text{+.10101}
\end{array}
\tag{7.1}
$$

Note that instruction SRO 00 merely clears register Q; thus, the dividend becomes $-.1000100000$.

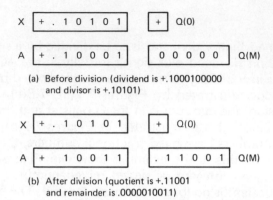

(a) Before division (dividend is +.1000100000
and divisor is +.10101)

(b) After division (quotient is +.11001
and remainder is .0000010011)

Fig. 7.7 Location of the binary points before and after division for
signed fractional numbers

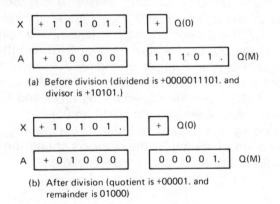

(a) Before division (dividend is +0000011101. and
divisor is +10101.)

(b) After division (quotient is +00001. and
remainder is 01000)

Fig. 7.8 Location of the binary points before and after division for
signed integers

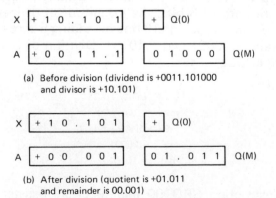

(a) Before division (dividend is +0011.101000
and divisor is +10.101)

(b) After division (quotient is +01.011
and remainder is 00.001)

Fig. 7.9 Location of the binary points before and after division for
signed mixed numbers

If the magnitudes of dividend X and divisor Y are both 5-bit integers, the magnitude of dividend X must again be expanded into a magnitude of 10 bits. Let X and Y be, respectively, −01110 and +00100. Division of X by Y requires the following instructions,

$$
\begin{array}{lll}
\text{m0} & \text{LDA} & \text{m3} \\
\text{m1} & \text{SRE} & \text{05} \\
\text{m2} & \text{DIV} & \text{m4} \\
\text{m3} & \text{−01110} & \\
\text{m4} & \text{+00100} &
\end{array}
\qquad (7.2)
$$

Note that instruction SRE 05 expands the 5-bit magnitude of the dividend into 10 bits, and the dividend becomes −0000001110.

If dividend X is an 11-bit signed integer −1010101110 stored at locations m4 and m5 and divisor Y is a 6-bit signed integer +00100 stored at location m6, division of X by Y requires the following instructions,

$$
\begin{array}{lll}
\text{m0} & \text{LDA} & \text{m5} \\
\text{m1} & \text{SRE} & \text{05} \\
\text{m2} & \text{LDA} & \text{m4} \\
\text{m3} & \text{DIV} & \text{m6} \\
\text{m4} & \text{−10101} & \\
\text{m5} & \text{001110} & \\
\text{m6} & \text{+00100} &
\end{array}
\qquad (7.3)
$$

Notice that the 11-bit signed number is loaded into the AQ casregister by the first three instructions.

If the dividend and the divisor are signed mixed numbers, scaling is required to avoid division overflow (division overflow is to be shown subsequently). Let dividend X and divisor Y be, respectively, +11.101 and +10.101. Division of X by Y requires,

$$
\begin{array}{lll}
\text{m0} & \text{LDA} & \text{m3} \\
\text{m1} & \text{SRO} & \text{02} \\
\text{m2} & \text{DIV} & \text{m4} \\
\text{m3} & \text{+11.101} & \\
\text{m4} & \text{+10.101} &
\end{array}
\qquad (7.4)
$$

After the division, the quotient is +01.011 which is not normally located.

7.2 USE OF THE ARITHMETIC INSTRUCTIONS

The first example shows the use of arithmetic instructions ADD,

SUB, MPY, and DIV together with instructions LDA, UNO, SRE, and STP. The problem is to compute

- a. 8 + 12
- b. 12 – 14
- c. 12 × 14
- d. –14 ÷ 3

and to show the results in the accumulator after each computation.

7.2.1 Symbolic Program

Both the symbolic and binary programs are shown in Figure 7.10.

Symbolic Program			Binary Program		
Instruction Address	Operation Code	Operand* Address	Instruction Address†	Operation Code	Operand Address
a0	LDA	m0	0000000(00)	10000	0100000
a2	ADD	ml	0000010(02)	10010	0100001
a4	UNO	a6	0000100(04)	001011	000011
a6	LDA	ml	0000110(06)	10000	0100001
a10	SUB	m2	0001000(10)	10011	0100010
a12	UNO	a14	0001100(12)	001011	000111
a14	LDA	ml	0001110(14)	10000	0100001
a16	MPY	m2	0010000(16)	10110	0100010
a20	UNO	a22	0010100(20)	001011	001011
a22	LDN	m2	0010110(22)	10001	0100010
a24	SRE	05	0011000(24)	110100	000101
a26	DIV	m3	0011010(26)	10111	0100011
a30	STP	00	0011110(30)	11111	0000000

Operand Address	Data words (Decimal numbers)	Operand Address†	Data words
m0	8	0100000(32)	001000
m1	12	0100001(33)	001100
m2	14	0100010(34)	001110
m3	3	0100011(35)	000011

Fig. 7.10 Program showing the use of arithmetic instructions

*m's in this column are operand addresses, but a's are instruction addresses because of jump instructions.

†The numbers in the parentheses are octal.

The instruction part consists of 13 instructions, and the data part of 6 data words. The first three instructions compute the addition problem, and the second, third, and fourth groups of three instructions compute, respectively, the subtraction, multiplication, and division problems. For the addition problem, the first instruction LDA loads number 8_{10} into the accumulator and the second instruction ADD adds number 12_{10} to it leaving the result in the accumulator. The JS switch on the panel should have been at the ON position. The third instruction UNO, which is a jump instruction, causes the computer to stop and the result (010100 or $+20_{10}$) in register A can be observed from lights LTA on the panel.

When the operator turns on the START switch, the computer continues to execute the next instruction. The operation of the next three instructions (LDA, SUB, UNO) is identical to the first three instructions, except a subtraction instead of an addition is executed. Since the result is 100010 or -2_{10}, bit A(0) which represents the sign is 1 to indicate that the difference is a negative number.

When the START switch is turned on again, the third set of three instructions (LDA, MPY, UNO) is executed. The multiplication leaves the result (00010101000 or $+168_{10}$) in the AQ register; the ten-bit product plus a sign bit are displayed on the panel.

When the operator turns on the START switch again, the next three instructions are executed. The first instruction LDN loads dividend -14_{10} into the accumulator. Since both the dividend and the divisor are 5-bit integers, the dividend should be scaled into a 10-bit integer so that the quotient and the remainder should also be integers. The second instruction SRE accomplishes this scaling by shifting the 5-bit dividend to the Q(M) register. The quotient will be in the Q register and the remainder in the A(M) register. Thus, the division ($-14/3$) should give a quotient of -4 and a remainder of -2. Lights LTA and LTQ exhibit numbers 100010 (or -2_{10}) and 100100 (or -4_{10}), respectively. After the division, the computer executes instruction STP and stops.

7.2.2 Binary Program

The binary program in Figure 7.1 consists of 26 instruction words and 6 data words. It is loaded with the first instruction in the first memory location. Since each instruction occupies two memory words, the memory addresses (00_8 to 30_8) for the instruction words are all even; but those (32_8 to 37_8) for the data words are either even or odd. The operation code is either a five-bit or a six-bit code.

Whenever it is a six-bit code, its address field can hold only a six-bit address. Jump instructions have a six-bit operation code and leave room only for 6 bits of an instruction address. But this instruction address can be reduced into a six-bit address because it is always even (i.e., the least significant bit of the address is always 0). For this reason, memory addresses a6, a14, and a22 which are, respectively, 0000110 (06_8), 0001110 (14_8), and 0010110 (22_8) become 000011 (3_8), 000111 (7_8), and 001011 (13_8) when they are placed in the address fields of these jump instructions. (See the third, sixth, and ninth lines of the binary program.)

7.2.3 Error Indication

As mentioned previously, addition overflow may occur during the addition and division overflow during the division. If the ERROR STOP switch is at the NOBP position, LTAV or LTDV will be turned on and the computer will stop when an addition overflow or a division overflow occurs. If the ERRORSTOP switch is at the BP position, the light will be turned on, but the computer will not stop. If the ERRORSTOP switch is at the AVBP position, the computer will not stop if addition overflow occurs.

7.2.4 Manual Loading and Running

After the binary program is prepared, it is loaded into the memory. This operation is called *loading*. The steps for manual loading are:

Step 1. Set switch CLEAR to the ON position.

Step 2. Set switch INPUT to the ON position.

Step 3. Set register M to the address of the first word to be loaded.

Step 4. Set switch START to the ON position. The computer will be waiting while showing 0101_2 in the D register.

Step 5. Load manually the first word into register X and press the START switch.

Step 6. Repeat step 5 to load the second, third, etc., until all the words are loaded.

The above steps load the words into the consecutive locations of the memory. If words are to be loaded nonconsecutively, register M must be set to the desired address before the START switch is turned on. Loading and unloading will be further described in Chapter 12.

After loading, the following steps are required to run the program:

Step 1. Set switch ERRORSTOP to NOBP, switch JS to OFF, switch MR to OFF, and switch MODE to PM.

Step 2. Set switch CLEAR to the ON position.

Step 3. Set register P to the starting address.

Step 4. Set switch START to the ON position.

After the fourth step, the program will be executed.

If the MODE switch is on the PM position and the ERRORSTOP switch on the BP position, the computer will stop when it reaches a STP instruction, or a manual input-output instruction (MNI and MNO), or a jump instruction (SBO, UNO, NAO, and NZO) when the JS switch is at the ON position, or an instruction error. If the MODE switch is on the IM, AEM, or DM position, it will also stop, respectively, when execution of an instruction is completed, when execution of a fetch sequence or an execution sequence is completed, or at the end of a clock period. If the MR switch is at the ON position, the execution of an instruction, a sequence, or micro-operations in one clock period is repeated according to whether the MODE switch is at the IM, AEM, or DM position, respectively.

7.3 OVERFLOWS

There are two overflows: addition overflow and division overflow. When an addition overflow occurs, light LTAD is turned on. When a division overflow occurs, light LTDV is turned on. In either case, computer operation stops.

7.3.1 Addition Overflow

Addition overflows occur whenever the result exceeds the size of the accumulator which is 5 bits. If the numbers are normally located, the largest number is +.11111 and the smallest number is −.11111. If the numbers are integers, the largest number is +11111 and the smallest is −11111.

7.3.2 Division Overflow

If X,Y,Q, and R are respectively the dividend, the divisor, the quotient, and the remainder, the division instruction DIV finds the unknown Q and R from the known X and Y so that the following relation is satisfied,

$$\frac{X}{Y} = Q + \frac{R}{Y} \qquad (7.5)$$

where R is less than Y. Divisor Y can be too small with respect to dividend X so that quotient Q becomes too large to be held in the quotient register Q. When this happens, division overflow occurs.

7.3.3 Division Overflow Condition

If dividend X and divisor Y are normally located, then the condition that the magnitude of dividend X must be larger than or equal to the magnitude of divisor Y or

$$/X/ \geqslant /Y/ \qquad (7.6)$$

is called the *division overflow condition.* If this condition is met, division overflow occurs. If this condition is not met, division proceeds and, after the division, the quotient is normally located.

As an example, let the normally located dividend X and divisor Y be, respectively, .1000100000 and .10101. Division of X by Y gives

$$\frac{X}{Y} = \frac{.1000100000}{.10101} = .11001 + \frac{.0000010011}{.10101} \qquad (7.7)$$

Since the magnitude of the dividend /.10001/ is less than the magnitude of the divisor /.10101/, condition (7.6) is not satisfied. Division proceeds. Note that quotient magnitude .11001 is 5-bit and normally located.

As another example, let dividend X and divisor Y be, respectively, .1110100000 and .10101. Division of X by Y gives

$$\frac{X}{Y} = \frac{.1110100000}{.10101} = 1.01100 + \frac{.0000000100}{.10101} \qquad (7.8)$$

Since the magnitude of the dividend /.11101/ is larger than the magnitude of the divisor /.10101/, condition (7.6) is satisfied. Division overflow occurs as the quotient magnitude 1.01100 is 6-bit and thus exceeds the size of register X. It is important to note that, if the comparisons in the above two examples are made on the five most significant bits of the normally located dividend, the tested result is the same even though any of the five least significant bits is nonzero.

If either the dividend or the divisor or both are not normally located, condition (7.6) cannot be directly applied. But it can be restated as follows. The condition that the magnitude of the five most significant bits of the 10-bit magnitude of the division must be larger than or equal to the five magnitude bits of the divisor. The five most significant bits of the 10-bit magnitude of the dividend is sufficient for the test to determine whether the quotient is 5-bit or 6-bit. Furthermore, the binary points of the dividend and the divisor are ignored during the test because they determine the binary point but not the magnitude of the quotient. Since the five most significant bits of the dividend are in subregister $A(M)$ and the magnitude of the divisor is in subregister $X(M)$, the division overflow condition can be stated as follows. If the following condition is true,

$$/A(M) \geqslant /X(M)/ \tag{7.9}$$

then division overflow occurs and computer operation stops.

Condition (7.9) agrees with condition (7.6); this is illustrated by the examples in division (7.7) and (7.8) where tests for the five most significant bits are indeed sufficient for normally located numbers. As will be described in Chapter 11, condition (7.9) is actually implemented by hardware for testing division overflow in the division sequence.

7.3.4 Examples of Division Overflow

Several examples are now shown to illustrate evaluation of condition (7.9). Let dividend X and divisor Y be, respectively, 0000011101 and 10101 which are integers. Division of X by Y gives

$$\frac{X}{Y} = \frac{0000011101}{10101} = 00001 + \frac{01000}{10101} \tag{7.10}$$

Since the five most significant bits of the dividend /00000/ is smaller than the five magnitude bits of the divisor /10101/, condition (7.9) is not satisfied. Division overflow does not occur, and division proceeds. The quotient magnitude is 5-bit and fits the quotient subregister $Q(M)$. Note that satisfaction of condition (7.9) gives an integer quotient when the dividend and the divisor are both integers.

Let dividend X and divisor Y be, respectively, 1110000000 and 10101 which are integers. Division of X by Y gives

$$\frac{X}{Y} = \frac{1110000000}{10101} = 101010 + \frac{00111}{10101} \qquad (7.11)$$

Since the five most significant bits of the dividend /11100/ is larger than the five magnitude bits of the divisor /10101/, condition (7.9) is met. Division overflow occurs as the quotient magnitude is a six-bit integer which overflows the quotient subregister Q(M).

Let dividend X and divisor Y be, respectively, 0000101.011 and 10.101 which are mixed numbers. Division of X by Y gives

$$\frac{X}{Y} = \frac{00101.01100}{10.101} = 010.00 + \frac{.00100}{10.101} \qquad (7.12)$$

The test of division overflow compares the five most significant bits of the dividend /00101/ with the five magnitude bits of the divisor /10101/; the binary points of the dividend and the divisor are ignored. Since /00101/ is smaller than /10101/, condition (7.9) is not met. Division overflow does not occur and division proceeds. Note that the quotient magnitude is 5-bit and normally located, and fits the quotient subregister Q(M).

Let dividend X and divisor Y be, respectively, 110.0101010 and 1010.1 which are mixed numbers. Division of X by Y gives

$$\frac{X}{Y} = \frac{110.0101010}{1010.1} = .100110 + \frac{.0000100}{1010.1} \qquad (7.13)$$

The comparison is again made between /11001/ and /10101/ as the binary points are ignored. Since /11001/ is larger than /10101/, condition (7.9) is satisfied. The quotient magnitude is 6-bit and overflows the quotient subregister Q(M). Division overflow occurs and computer operation stops.

7.4 FLOW CHARTING

The second example shows the use of a flow chart to describe the computation process and the use of manual input-output instructions to receive inputs and to deliver outputs.

The problem is to compute the slope of a straight line S in two dimensions, given two points (X_1, Y_1) and (X_2, Y_2), by the expression

$$S = \frac{X_2 - X_1}{Y_2 - Y_1} \qquad (7.14)$$

It is assumed that the values of X's and Y's are all integers and their magnitudes are equal to or less than 31. But the numerical value of the slope may consist of an integral part S_i and a fractional part S_f or

$$S = S_i + S_f \tag{7.15}$$

For example, if the two points are (6,5) and (3,3), then S is equal to 1.5. Thus, S_i is 1 and S_f is .5. As will be seen, S_i and S_f are computed separately.

7.4.1 Flow Chart

A computation process may consist of many steps and these steps may be "branched" and "looped." It is often desirable to diagram this process so that the process can be visualized. The resulting diagram is called a *flow chart*. As an example, the computation process to find the above defined slope, though simple, is flow charted and shown in Figure 7.11.

Each rectangular box in the flow chart denotes a computational step such as "input X's and Y's" and "compute $(Y_2 - Y_1)$." It has one output but may have more than one input. Each oval box indicates a testing step such as "Is $(Y_2 - Y_1) = 0$?" It has two or more outputs, and the condition of branching should be indicated on each of the outputs. The lines connecting the "stop" boxes to the start line form the loops.

In Figure 7.11, the numbers for X's and Y's are first inputted. Quantity $(Y_2 - Y_1)$ is next computed and tested for 0. If it is 0, it indicates that the slope is infinite; the computer is instructed to stop and is then returned to the start point. If $(Y_2 - Y_1)$ is not 0, $(X_2 - X_1)$ is computed. Then, division $(X_2 - X_1)/(Y_2 - Y_1)$ is performed. This division gives an integer quotient (if it exists) which is S_i and a remainder which is divided by $(Y_2 - Y_1)$ to produce S_f. Finally, the values of the differences and S_i and S_f are outputted and the computer stops. If the JS switch is turned on, control returns to the start point for computing the slope for the next set of input numbers.

7.4.2 Symbolic Program

The symbolic program is shown in Figure 7.12. To receive manual input, instruction MNI is used; it is preceded by instruction LCT to load counter C. The four input numbers are stored in locations m1 through m4. Instructions LDA, SUB, and STA compute $(X_2 - X_1)$

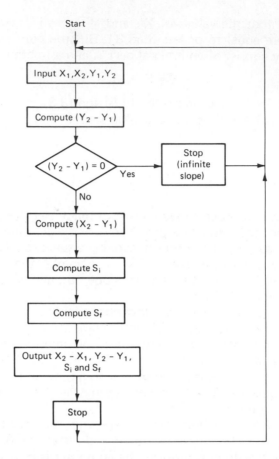

Fig. 7.11 Flow chart for computing a slope

and store the result in location m4. Instruction STP stops the computer operation, and upon turning on the START switch the computer operation resumes from the first instruction, because the address of the STP instruction is a0. Instructions LDA, SUB, and STA are employed again to compute $(Y_2 - Y_1)$ and store the result in location m5. Instructions LDA, SRO, DIV, and STQ perform the division and store the quotient (i.e., S_i) in the Q register, in location m6; the remainder is in the accumulator. Instructions SRO, DIV, and STQ divide the remainder by the divider again to give S_f which is stored in location m7. By leaving the remainder in the accumulator instead of shifting it right to the Q register as was done previously increases the remainder by a factor of 2^5. The quotient thus obtained should be decreased by a factor of 2^5 given the fractional

Memory Address	Operation Code	Operand Address	Comments
a0	LCT	3	Load 3 to counter C
a2	MNI	m0	manual input X_1, X_2, Y_1, Y_2
a4	LDA	m1	load X_2 into register A
a6	SUB	m0	$X_2 - X_1$
a10	STA	m4	store $(X_2 - X_1)$ in m4
a12	NZE	a16	test A for 0
a14	STP	a0	stop, infinite slope
a16	LDA	m3	Y_2
a20	SUB	m2	$Y_2 - Y_1$
a22	STA	m5	store $(Y_2 - Y_1)$ in m5
a24	LDA	m4	load dividend into A
a26	SRO	5	shift AQ(M) right 5-bit positions
a30	DIV	m5	compute S_i
a32	STQ	m6	store S_i in m6
a34	SRO	0	clear register Q
a36	DIV	m5	compute S_f
a40	STQ	m7	store S_f in m7
a42	LCT	3	load 3 to counter C
a44	MNO	m4	manual output m4,m5,m6, and m7
a46	UNO	a0	transfer to a0
m0		X_1	
m1		X_2	
m2		Y_1	
m3		Y_2	
m4		$X_2 - X_1$	
m5		$Y_2 - Y_1$	
m6		S_i	
m7		S_f	

Fig. 7.12 Program for computing a slope

part, S_f. Since S_i and S_f are stored and displayed separately, this decrease by a factor of 2^5 is thus understood and no further step is necessary. Instructions LCT and MNO display the results in m4 through m7, and instruction UNE transfers the computation back to the start point upon turning on the JS switch.

7.4.3 Operation Remarks

The MODE switch is set to the PM position, the MR switch to the

OFF position, the ERRORSTOP switch to the NOBP position, and the JS switch to the ON position. When the numbers are loaded into the X register, they are set in the order of X_1, X_2, Y_1, and Y_2. When the numbers are displayed in the X register, they are exhibited in the order of $(X_2 - X_1)$, $(Y_2 - Y_1)$, S_i and S_f.

7.5 ITERATIVE SOLUTION

This example shows how to obtain a solution by iteration. The problem is to compute the square root of a positive number N or,

$$R = \sqrt{N} \tag{7.16}$$

where R is the integral part of the square root and the maximum value of N is 31.

7.5.1 Iterative Process

An interative process often involves a guess of initial value, a method of terminating the process, and a change of the value of a parameter. To formulate the iterative process for finding the square root, the above equation is rewritten

$$\left[\frac{N}{R}\right] - R = 0 \tag{7.17}$$

The DIV instruction divides an integral dividend in the AQ register and gives an integral quotient in the Q register. Let $[N/R]$ denote the integral part of the quotient of N/R, and F be the fractional part. We then have

$$F = \left[\frac{N}{R}\right] - R \tag{7.18}$$

The iterative process here first selects initial value of R to be N. It then computes F and tests F for termination. For the first iteration, F is negative except when N is 1. In this case, F is 0 and R is the right answer. If F is negative, R is decremented by 1; R is the parameter. F is again computed and, if negative, R is again decremented. The process is iterated until F is either 0 or positive. The value of R at that time is taken as the approximate value of number N.

7.5.2 Flow Chart

The above iterative process is described in the flow chart in Figure

7.13. In order to illustrate this process, an example is shown. Let N be 9. We then have,

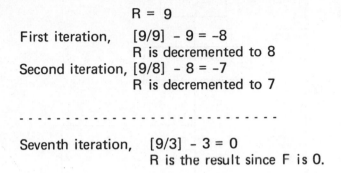

$$R = 9$$

First iteration, $[9/9] - 9 = -8$
R is decremented to 8
Second iteration, $[9/8] - 8 = -7$
R is decremented to 7

- -

Seventh iteration, $[9/3] - 3 = 0$
R is the result since F is 0.

This iterative process gives R a value of 3. As another example, let N be 12. We then have,

$$R = 12$$

First iteration, $[12/12] - 12 = -11$
R is decremented to 11

- -

Ninth iteration, $[12/4] - 4 = -1$
R is decremented to 3
Tenth iteration, $[12/3] - 3 = +1$
R is the result since F is positive.

This iterative process gives R a value of 3.

7.5.3 Symbolic Program

Figure 7.14 shows the symbolic program for finding the square root R of a positive integer N. Locations n1 and n2 store N and R, respectively. Instruction MNI inputs a number N in location n1. No prior LCT instruction is required here because counter C will have been reset to 0 by the CLEAR switch. The initial value of R is chosen to be N and is loaded into location n2 by instruction LDC. The next three instructions compute [N/R] which is left in the Q register. Instruction SLE shifts [N/R] to the accumulator and instruction SUB computes fraction F. Instruction NAE tests the fraction. If the fraction is negative, R in n2 is decremented by

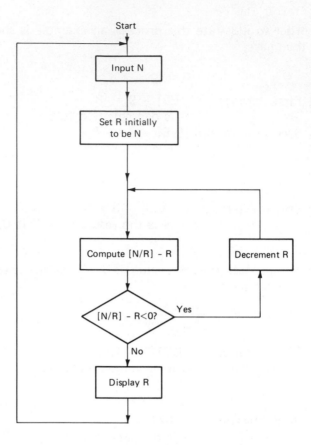

Fig. 7.13 Flow chart for finding the square root of a positive integer

instruction RSU. This completes one iteration, and the next iteration begins at the division. This process of iteration continues on until F is either 0 or positive; at this time, R is loaded in the accumulator for display by lights LTA.

7.5.4 Remarks

The above program can be extended to find the fractional part of the square root as well. If the initial value of R is taken to be N/2, the number of iterations can be reduced. In either case, the flow chart will become more complicated and the program longer.

Memory Address	Operation Code	Operand Address	Comments
a0	MNI	n1	input N
a2	LDC	n1	load initial value of R into n2
a4	LDA	n1	
a6	SRE	5	
a10	DIV	n2	[N/R] in register Q
a12	SLE	5	
a14	SUB	n2	[N/R] – R
a16	NAE	a24	test acc being not negative
a20	STA	n2	
a22	UNE	a0	
a24	RSU	n2	decrement R
a26	UNE	a4	
n1	N		
n2	R		

Fig. 7.14 Program for finding the square root of a positive integer

7.6 INDEXING

This example illustrates the indexing technique which has led to the implementation of index registers in many of today's computers. Indexing means incrementing (or sometimes decrementing) the address in the address field of an instruction. The usefulness of indexing will be obvious if we consider the simple problem of adding N numbers.

7.6.1 Addition of N Numbers

Assume that there are ten numbers stored in locations m1 through m10. To add these ten numbers, the following ten instructions are required:

```
LDA    m1
ADD    m2
ADD    m3
- - - - - - - - -
ADD    m10
```

If there are 100 or 1000 numbers, there need 100 or 1000 instructions which are obviously too lengthy and wasteful of the memory space. Now if, after the execution of the second instruction, address m2 in this instruction is changed to m3, the third instruction is not needed. Similarly, if address m3 is again changed to m4, the fourth instruction is not needed. It is apparent that, by changing m2 to m3, then to m4, then to m5, etc., only one ADD instruction is required. These address m's bear the following relations:

$$m3 = m2 + 1,$$
$$m4 = m3 + 1,$$
$$- - - - - - - - - - -$$
$$m10 = m9 + 1$$

Therefore, m3 can be obtained by incrementing m2; m4 by incrementing m3, etc.

By making use of these relations, the above ten instructions are changed into the following five instructions:

```
a1  LDA  m1
a2  ADD  m2
    STA  m1
    RAU  a3
    UNE  a1
```

The above RAU instruction increments the address m2 to m3, to m4, to m5, etc. Since the RAU instruction uses the accumulator, the partial sum in the accumulator must first be stored somewhere. For this reason, instruction STA stores the partial sum in location m1. The jump by instruction UNE to instruction LDA forms a loop. However, this loop, once started, cannot be stopped. Therefore, a counter to count and then to test the required number of iterations is required.

Let the count be stored in location m0 and the count is decremented each time the address is decremented. The count is then tested. When the count reaches 0, the addition is completed and the loop branches to the normal sequence. The above five instructions are changed into the following six instructions:

```
a0  LDA  m1
a2  ADD  m2
    STA  m1
    RAU  a3
    RSU  m0
    NZE  a0
```

The above first three instructions again compute the partial sum. Instruction RAU increments address m2. Instruction RSU decrements the count in location m0. And instruction NZE tests the count and performs the branching.

7.6.2 Flow Chart

A flow chart for adding N numbers by using indexing is shown in Figure 7.15. The inner loop consists of four boxes which specify the

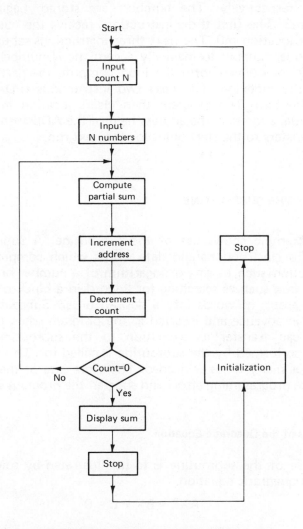

Fig. 7.15 Flow chart for adding N numbers

four tasks required in the indexing. The outer loop performs the function of acquiring count N and the N numbers for the addition, displaying the sum after the addition is completed and initializing for the next run.

7.6.3 Symbolic Program

The symbolic program for adding the N numbers is shown in Figure 7.16. The count, sum, and constant 0 are stored in m0, m1, and m2, respectively. The numbers are stored, beginning from location m3. The first three instructions receive the number N and store it in location m0. The next three instructions set up counter C with a proper number to manually accept the N numbers. The next six instructions which form the loop compute the partial sum and perform the indexing. The next two instructions (LDA and STP) display the sum. The program then clears location m1, puts the proper initial address in the address field of the ADD instruction, and finally transfers to the start point for the next run.

7.7 USE OF THE SUBROUTINE

This example shows use of the subroutine. A subroutine is a sequence of instructions and data words which compute an often used function such as sine or logarithm of a number or performs a recurring task such as searching for a word in a block of words and sorting a group of words into a desired order. Subroutines can be prepared in advance and inserted in the program when needed. The program can transfer its execution to the subroutine when the function performed by the subroutine is called for. This transfer can be made as many times as needed. Therefore, use of the subroutine can reduce programming effort and shorten the program size.

7.7.1 Roots of the Quadratic Equation

The use of the subroutine is to be illustrated by solving for the roots of a quadratic equation,

$$AX^2 + BX + C = 0 \qquad (7.19)$$

Memory Address	Operation Code	Operand Address	Comments
a0	MNI	all	input count N
a2	LDA	all	
a4	STA	m0	set up counter in m0
a6	RSU	all	set up for N counts
a10	LCT		load (N–1) to counter C
a12	MNI	m3	input N numbers into m3 through m3+(N–1)
a14	LDA	m1	
a16	ADD	m3	compute partial sum
a20	STA	m1	store partial sum into m1
a22	RAU	a17	increment operand address in a17
a24	RSU	m0	decrement count in m0
a26	NZE	a14	test count
a30	LDA	m1	display sum
a32	STP	a34	
a34	LDA	m2	
a36	STA	m1	reset location at m1 to 0
a40	LDA	a13	
a42	STA	a17	set up initial operand address
a44	UNE	a0	transfer to a0
m0		"count"	
m1		"sum"	
m2		000000	
m3		"first input number"	
—			
—			
m3 + (N – 1)		"last input number"	

Fig. 7.16 Program for adding N numbers

The solution to this equation is well known. When coefficient A is zero there is only one root X or

$$X = -C/B \qquad (7.20)$$

Let us define

$$D = B^2 - 4 A C \qquad (7.21)$$

$$E = D \qquad (7.22)$$

$$F = -D \qquad (7.23)$$

When D is equal to 0, the two roots are equal or

$$X1 = X2 = -B/(2 A) \qquad \text{for } D = 0 \qquad (7.24)$$

When D is larger than 0, the two roots are both real or

$$X1 = \frac{-B + E}{2A}$$

$$X2 = \frac{-B - E}{2A}$$

(7.25)

When D is smaller than 0, the two roots are complex. The real and imaginary parts of these two roots are:

$$XR = \frac{-B}{2A}$$

$$XI = \frac{+F}{2A}$$

(7.26)

7.6.2 Flow Chart

A flow chart for computing the roots of the quadratic equation is shown in Figure 7.17. Coefficient A is first tested. If it is 0, the single root $-C/B$ is computed and the program is returned to the start point. If it is not 0, quantity D is computed. If D is 0, roots X1 and X2 are computed from expression (7.24). If D is positive, roots X1 and X2 are computed from expressions (7.25). If D is negative, the real and imaginary parts of the roots are computed from expressions (7.25). After the roots are computed, the program is returned to the start point.

7.6.3 Symbolic Program

Figure 7.18 shows the symbolic program for solving for the roots of the quadratic equation. It is assumed that A and D are both not equal to 0 in order that the program is small enough to be stored in the memory. The square root subroutine is located from addresses a144 through a171 and its data words are located at addresses m9 and m10. This subroutine is identical to the symbolic program in Figure 7.14 except the first instruction MNI in Figure 7.14 is replaced by instruction STA and instruction STA near the end in Figure 7.14 is omitted. This subroutine is called by instructions SBE located at addresses a50 and a102. Since instruction SBE stores the contents of register P in the location at address 1, the first two

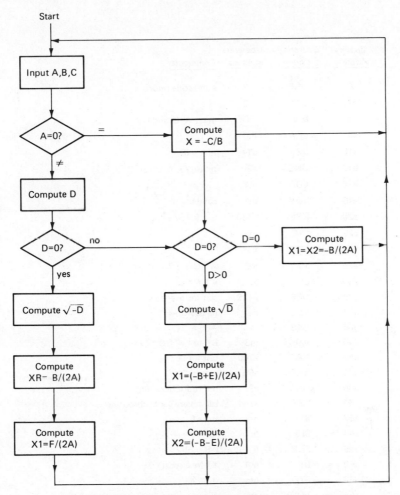

Fig. 7.17 Flow chart for solving a quadratic equation. Note:

$$E = \sqrt{D} = \sqrt{B^2 - 4AC}$$

$$F = \sqrt{-D} = \sqrt{4AC - B^2}$$

memory words store a UNE instruction for returning the program to the normal sequence after the subroutine has been executed. This situation is illustrated by the diagram in Figure 7.19. As shown, instruction SBE a144 located at address a50 transfers to the first instruction of the subroutine located at address a144. When the subroutine reaches its last instruction, it transfers to instruction UNE at location a0 which transfers to the instruction located at address a52 from which the program resumes its normal sequence. Similar transfers occur for subroutine instruction SBE located at address a102.

Memory Address	Operation Code	Operand Address	Comments
a0	UNE	2	subroutine return
a2	LCT	2	
a4	MNI	m0	input A, B, and C
a6	LDA	m0	A
a10	NZE	a14	Is A = 0?
a12	UNE	a2	return for next run
a14	LDA	m1	
a16	MPY	m1	compute B^2
a20	NZE	a130	test for overflow
a22	STQ	m3	
a24	LDA	m0	
a26	MPY	m2	A * C
a30	SLE	2	4 * A * C
a32	NZE	a130	test for overflow
a34	SLE	5	no overflow
a36	CAS		−4 * A * C
a40	ADD	m3	B^2 −4 * A * C = D
a42	NAE	a100	test for D
a44	NZE	a50	case of D > 0
a46	UNE	a2	return for next run
a50	SBE	a144	call square root subroutine
a52	STA	m4	store E
a54	SUB	m1	−B + E
a56	SRE	6	(−B + E)/2
a60	DIV	m0	X1 (real root)
a62	STQ	m5	store X1
a64	LDN	m4	−E
a66	SUB	m1	− B− E
a70	SRE	6	(− B− E)/2
a72	DIV	m0	X2 (real root)
a74	STQ	m6	store X2
a76	UNE	a2	
a100	CAS		case of D < 0, 4 * A * C − B^2 = F
a102	SBE	a144	call square-root subroutine

Fig. 7.18 Program for solving a quadratic equation

Memory Address	Operation Code	Operand Address	Comments
a104	STA	m4	store F
a106	LDN	m1	–B
a110	SRE	6	–B/2
a112	DIV	m0	XR (real part of complex root)
a114	STQ	m7	store XR
a116	LDA	m4	F
a120	SRE	6	F/2
a122	DIV	m0	XI
a124	STQ	m8	store XI
a126	UNE	a2	
a130	STP	a2	overflow, stop
m0		A	
m1		B	
m2		C	
m3		B^2	
m4		E or F	
m5		X1 (real root)	
m6		X2 (real root)	
m7		XR (real part of complex root)	
m8		XI (imaginary part)	
m9		N (for square root subroutine)	
m10		R (for square root subroutine)	
a144	STA	m9	beginning of subroutine
a146	LDC	m9	
a150	LDA	m9	
a152	SRE	5	
a154	DIV	m10	
a156	SLE	5	
a160	SUB	m10	
a162	MAE	a170	
a164	RSU	m10	
a166	UNE	a150	
a170	UNE	a0	end of subroutine

Fig. 7.18 (continued)

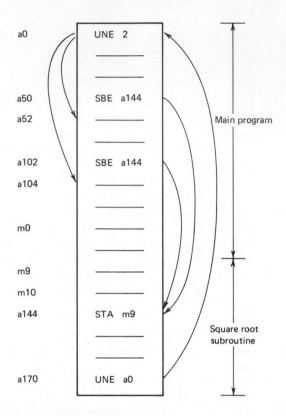

Fig. 7.19 Diagram showing the instruction transfers due to the two subroutine instructions SBE

In the symbolic program, instructions located at a2 and a4 input the values of coefficients A,B, and C. Coefficient A is tested by instructions located at a6 and a10. D is computed by instructions located from a14 through a40. Notice that an overflow is tested after each multiplication because, if the product exceeds 5 bits, the A register cannot hold it (unless double precision arithmetic is employed). D is tested by two jump instructions NAE and NZE in order to have three branches. When D is 0, positive, and negative, the program branches to the instruction located at a46, a50, and a100, respectively. Instructions located from a50 through a76 compute the two real roots. Instructions located from a100 through a126 compute the real and imaginary parts of the complex roots. Instructions located at a12,a46,a76, and a126 all return to the instruction located at a2, the start point. The data of the program are located at addresses m0 through m8.

PROBLEMS

7.1   Given the following pairs of binary multiplicands and multipliers,
      (a) 101.01 X 010.10
      (b) 101.01 X 0101.0
      (c) .10101 X .01010
      where is the location of the binary point in the AQ register after the
      multiplication in each case? In which case does the product overflow (i.e.,
      the integral part of the product exceeds 5 bits)?

7.2   Given the following pairs of binary dividends and divisors,
      (a) 101.01 + 010.10
      (b) 101.01 + 0101.0
      (c) .10101 + .01010
      where is the location of the binary point in the Q register after division in
      each case?

7.3   Compute, $Z = ((A + B) \times C) + D$

      where   A = 101.01
                 B = 100.10
                 C = 10.111
                 D = 11.011

      (a) Where is the location of the binary point in the Q register after the
           division?
      (b) What is the value of Z?

7.4   By using the same values of A,B,C, and D as those in Prob. 7.3, compute,

$$Z = (A + B) * C + D$$

      A two-bit accuracy should be maintained.

7.5   In the iterative solution of finding the square root of a positive integer N
      in the program in Figure 7.14, the initial value of root R is taken to be N.
      Draw a flow chart and write a symbolic program if the initial value of R is
      taken to be N/2.

7.6   In the iterative solution of finding the square root of a positive integer N,
      if both the integral and fractional parts of the square root are required,
      draw a flow chart and prepare a symbolic program.

7.7   Given m numbers, N1,N2,N3,N4,. . .,Nm, by means of indexing draw a
      flow chart and prepare a symbolic program to compute:

$$SUM = N1 - N2 + N3 - N4 + N5 \text{------} Nm$$

7.8   Given three six-bit signed binary numbers, compare these three numbers
      and place the largest, the middle, and the smallest in the X, A, and Q
      register, respectively. Both flow chart and symbolic diagram are required.

7.9 Let N be an integer of 1,2, ... , or 6. Draw a flow chart and write a symbolic program to find factorial N. A ten-bit product should be preserved.

7.10 Load manually "hundreds" in the X register, "tens" in the A register, and "units" in the Q register. The contents of these registers can be only 00000, 00001, ... ,01001 to represent the ten decimal digits 0,1, ... ,9, respectively. (Decimal number represented by decimal digits of such a representation is called BCD number or binary coded decimal number.) Convert this BCD number into a ten-bit binary number stored in the AQ(M) subregister. Draw a flow chart and prepare a symbolic program to make the conversion.

7.11 Forty numbers ranging from −31 to +31 are manually loaded into the memory in whatever order they happen to be. Draw a flow chart and write a symbolic program to sort these numbers into descending order.

7.12 Reprogram the symbolic program in Figure 7.18 for solving a quadratic equation so that coefficients A and D may become 0. Assume that the memory has more than 128 words.

8

Generation of
Timing and
Control
Signals

Chapter 6 presents the configuration of the computer which consists of the registers, memory, switches, lights, and the others; they are described by declaration statements. This chapter describes the clock pulse, timing signals, command signals, and control signals by means of which the labels of the execution statements are formed. With these labels, micro-operations are sequenced to carry out the sequential steps required for the instructions.

8.1 TWO-PHASE CLOCK

This computer uses a two-phase clock. The configuration, shown in the diagram of Figure 8.1, is described by the statements

Clock,	CP
Delay,	$\Delta = 15$
Register,	RUN2
Terminal,	CP1=CP*RUN2
	CP2=ΔCP1

(8.1)

The two-phase clock whose clock pulses are CP1 and CP2 is generated by a single-phase clock CP in conjunction with a delay element. Register RUN2, which is the previously mentioned start flipflop, controls the generation of CP1 and CP2. When RUN2 is l, CP1 and CP2 are being generated; otherwise, they are not. (See start logic in Chapter 12.) The period of clock CP is 50 microseconds or a rate of 20,000 pulses per second. Delay operator Δ denotes a 15-microsecond delay.

8.2 ADD-CONTROL CLOCK PULSES

The above clock pulses CP1 and CP2 control all the micro-operations except when a three-step add subsequence occurs. (The add subsequence will be described in a later chapter.) When the add subsequence occurs, generation of clock pulses CP1 and CP2 is "stopped"; instead, a sequence of three clock pulses T(1),T(2), and T(3) is generated for controlling the add subsequence. At the end of this three-clock pulse sequence, generation of clock pulses CP1 and CP2 is resumed. The generation of the three clock pulses T(1-3) is controlled by the previously described add-control register AC.

The configuration for generating these clock pulses is also shown by the diagram in Figure 8.1 and described by the statements

Register,	AC(1-0)
Decoder,	N(0-3)=AC
Terminal,	T(0-3)=N(0-3)*CP1
	TD=N(0)*CP2

(8.2)

Normally, register AC contains 0 and decoder terminal N(0) is 1; pulses T(0) and TD actually control the micro-operations instead of pulses CP1 and CP2. Register AC is a counter. When register AC increments from 0 to 1, namely,

$$AC \leftarrow countup \ AC$$ (8.3)

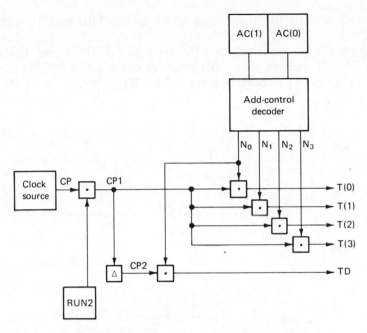

Fig. 8.1 Generation of clock pulses CP, T, and TD

decoder terminal N(0) becomes 0 and pulses T(0) and TD cease to occur. But N(1) now becomes 1 and pulse T(1) thus appears. Pulse T(1) is made to increment register AC from 1 to 2 or,

$$/T(1)/ \quad AC \leftarrow \text{countup } AC \tag{8.4}$$

Thus, decoder terminal N(1) becomes 0 and T(1) ceases to occur. (T(1) appears only once.) But N(2) now becomes 1 and T(2) now appears. Similarly, T(2) is made to increment register AC from 2 to 3 or,

$$/T(2)/ \quad AC \leftarrow \text{countup } AC \tag{8.5}$$

T(2) then ceases to occur and T(3) now appears. When T(3) is made to increment register AC from 3 to 0 or,

$$/T(3)/ \quad AC \leftarrow \text{countup } AC \tag{8.6}$$

pulses T(0) and TD occur again. They continue to occur as long as register AC contains 0. In short, by making the AC register count from 0 to 3, a sequence of three clock pulses T(1), T(2), and T(3) is generated, and in the meantime clock pulses T(0) and TD cease to occur.

Figure 8.2 shows the decoder terminals N(0–3) and the clock pulses T(0–3). Notice that T(0) and TD occur when N(0) is 1, while T(1), T(2), or T(3) occurs only when N(1), N(2), or N(3) is 1, respectively.

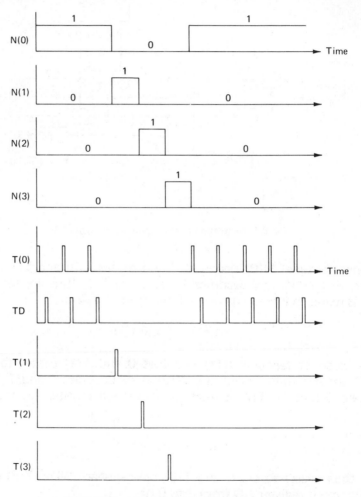

Fig. 8.2 Generation of clock pulses (T's)

8.3 TIMING SIGNALS

In the subsequent description of the fetch and execution sequences, a sequence of 16 control signals is required for up to 16 sequential steps. Therefore, it is necessary to convert a two-phase clock into a sequence of 16 pulses to be called *timing signals*. This sequence can be obtained by using counter D and a decoder in the manner shown in the diagram of Figure 8.3. This configuration is described by the statements,

$$
\begin{aligned}
&\text{Register,} && D(3-0) \\
&\text{Decoder,} && B(0-15)=D && (8.7) \\
&\text{Terminal,} && DP(0-15)=B(0-15)*T(0)
\end{aligned}
$$

The above configuration is similar to the one described in Figure 4.7. The output terminals of the decoder are named B's, and the timing signals are named DP's. The operation of this timing signal generator is illustrated by the diagram in Figure 8.4. Each time pulse T(0) occurs, a DP timing signal appears. As counter D increments, each of terminals DP(0-15) is activated in turn. In short, by means of the Distributor decoder, Distributor register D distributes the sequence of pulses T(0) to terminals DP(0-15) in turn.

After the occurrence of each T(0), pulse TD increments the D register, namely,

$$
/TD/ \quad D \leftarrow \text{countup } D \qquad (8.8)
$$

Because the period of clock pulse T(0) is 50 microseconds and TD occurs only 15 microseconds later, counter D is advanced during each clock period. This shows how a two-phase clock generates a sequence of many timing signals.

Terminals DP(0-15) will appear in the labels of the execution statements in the subsequent chapters. As shown in Figure 8.1 and statements (8.1) and (8.2), whenever register RUN2 is set to 1, pulse T(0) stops. As a result, none of the DP pulses occurs, and no execution statement whose label is made up of a DP signal is executed. If all the labels of the execution statements which specify a computer are formed with a DP signal, the computer ceases to operate.

8.4 COMMAND SIGNALS

A command signal orders a particular execution sequence. Therefore, command signals are derived from the operation code of an instruction. As will be described in the next chapter, the operation code is transferred to the I register during the fetch

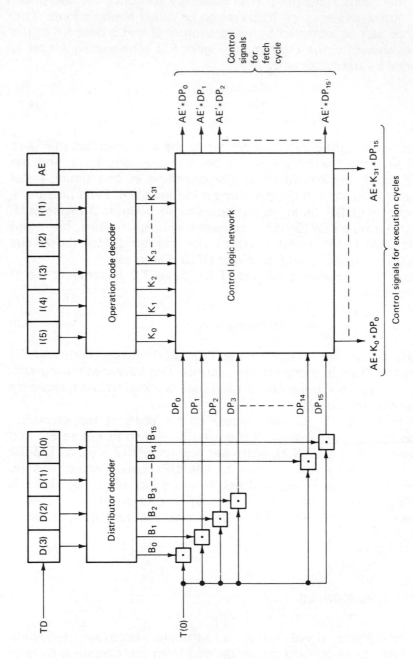

Fig. 8.3 Generation of timing and control signals

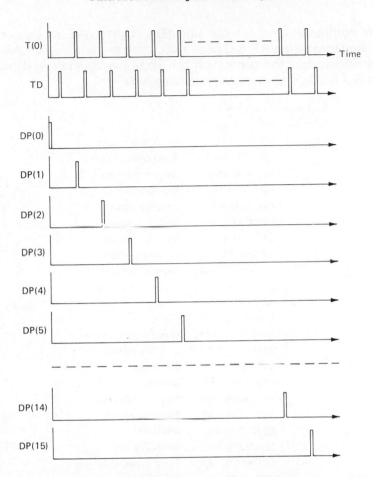

Fig. 8.4 Generation of timing signals DP(0–15)

sequence. Its contents are decoded by the Operation-code decoder to produce a signal at one of the decoder terminals K(0–31).

The instruction formats in Figure 6.1 show that there can be either a 5-bit code or a 6-bit code. The 6-bit codes are for the jump and shift instructions. When the op-codes for these instructions in Table 6.2 are examined, it is clear that, for the jump instructions, the extra bit in the op-code indicates the dependence on or independence of the position of the JS switch. And in the case of the shift instructions, the extra bit indicates the need of an additional micro-operation or not during the respective execution sequence. Therefore, the op-code is basically a 5-bit code. Since these bits are transferred to subregister I(5–1), the decoder is required to decode only these 5 bits as shown in Figure 8.3.

The computer employs the single-bit register AE to denote the fetch sequence when AE is 0 or an execution sequence when AE is 1. The configuration for generating the command signals is shown in Figure 8.3 and is described by the statements

Register,	I(5–0),AE	
Decoder,	K(0–31)=I(5–1)	
Terminal,	SB=K(4)*AE,	$subroutine jump
	UN=K(5)*AE,	$unconditional jump
	NA=K(6)*AE,	$negative accumulator
	NZ=K(7)*AE,	$non-zero jump
	MNI=K(8)*AE,	$manual input
	MNO=K(9)*AE,	$manual output
	EXI=K(10)*AE,	$external input
	EXO=K(11)*AE,	$external output
	LDA=K(16)*AE,	$load accumulator
	LDN=K(17)*AE,	$load acc negative
	ADD=K(18)*AE,	$add
	SUB=K(19)*AE,	$subtract
	RAU=K(20)*AE,	$replace absolute unity
	RSU=K(21)*AE,	$replace subtract unity
	MPY=K(22)*AE,	$multiply
	DIV=K(23)*AE,	$divide
	STA=K(24)*AE,	$store accumulator
	STQ=K(25)*AE,	$store Q register
	SR=K(26)*AE,	$shift AQ right
	SL=K(27)*AE,	$shift AQ left
	LDC=K(28)*AE,	$load consecutive
	LCT=K(29)*AE,	$load counter
	CAS=K(30)*AE,	$change accumulator sign
	STP=K(31)*AE	$stop

(8.9)

For better readability, the symbolic names of the instructions are used as the names of the above command signals except those of jump and shift instructions which depend on bit I(0). With reference to the op-code in Table 6.2 the command signals for the jump and shift instructions could be those described by the statement:

Terminal,	UNE=UN*I(0)',
	UNO=UN*I(0),
	NAE=NA*I(0)',
	NAO=NA*I(0),
	NZE=NZ*I(0)',
	NZO=NZ*I(0),

(8.10)

$$SBE = SB*I(0)',$$
$$SBO = SB*I(0),$$
$$SRE = SR*I(0)',$$
$$SRO = SR*I(0),$$
$$SLE = SL*I(0)',$$
$$SLO = SL*I(0).$$

Nevertheless, as will be shown in the later chapters, these command signals are not needed. Thus, the command signals require only 24 decoder terminals. Decoder terminals K(0–3) and K(12–15) are not used. These terminals, however, may be used for detecting the instruction error by defining terminal DIE,

$$\text{Terminal,}\quad DIE = K(0) + K(1) + K(2) + K(3) + K(12) + K(13) + K(14) + K(15) \quad (8.11)$$

If terminal DIE is 1 at the appropriate time, it indicates an illegal op-code. Register IE will be set to 1 and light LTIE will be turned to the ON condition.

8.5 CONTROL SIGNALS

Control signals are those represented by the labels of execution statements. Most of the control signals are either those for the fetch sequence or those for the execution sequences. The control signals for the fetch sequence are a sequence of timing signals DP(0–15) when register AE is 0 or,

$$AE'*DP(0-15)$$

The control signal for an execution sequence is also a sequence of timing signals DP(0–15) when there is a command signal. Since there are 24 command signals, there are 24 sets of control signals for the execution sequences. Examples of the control signals for the command signals UN and LDA are,

$$UN*DP(0-15)$$

and   (8.12)

$$LDA*DP(0-15)$$

Note that the control signals for the command signal UN are for both instructions UNE and UNO.

As shown in Figure 8.3, the fetch sequence alternates with an execution sequence. This alternation can be readily accomplished by complementing register AE during the timing period DP(15) as described below,

$$
\begin{array}{lll}
\text{/CLEAR(ON)/} & \text{AE} \leftarrow 0 \\
\text{/DP(15)/} & \text{AE} \leftarrow \text{AE}' & (8.13)
\end{array}
$$

In the above, register AE is initially reset to 0 by the CLEAR switch. Figure 8.5 shows the control signals of the fetch and execution sequences and illustrates the alternation of the fetch sequence with an execution sequence.

There are occasions where local two-step control signals are needed. They are obtained by using a delay element. Some cases of two-step control signals with a 15-microsecond delay are:

a. $\text{AE}' * \text{DP}(0)$ and $\Delta(\text{AE}' * \text{DP}(0))$
b. $\text{SB} * \text{DP}(0)$ and $\Delta(\text{SB} * \text{DP}(0))$
c. $\text{MNI} * \text{DP}(9)$ and $\Delta(\text{MNI} * \text{DP}(9))$

Some cases of two-step control signals with a 30-microsecond delay are:

d. $\text{SR} * \text{DP}(10)$ and $2\Delta(\text{SR} * \text{DP}(10))$
e. $\text{MNO} * \text{DP}(13)$ and $2\Delta(\text{MNO} * \text{DP}(13))$
f. $\text{MPY} * \text{DP}(14)$ and $2\Delta(\text{MPY} * \text{DP}(14))$

Figure 8.6 shows the generation of the local control signals for the cases (a) and (d), where delay Δ denotes a 15-microsecond delay.

PROBLEMS

8.1 If the sequence of the add-control pulses is not required, what elements can be eliminated?

8.2 Is it possible to generate the timing signals DP(0–15) by using a single-phase clock instead of the two-phase clock. If it is, describe it by statements and by a diagram.

8.3 Draw a logic diagram for the control logic network in Figure 8.3.

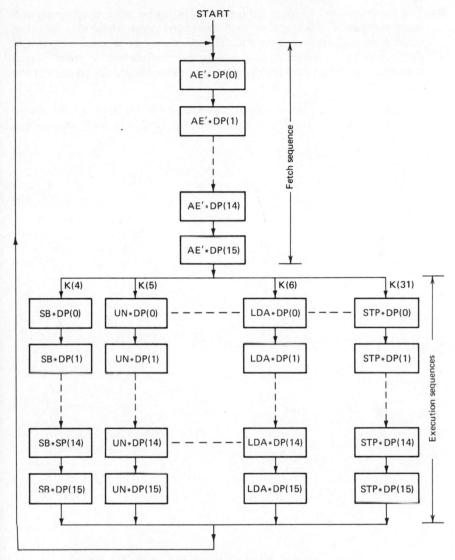

Fig. 8.5 Control signals for the fetch and execution sequences

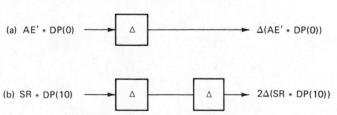

Fig. 8.6 Generation of local control signals

8.4 The configuration in Figure 8.3 generates sequences of control signals of a fixed number of 16 steps. If each command signal requires a different number of steps ranging from 8 to 16 steps, show how sequences of control signals can be generated in such a way that the number of steps in each sequence is different (but fixed) for each command signal (or op-code of the instruction).

8.5 Decoder K decodes the 5 bits of subregister I(5–1). How are the six-bit op-codes in Figure 6.11(b) and (c) for the jump and shift instructions decoded?

9

Fetch

Sequence

The operation of a stored program computer is essentially the sequencing of various sequences which constitute the functional capability of the computer. This chapter describes the fetch sequence, while Chapters 10 through 13 describe the execution sequences.

9.1 CONTROL CYCLE

As described in Chapter 6, before an instruction in the random access memory can be executed, it is necessary to carry out a sequence of micro-operations such as the fetch (or acquisition) of an instruction from the memory, the decoding of the op-code of the instruction, the testing of illegal op-codes, the transfer of the operand address of the instruction to the address register of the memory, and the formation of the next instruction address. These micro-operations which make ready for the execution of the instruction form a sequence called the *fetch sequence.* After the fetch sequence is executed, it is followed by an execution sequence; the execution sequence carries out the micro-operations that are required by the instruction. There is only one fetch sequence because the micro-operations required for preparing the execution of any instruction are the same. But execution sequences are different; usually there are as many execution sequences as the number of the instructions in the instruction set. After an execution sequence is executed, it is followed by the fetch sequence. This alternate execution of the fetch and execution sequences forms a cycle which has been shown in Figures 6.3 and 8.5. This cycle is called the *control cycle.* After a program is loaded into the memory and the execution of the program is initiated, instruction after instruction of the program is executed; each instruction is carried out in one control cycle. The computer merely carries out one control cycle after another until it is instructed or activated to stop.

9.2 CONFIGURATION

The computer elements that are involved in the execution of the fetch sequences are described below.

```
Comment, configuration of fetch sequence begins here.
Register,    M(6-0),      $memory address register
             X(0-5),      $memory buffer register
             P(6-1),      $program address register
             I(5-0),      $instruction register
             D(3-0)       $distributor register
             AE,          $fetch-execution control register
             IE,          $instruction error indicator
             RUN1,        $stop control register
             EL,          $I/O data transfer indicator
             OV,          $overflow indicator
             LZ,          $logic zero indicator                        (9.1)
             SI           $sign indicator
Subregister, M(P)=M(6-1) $program address part of register M
Memory,      MEM(M)=MEM(0-127,0-5)
Switch,      ERRORSTOP(NOBP,AVBP,BP)   $three-position errorstop switch
             MR(ON,OFF),               $mode repeat switch
             JS(ON,OFF),               $sense switch
             MODE(DM,AEM,IM,PM)        $mode switch with four positions
Terminal,    READ                      $initiate memory read
             DIE=K(0)+K(1)+K(2)+K(3)+K(12)+K(13)+K(14)+K(15),
             DMR=MODE(DM)*MR(ON),
             AEMR=MODE(AEM)*MR(ON),
             IMR=MODE(IM)*MR(ON)
```

In the above description, random access memory MEM whose address register is M and buffer register is X is where the program is stored. Program register P stores the address of the next instruction.

Instruction register I stores the op-code part of the instruction. Terminal DIE detects and register IE indicates the illegal op-codes. Register AE controls the alternate execution of the fetch and execution sequences of the control cycle. Switches ERRORSTOP, MR, and MODE are sensed during the fetch sequence. Terminal DMR denotes the condition that the MODE switch is at the DM position and MR switch is at the ON position; this is the condition to repeat the execution of those micro-statements that are being activated by the current clock signal T(i). Terminal AEMR is similar to terminal DMR except that the MODE switch is at the AEM position; this is the condition that the current sequence be repeated whether it is the fetch or an execution sequence. Terminal IMR is also similar to terminal DMR except that the MODE switch is at the IM position; this is the condition that the current instruction be repeated.

9.3 SPECIAL MICRO-OPERATIONS

There are micro-operations which occur during every fetch sequence or every execution sequence. These micro-operations occur at timing signals DP(14) and DP(15) as described below,

$$
\begin{aligned}
&/DP(14)/ \quad OV \leftarrow 0, \\
&\qquad\qquad\; LZ \leftarrow 0, \\
&\qquad\qquad\; SI \leftarrow 0 \qquad\qquad\qquad\qquad\qquad (9.2)\\
&/DP(15)/ \quad EL \leftarrow 0 \\
&\qquad\qquad\; IF(AEMR=0)\ THEN\ (AE \leftarrow AE')
\end{aligned}
$$

The micro-operations which occur at DP(14) reset registers OV, LZ, and SI to 0. The micro-operations which occur at DP(15) reset register EL to 0 and, if terminal AEMR is equal to 0, complement the contents of register AE so as to alternate the execution of the fetch and execution sequences.

Another important micro-operation which occurs at every clock cycle is

$$
/TD/ \quad IF\ (DMR = 0)\quad THEN\quad (D \leftarrow countup\ D) \qquad (9.3)
$$

This incrementing-register-D micro-operation is the one described previously in statement (8.8) except the condition for its execution is now specified.

9.4 FETCH SEQUENCE

The sequential operations of the fetch sequence are now described by the sequence chart and then by statements. The fetch sequence begins by transferring the next instruction address to the memory address register M and ends after the operand address of the instruction is transferred to the memory address register M. Since each instruction consists of two memory words, two memory accesses are required during the fetch sequence.

9.4.1 Sequence Chart

The sequence chart for the fetch sequence is shown in Figure 9.1. The address of the next instruction is in the P register; this address is transferred to address register M. Since the 6-bit instruction address in the P register is an even address of the memory, the contents of register P is transferred to the subregister M(P) and bit M(0) is reset to 0. The op-code part of the instruction is next read out of the memory and transferred to buffer register X and then to instruction register I. The op-code is tested for illegal op-codes. If it is an illegal op-code, register IE is set to 1 and, if additionally switch ERRORSTOP is at the NOBP position, register RUN1 is set to 1 to stop the operation of the computer. If the op-code is legal (or if the op-code is illegal but switch ERRORSTOP is not at the NOBP position), terminals AEMR and IMR are sensed to see if they are both zero. If they are both zero (this means that the current sequence or the current instruction is not to be repeated), register P is incremented. Since the instruction consists of two memory words, the second memory word which is the six-bit address part of the instruction has to be fetched. The address for the second memory word can be readily obtained by setting bit M(0) to 1. The second memory word is next read out of the memory and transferred to register M(5–0), while bit I(0) which is the leftmost bit of the 7-bit operand address is transferred to bit M(6). The operand address of the instruction is now in address register M.

9.4.2 Sequence Description

The description of the fetch sequence which is obtained from the sequence chart is now shown below.

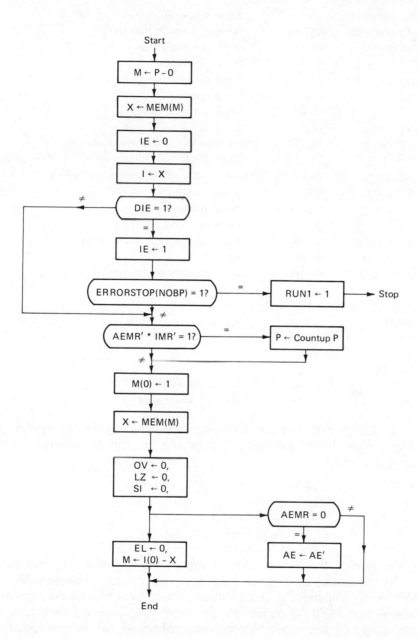

Fig. 9.1 Sequence chart for the fetch sequence

Comment, fetch sequence begins here

/AE'*DP(0)/	M←0	$clear register M
/Δ(AE'*DP(0))/	M(P)←P	$transfer next inst. address
/AE'*DP(1)/	READ←1	$initiate memory read
	X←0	$clear register X
/Δ(AE'*DP(1))/	X←MEM(M)	$read op-code from memory
/AE'*DP(2)/	I←0,	$clear register I
	IE←0	$clear inst. error indicator
/AE'*DP(3)/	I←X	$transfer op-code to register I
/AE'*DP(4)/	IF (DIE=1) THEN (IE←1) $set error indication	
	IF (DIE*ERRORSTOP(NOBP)=1) THEN (RUN1←1) $initiate stop	
/AE'*DP(5)/	IF (AEMR'*IMR'=1) THEN (P←countup P) $increment P	
/AE'*DP(10)/	M(0)←1	$increment M
/AE'*DP(11)/	READ←1	$initiate memory read
	X←0	$clear register X
/Δ(AE'*DP(11))/	X←MEM(M)	$read operand address from memory
/AE'*DP(15)/	M←0	$clear M
/Δ(AE'*DP(15))/	M←I(0)–X	$transfer operand address to register M

$$(9.2)$$

Comment, fetch sequence ends here

/DP(14)/	OV←0,	
	LZ←0,	
	SI←0	
/DP(15)/	EL←0,	
	IF (AEMR=0) THEN (AE←AE')	
/TD/	IF (DMR=0) THEN (D←countup D)	

In Chapter 8, the local two-step control signals are introduced. The above fetch sequence makes use of the following two-step control signals,

(a)   AE'*DP(0)   and   Δ(AE'*DP(0)),
(b)   AE'*DP(1)   and   Δ(AE'*DP(1)),
(c)   AE'*DP(11) and   Δ(AE'*DP(11)),
(d)   AE'*DP(15) and   Δ(AE'*DP(15))

Each pair of the above control signals are 15 microseconds apart.
In the above description, the first two micro-operations, M ← 0, M(P) ← P, transfer the next instruction address to address register M where bit M(0) is reset to 0; these two micro-operations are sequenced by the above two-step control signals (a). Micro-operation, READ ← 1, initiates memory read operation for fetching the instruction. Micro-operations, X ← 0 and X ← MEM(M), which are sequenced by the above two-step control signals (b), read a word

from the memory. Register IE is cleared at DP(2) and conditionally set to 1 at DP(4). Register I is cleared at DP(2) and the op-code part of the instruction in register X is transferred to register I at DP(3). Testing of illegal op-codes is done at DP(4). If execution of the current sequence or the current instruction is not repeated, register P is incremented at DP(5); register P now contains the address for the next instruction. Micro-operation, $M(0) \leftarrow 1$, at DP(10) generates the address for the second memory word of the instruction. During the next clock cycle, the second memory word of the instruction is read out of the memory by the above two-step control signals (c). Finally, micro-operations $M \leftarrow 0$, $M(5-0) \leftarrow X$, and $M(6) \leftarrow I(0)$ transfer the 7-bit operand address to address register M; these micro-operations are sequenced by the above two-step control signals (d).

The above description also includes the description of the special micro-operations which occur in every sequence and the incrementing-D-register micro-operation. As shown, registers OV, LZ, and SI are reset to 0 at DP(14). Register EL is reset to 0 and register AE is conditionally complemented, both at DP(15). Complementing of register AE at this time causes the next sequence to be an execution sequence. And register D is incremented by pulse TD if the condition to repeat the execution of the micro-operations of the current execution statement is not true; this increment causes the advancing of timing signal DT(i).

9.5 DISPLAY OF THE SEQUENTIAL OPERATIONS

The operations of the fetch sequence can be observed, step by step, on the control panel of the computer. Such observations give readers a visual and realistic perception of the computer operation. A series of photos was taken to show the conditions of the lights and the positions of the switches on the control panel at the end of each clock cycle. This series of photos is shown in Appendix A.

PROBLEMS

9.1 If the word length of the memory is 12 bits so that only one access of the memory is sufficient to fetch the instruction,
 (a) what computer elements in statements (9.1) have to be changed?
 (b) Simplify the sequence description in statements (9.2).

9.2 If terminal DMR is 1, does the timing signal DT(i) advance at each TD? If not, how can timing signals DT(i) be advanced?

9.3 If switch ERRORSTOP is not at NOBP position and if an illegal op-code is detected, will the fetch sequence continue? If it will, what will happen?

9.4 If terminal AEMR is 1, will the sequence continue? If it will, what will happen to the next sequence? Why?

9.5 Are the following micro-operations needed?
(a) $M \leftarrow 0$ at DP(0),
(b) $X \leftarrow 0$ at DP(1),
(c) $I \leftarrow 0$ at DP(2),
(d) $IE \leftarrow 0$ at DP(2),
(e) $M(0) \leftarrow 1$ at DP(10)
(f) $OV \leftarrow 0$, at DP(14)
(g) $EL \leftarrow 0$, at DP(15)
If yes, why? If not, how can they be eliminated?

9.6 Suggest a solution to remove the use of the local two-step control signals in statements (9.2).

9.7 As shown in Figure 6.11, the format for the jump instructions consists of a six-bit op-code and a six-bit address. How do the micro-operations at DP(15) which set up a 7-bit address affect the execution of the jump instruction?

9.8 Repeat problem 9.7 but considering the formats of
(a) the shift instructions in Figure 6.11(c),
(b) the load-C instruction in Figure 6.11(d),
(c) the change-accumulator-sign instruction in Figure 6.11(e), and
(d) the stop instruction in Figure 6.11(f).

10

Addition and

Subtraction

Sequences

Each instruction of the instruction set is implemented by a sequence. As mentioned, such a sequence is called an execution sequence. This chapter presents the sequences for instructions ADD, SUB, LDA, LDN, RAU, and RSU, all of which involve the use of the parallel adder. The elements involved in these sequences and the logic of the parallel adder are first described. The addition algorithm is next shown. The descriptions of these execution sequences then follow.

10.1 CONFIGURATION

The configuration for executing addition and subtraction sequences, except for the parallel adder, was shown when the arithmetic unit was described in Chapter 6. For the sake of convenience, the elements involved in the addition and subtraction sequences, including the parallel adder, are described again below.

Register,   X(0-5),

              A(0-5),

              SI,   (10.1)

              OV,

```
                 LZ,
                 RUN1,
                 AV,
Subregister,     A(M)=A(1-5),
                 X(M)=X(1-5),
Memory,          MEM(0-127,0-5),
Switch,          ERRORSTOP(NOBP,AVBP,BP),
                 MODE(DM,AEM,IM,PM),
                 MR(ON,OFF),
Light,           LTAV,
Terminal,        DMR=MODE(DM)*MR(ON),                        (10.1)
                 AEMR=MODE(AEM)*MR(ON),
                 T(0-3)=N(0-3)*CP1,
Terminal,        C(4)=A(5)*X(5),
                 C(3)=G3,
                 C(2)=A(3)*X(3),
                 C(1)=G1+G3*P3,
                 C(0)=P1*G1+P1*P3*G3,
                 G3=X(4)*X(5)*A(5)'+X(5)*A(4)'*A(5)'+X(4)*A(4)',
                 G1=X(2)*X(3)*A(3)'+X(3)*A(2)'*A(3)'+X(2)*A(2)',
                 G0=A(1)*X(1),
                 P3=A(2)*A(3),
                 P1=A(1)
```

In the above description, terminals DMR and AEMR which denote the conditions for repeating executions of micro-statements or sequence have been explained in Chapter 8. Terminals T(1–3) are the control signals for the three-step parallel adder. The parallel adder is described by the last terminal statement above. The logic of the parallel adder is now described.

10.2 PARALLEL ADDER

Since the sign bit is not involved in the addition, the parallel adder consists of five bits. In order to illustrate the use of group carries, the five bits are divided into three groups; this is illustrated in Fig. 10.1. The first bit forms group 1, the second and third bits form group 2, and the fourth and fifth bits form group 3. Carries C(0), C(1), and C(3) in Fig. 10.1 are the group carries because they are the carries generated from one group to the next group. Carries C(2) and C(4), not shown in Fig. 10.1, are carries in groups 2 and 3, respectively.

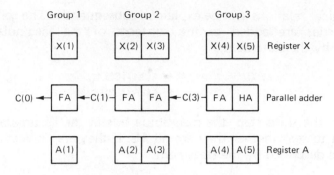

Fig. 10.1 Three groups of the parallel adder

10.2.1 Three-step Addition

The operation of the adder takes three steps which are activated by control signals $T(1-3)$, respectively. During the first step, local carries are generated, and addition is performed within each group. Thus, we have,

Terminal,	$C(4) = A(5)*X(5)$,	$local carry C(4)	
	$C(2) = A(3)*X(3)$,	$local carry C(2)	
/T(1)/	$A(5) \leftarrow A(5) \oplus X(5)$,	$sum bit of a half adder	
	$A(4) \leftarrow A(4) \oplus X(4) \oplus C(4)$,	$sum bit of a full adder	(10.2)
	$A(3) \leftarrow A(3) \oplus X(3)$,	$sum bit of a half adder	
	$A(2) \leftarrow A(2) \oplus X(2) \oplus C(2)$,	$sum bit of a full adder	
	$A(1) \leftarrow A(1) \oplus X(1)$	$sum bit of a half adder	

The above operation requires the use of one half adder each for the first, third, and fifth bits and one full adder each for the second and fourth bits. The logical relations for the sum and carry outputs of the half adder and full adder have been shown in Chapter 1. Notice the label is $T(1)$ as it is singly controlled by this clock signal.

During the second step, group carries $C(3)$ and $C(1)$ are generated. Their generations are described by the terminal statement,

Terminal,	$C(3)=G3$	
	$C(1)=G1+P3*G3$	
	$C(0)=P1*G1+P1*P3*G3$	
	$G3=X(4)*X(5)*A(5)'+X(5)*A(4)'*A(5)'+X(4)*A(4)'$	
	$G1=X(2)*X(3)*A(3)'+X(3)*A(2)'*A(3)'+X(2)*A(2)'$	(10.3)
	$G0=A(1)*X(1)$	
	$P3=A(2)*A(3)$	
	$P1=A(1)$	

These logical relations will be explained subsequently. The generated group carries are added to the contents of the accumulator as described by the statement,

$$/T(2)/ \qquad A(3,1) \leftarrow A(3,1) \oplus C(3,1),$$
$$A(2) \;\; \leftarrow A(2) \oplus (A(3) * C(3)) \qquad\qquad (10.4)$$

During the third step, the magnitude bits in the accumulator are examined to see whether they are all 1's. If they are, indicator LZ is set to 1 as described by the statement,

$$/T(3)/ \quad \text{IF } (A(M)=37) \quad \text{THEN} \quad (LZ \leftarrow 1) \qquad (10.5)$$

Indicator LZ will be later examined to determine whether negative zero has occurred. If it has, it will be changed into positive zero.

It should be noted that the parallel adder always performs an addition of two unsigned binary numbers, even when it is involved in the addition or subtraction of signed binary numbers.

As an example, assume that unsigned numbers 00011 and 01101 are stored in registers X and A respectively as shown in Fig. 10.2(a). During the first step, addition within each group is performed; the result 01100 is shown in Fig. 10.2(b). During the second step, group carries are generated. In this case, both C(1) and C(3) are 1; they are added to the accumulator. The sum 10000 is in the accumulator as shown in Fig. 10.2(c). Notice that C(0) is 0 During the third step, the accumulator is examined. In this case, it is not negative zero and no action is taken. The contents in register A in Fig. 10.2(d) are thus the same as those in Fig. 10.2(c).

10.2.2 Group Carries

The generation of group carries is now described. The boolean expression for G3 in the terminal statement (10.3) is obtained from the truth table described in Table 10.1. The first four columns show the 16 possible states of bits X(4,5) and A(4,5) before clock signal T(1) occurs. When the sum of the binary numbers in X(4,5) and A(4,5) is 4, 5, or 6, group carry G3 occurs; in this case a 1 is entered in the ninth column. Bits X(4,5) do not change during clock period T(1); therefore, the first and second columns are respectively the same as the fifth and sixth columns. But bits A(4,5) in the third and fourth columns do change to those shown in the seventh and eighth columns. Since group carry occurs during clock period T(2), the boolean expression for G3 should be obtained from the fifth through eighth columns but not from the first through the fourth columns.

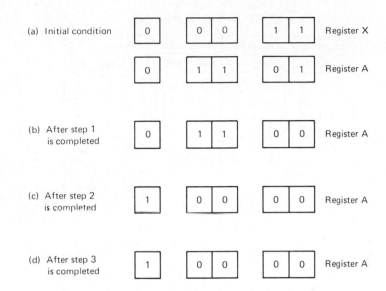

(a) Initial condition | 0 | 0 | 0 | 1 | 1 | Register X

0 | 1 | 1 | 0 | 1 | Register A

(b) After step 1
is completed | 0 | 1 | 1 | 0 | 0 | Register A

(c) After step 2
is completed | 1 | 0 | 0 | 0 | 0 | Register A

(d) After step 3
is completed | 1 | 0 | 0 | 0 | 0 | Register A

Fig. 10.2 An example of the 3-step addition

As shown in Table 10.1, G3 has a value of 1 when $X(4,5)-A(4,5)$ in the fifth through eighth columns are 0100, 1000, 1001, 1100, 1101, and 1110. Thus, we have,

$$G3=X(4)'*X(5)'*A(4)'*A(5)'+X(4)*X(5)'*A(4)'*A(5)'+X(4)$$
$$*X(5)'*A(4)'*A(5)+X(4)*X(5)*A(4)'*A(5)'+X(4)*X(5)*A(4)'$$
$$*A(5)+X(4)*X(5)*A(4)*A(5)'$$

After simplification, we have

$$G3=X(4)*X(5)*A(5)'+X(5)*A(4)'*A(5)'+X(4)*A(4)' \qquad (10.6)$$

which is the expression in statement (10.3). Note that G3 is the carry generated directly from bits $A(4,5)$ and $X(4,5)$ in group 3. It is not generated from carry $C(4)$ in order that the delays in the logic circuits due to generation of $C(4)$ can be avoided. (These delays are not significant in this parallel adder as the adder has a few groups and only two bits per group, but the delays become crucial for a parallel adder when there are many bits which can be as many as 60 or more bits.) Group carry $C(3)$ is the same as carry G3. We thus have

$$C(3) = G3 \qquad (10.7)$$

Carry G1 can be obtained from a truth table similar to the truth table in Table 10.1. We then have,

$$G1 = X(2)*X(3)*A(3)'+X(3)*A(2)'*A(3)'+X(2)*A(2)' \qquad (10.8)$$

Table 10.1 Truth table for group carry G3

Before clock $T(1)$ occurs				After clock $T(1)$ occurs				
X(4)	X(5)	A(4)	A(5)	X(4)	X(5)	A(4)	A(5)	G3
0	0	0	0	0	0	0	0	0
0	0	0	1	0	0	0	1	0
0	0	1	0	0	0	1	0	0
0	0	1	1	0	0	1	1	0
0	1	0	0	0	1	0	1	0
0	1	0	1	0	1	1	0	0
0	1	1	0	0	1	1	1	0
0	1	1	1	0	1	0	0	1
1	0	0	0	1	0	1	0	0
1	0	0	1	1	0	1	1	0
1	0	1	0	1	0	0	0	1
1	0	1	1	1	0	0	1	1
1	1	0	0	1	1	1	1	0
1	1	0	1	1	1	0	0	1
1	1	1	0	1	1	0	1	1
1	1	1	1	1	1	1	0	1

G1 is the carry generated directly from bits $X(2,3)$ and $A(2,3)$ in group 2, but not from carry $C(2)$.

Carry P3 which occurs when both $A(2)$ and $A(3)$ are 1,

$$P3 = A(2)*A(3) \tag{10.9}$$

indicates the condition that carry $C(3)$, if it occurs, is propagated through group 2 to become carry $C(1)$. Group carry $C(1)$ can be carry G1 generated from group 2 or can be carry $C(3)$ propagated through group 2. Thus, we have,

$$C(1) = G1 + P3*G3 \tag{10.10}$$

Since G0 is the generated carry from group 1, we have,

$$G0 = A(1)*X(1) \tag{10.11}$$

And since P1 is 1 when $A(1)$ is 1, we have,

$$P1 = A(1) \tag{10.12}$$

Group carry $C(0)$ is defined in statement (10.3) as either carry G1 propagates through group 1 or carry G3 propagated through groups 1 and 2. Thus, we have,

$$C(0) = P1*G1+P1*P3*G3 \qquad (10.13)$$

The derivation of group carries in statement (10.3) has now been shown.

10.2.3 Overflow

When two unsigned binary numbers are added by means of the parallel adder, overflow may occur. During the first step of the three-step addition, overflow occurs when G0 is 1. When this happens, register OV is set to 1. Thus we have

$$/T(1)/ \; IF \; (G0=1) \; THEN \; (OV \leftarrow 1) \qquad (10.14)$$

During the second step, overflow may also occur when C(0) is 1. Thus we have,

$$/T(2)/ \; IF \; (C(0)=1) \; THEN \; (OV \leftarrow 1) \qquad (10.15)$$

Since register LZ is set to 1 if negative zero occurs during the third step, both registers OV and LZ may be set to 1 during the three-step addition operation.

10.2.4 Logic Diagrams

The logic diagram of the parallel adder for the part active during the first step is shown in Fig. 10.3; this diagram is drawn from statement (10.2). The logic diagram of the parallel adder for the part active during the second step is shown in Fig. 10.4; this diagram is drawn from statements (10.3) and (10.4). In each of these two diagrams, D-type of flipflops are employed. As a result, lines for the data transfers are connected to the d inputs, while the lines for control signals T(1) and T(2) are connected to the c inputs.

Group carries C(0),C(1) and C(3) are shown in Fig.l0.4. Notice that C(3) is obtained through a two-level ·logic, C(1) through a three-level logic, and C(0) through a four-level logic. These carries would have more levels if the gated carry such as that shown in Fig. 3.19 were used. This is a matter of great importance for a practical parallel adder, because there is a longer delay when a signal has to go through the logic circuits of more levels. The longer is the delay, the

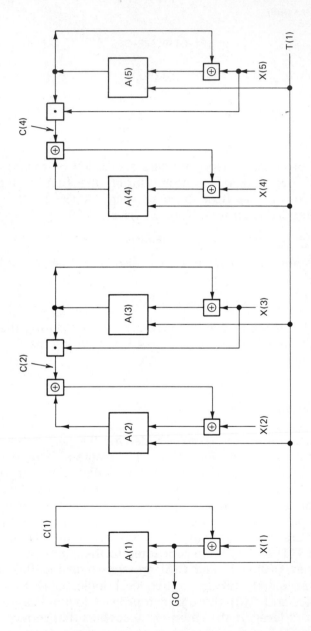

Fig. 10.3 Logic diagram of the parallel adder for the part active during control signal T(1)

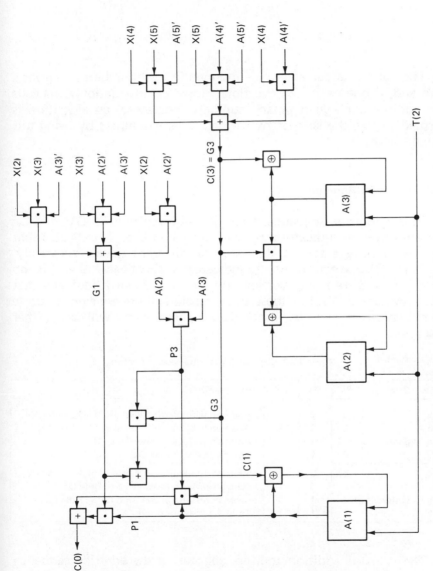

Fig. 10.4 Logic diagram of the parallel adder for the part active during control signal T(2)

longer is the addition time and often the longer are the multiplication and division times. Addition time is an important measure of the speed of operation of a digital computer.

10.3 ADDITION ALGORITHM

The parallel adder adds two unsigned five-bit numbers and gives a sum and, if one exists, an overflow. However, instruction ADD calls for addition of signed binary numbers. Therefore, an algorithm is formed to give the sum of two signed binary numbers by using this parallel adder.

10.3.1 Rules for Addition

In the addition sequence, three single-bit registers SI, OV, and LZ are employed as indicators. Register SI, when 0 or 1, indicates that the two numbers are of the same or different signs respectively. Register OV, when 0 or 1, indicates, respectively, there is no overflow or there is an overflow. Register LZ, when 1, indicates that bits A(M) are all 1's. For these three registers, there are eight possible combinations shown in Table 10.2. These cases will be further discussed.

Table 10.2 Explanation of three add indicators

Case	Sign	SI	OV	LZ	Explanation
a		0	0	0	Addition with no overflow. Rule (1)
b		0	0	1	Addition with sum bits being all 1's. Rule (1).
c	Same	0	1	0	Addition with overflow. Rule (1)
d		0	1	1	This case does not occur.
e		1	0	0	Subtraction requiring 1's compl. of A. Rule (2c)
f		1	0	1	Subtraction with negative zero. Rule (2b)
g	Different	1	1	0	Subtraction with end-around carry. Rule (2a)
h		1	1	1	This case does not occur.

The rules of addition that are adopted in the addition sequence are enumerated below,

1. When the signs are the same, add the magnitudes of the two numbers and retain the sign of the augend in the A register. Indicate the overflow if it occurs.

2. When the signs are different, complement each magnitude bit of the addend in the X register, and then add these magnitude bits to those of the augend in the A register. Retain the sign in the A register. Call this sum the first sum. Three cases arise:
   a. If an end-around carry occurs, add one to the least significant bit of the first sum to form the final sum.
   b. If an end-around carry does not occur but the magnitude of the first sum being all 1's (i.e., negative zero) occurs, the final sum is zero. The A register including the sign bit is then reset to 0.
   c. If neither the end-around carry nor the magnitude of the first sum being all 1's occurs, the final sum is obtained by 1's complementing the first sum (including the sign bit) of the A register.

The rules of addition are now illustrated by ten examples, each of which represents one of ten possible cases. For the sake of convenience and clarity, the numbers in these examples are all integers. This does not prevent one from regarding the binary point at the other locations so that the numbers become fractional or mixed. It is only necessary that the binary points of the two numbers are lined up.

10.3.2 Addition When SI is Zero

When the two numbers have the same sign, register SI is reset to 0 and the numbers in the X register (addend) and in the A register (augend) are added. The addition is carried out in the following manner. The magnitude bits in the X and A registers are added, and the sign in the A register is retained. When an overflow occurs, register OV is set to 1. When SI is 0, negative zero does not occur; therefore, the case where SI and LZ are both 1 in Table 10.2 does not occur. (This case can occur by statement (10.5), but it is not regarded as negative zero since SI is 0.) The following four examples show the cases where SI is 0 and OV is either 0 or 1.

Example 10.1 Both numbers are positive

	Binary	Decimal
Register A (augend)	+10001	+17
Register X (addend)	+00101	+05
Register A (sum)	+10110	+22

SI = 0,
OV = 0,
LZ = 0.

The sum in the A register is binary 010110. There occurs neither an overflow nor negative zero. Registers SI, OV, and LZ are all 0.

Example 10.2 Both numbers are negative

	Binary	Decimal
Register A	−10001	−17
Register X	−00101	−05
Sum in A	−10110	−22

SI = 0,
OV = 0,
LZ = 0.

The sum in the A register is binary 110110. Similar to the last example, registers SI, OV, and LZ are all 0.

Example 10.3 Overflow occurs

	Binary	Decimal
Register A	+10001	+17
Register X	+10100	+20
	+(1)00101	+37

Overflow

SI = 0,
OV = 1,
LZ = 0.

Overflow occurs and the sum binary 000101 is thus incorrect. Register OV is set to 1. If both numbers are negative, overflow will again occur.

Example 10.4 Sum is +11111

	Binary	Decimal
Register A	+10101	+21
Register X	+01010	+10
Sum in A	+11111	+31

→ Not negative zero

$$SI = 0,$$
$$OV = 0,$$
$$LZ = 1.$$

The sum +11111 is not negative zero but decimal +31. Registers SI and OV are 0, but LZ is 1. If both numbers are negative, the sum is – 11111 which is not negative zero but decimal – 31.

10.3.3 Subtraction When SI Is One

When the two numbers are of different signs, register SI is set to 1 and the number in the X register is subtracted from the number in the A register. Instead of subtraction, addition of 1's complement of the subtrahend is performed. To carry out this addition, the magnitude bits in the X register (subtrahend) are 1's complemented and then added to the magnitude bits in the A register (minuend). The result in the A register at this time is called the first sum. The first sum may have an overflow (which is not an overflow but a so-called end-around carry) or may produce a negative zero. The handling of the end-around carry and negative zero is illustrated in the following six examples.

Example 10.5 Minuend is positive and has a larger magnitude

	Binary	Decimal
Register A (minuend)	+10001	+17
Register X (subtrahend)	– 00101	–05
		+12

Instead of subtraction, the magnitude bits in the X register (i.e., 00101) are 1's complemented and then added to those in the A register as shown below,

Register A (augend)	+10001
Register X (addend)	– 11010
Register A (first sum)	+(1)01011
add end-around carry	1
Register A (final sum)	+01100

SI = 1,
OV = 1,
LZ = 0.

Because of addition of 1's complement, end-around carry may occur. Here, it does occur. Register OV (now it becomes a misnomer) is set to 1 and the carry is added to the least significant bit to produce the final sum which is binary 001100.

Example 10.6 Minuend is negative and has a larger
                magnitude

	Binary	Decimal
Register A (minuend)	– 10001	– 17
Register X (subtrahend)	+00101	+05
		– 12

Again, the magnitude bits in the X register are 1's complemented and added to those in the A register as shown below,

Register A (augend   – 10001
Register X (addend)   +11010
Register A (first sum) – (1)01011

add end-around carry ————➤ 1
Register A (final sum)   –01100

SI = 1,
OV = 1,
LZ = 0.

Although the minuend is negative instead of positive, this example is similar to the last one in that an end-around carry occurs. The final sum is binary 101100.

Example 10.7 Minuend is positive and has a
                smaller magnitude

	Binary	Decimal
Register A (minuend)	+00101	+ 5
Register X (subtrahend)	– 10001	– 17
		– 12

Again, the magnitude bits in the X register are 1's complemented and added to those in the A register as shown below,

Register A (augend)   +00101
Register X (addend)   −01110
Register A (first sum)   +10011

1's complement

Register A (final sum)   −01100

SI = 1,
OV = 0,
LZ = 0.

No end-around carry occurs; this indicates that the magnitude of the addend is larger than that of the augend. The first sum and the sign bit are both 1's complemented. The final sum is binary 101100.

Example 10.8 Minuend is negative and has a smaller magnitude

	Binary	Decimal
Register A (minuend)	−00101	− 5
Register X (subtrahend)	+10001	+17
		+12

Again, the magnitude bits in the X register are 1's complemented and added to those in the A register as shown below,

Register A (augend)   −00101
Register X (addend)   +01110
Register A (first sum)   −10011

1's complement

Register A (final sum)   +01100

SI = 1,
OV = 0,
LZ = 0.

Although the minuend is negative, this example is similar to the last example. No end-around carry occurs. The final sum, obtained by 1's complementing the first sum and the sign bit, is binary 001100.

Example 10.9 Minuend is positive and has the
                  same magnitude

	Binary	Decimal
Register A (minuend)	+10001	+17
Register X (subtrahend)	-10001	-17
		0

Again, the magnitude bits in the X register are 1's complemented and added to those in the A register as shown below,

Register A (augend)	+10001
Register X (addend)	-01110
Register A (first sum)	+11111

Clear register A

Register A (final sum)   +00000

SI = 1,
OV = 0,
LZ = 1.

Since magnitude bits are all 1's, register LZ is set to 1. When registers SI and LZ are both 1, negative zero occurs. Register A including the sign bit is reset to 0, thus the final sum is binary 000000.

Example 10.10 Minuend is negative and has the
                    same magnitude

	Binary	Decimal
Register A (minuend)	-01010	-10
Register X (subtrahend)	+01010	+10
		0

Again, the magnitude bits in the X register are 1's complemented and added to those in the A register as shown below,

        Register A (augend)   −01010
        Register X (addend)   +10101
        Register A (first sum)   −11111

                                        Clear register A

        Register A (final sum)   +00000

                                  SI = 1,
                                  OV = 0,
                                  LZ = 1.

Although the minuend is negative, this example is similar to the last example. Negative zero occurs and the final sum is binary 000000.

The case in Table 10.2 where SI and OV and LZ are all 1 does not occur because, if the result is zero, the end-around carry cannot occur at the same time.

10.4 ADD AND SUB SEQUENCES

When a number Y is added to another number X by instruction ADD or when a number Y is subtracted from another number X by instruction SUB, number X must already be in the A register. Number X can be loaded into the A register by instruction LDA, or it is left there as a result of a previous instruction.

The ADD or SUB sequence is an execution sequence. The sequence chart for the ADD sequence is first shown, then the description of the ADD and SUB sequences follows.

10.4.1 ADD Sequence Chart

The ADD sequence is an implementation of the above addition algorithm. The sequence chart for the ADD sequence is shown in Fig. 10.5. As shown, the addend is first read out of the memory. The two sign bits X(0) and A(0) are then tested. If they are different, register

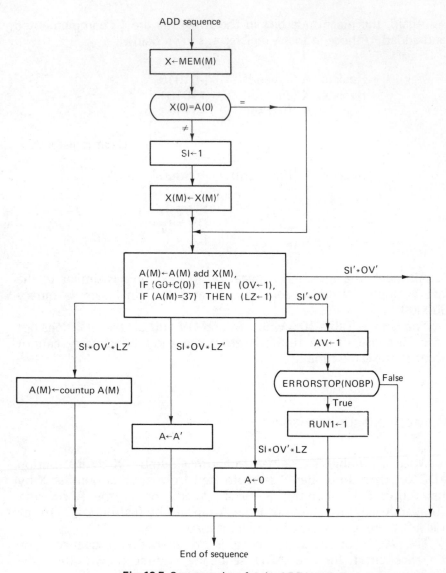

Fig. 10.5 Sequence chart for the ADD sequence

SI is set to 1 and magnitude bits X(M) is 1's complemented. Addition is next performed. If overflow occurs, OV is set to 1. If bits A(M) are all 1's, LZ is set to 1. Registers SI, OV, and LZ are tested. If both SI and OV are 0, rule (1) of the addition algorithm applies; nothing further is to be done. The ADD sequence ends. If SI is 0 but OV is 1, rule (1) with overflow applies. In this case, register AV is set to 0, and the ERRORSTOP switch is on the NOBP position, RUN1 is set to 1; the add overflow condition is thus indicated and the computer ceases to operate. If both SI and OV are 1 but LZ is 0, then rule (2a) applies. The end-around carry is added to the first sum in the A register. The ADD sequence is completed. If both SI and LZ are 1 but OV is 0, then rule (2b) applies. In this case, negative zero occurs; the first sum and the sign bit in the A register are both set to 0. The ADD sequence ends. If SI is 1 but both OV and LZ are 0, then rule (2c) applies. The first sum and the sign bit in the A register are both 1's complemented. The ADD sequence is completed.

10.4.2 ADD Sequence Description

The description of the ADD sequence which is obtained from the sequence chart is shown below. Note that this description includes the previously described three-step add subsequence, the special micro-operations which occur in every sequence, and the incrementing-D-counter micro-operation.

Comment, ADD sequence begins

/ADD∗DP(1)/	X←0,	$clear register X
	READ←1	$initiate memory read
/Δ(ADD∗DP(1))/	X←MEM(M)	$load addend to X
/ADD∗DP(3)/	IF (A(0)≠X(0)) THEN (SI←1)	$set SI
/ADD∗DP(4)/	IF (SI) THEN (X(M)←X(M)')	$1's complement of X
/ADD∗DP(5)/	IF (DMR=0) THEN (AC←countup AC)	$start add subsequence

Comment, ADD sequence begins here

/T(1)/	A(5,3,1)←A(5,3,1)⊕X(5,3,1),	$add within adder groups
	A(4,2)←A(4,2)⊕X(4,2)⊕C(4,2),	
	IF (GO=1) THEN (OV←1),	$set overflow
	IF (DMR=0) THEN (AC←countup AC)	$advance add control
/T(2)/	A(3,1)←A(3,1)⊕C(3,1),	$add group carries
	A(2)←A(2)⊕(A(3)∗C(3)),	
	IF (C(0)=1) THEN (OV←1),	$set overflow (10.16)
	IF (DMR=0 THEN (AC←countup AC)	$advance add control
/T(3)/	IF (A(M)=37) THEN (LZ←1),	$test A(M) being all 1's
	IF (DMR=0) THEN (AC←countup AC)	$advance add control

Comment, add subsequence ends here and returns to ADD sequence

/ADD∗DP(6)/	IF (SI∗OV'∗LZ') THEN (A←A')	$Rule (2c)
/ADD∗DP(7)/	IF (SI'∗OV) THEN (AV←1),	$Rule (1)
	IF(ERRORSTOP(NOBP)) THEN (RUN1←1)	
	IF (SI∗OV'∗LZ) THEN (A←0),	$Rule (2b)
	IF (SI∗OV∗LZ') THEN (A(M)←countup A(M))	$Rule (2a)

Comment, ADD sequence ends here

Comment, the following occurs at every sequence

/DP(14)/	OV←0, LZ←0, SI←0	$clear OV, LZ, and SI
/DP(15)/	EL←0	$clear EL
	IF (AEMR=0) THEN (AE←AE′)	$switch to fetch sequence
/TD/	IF (DMR=0) THEN (D←countup D)	$increment D

In the above description, the addend is read out of the memory during DP(1). The two sign bits are tested during DP(3); register SI is set to 1 if they do not agree. During DP(4), X(M) is 1's complemented if SI is 1 in preparation for an addition of 1's complement of X(M). During DP(5), add subsequence is started by incrementing-register-AC micro-operation (AC ← countup AC) if the condition DMR (which means that the MODE switch is at the DM position and the MR switch is at the ON position) is not true.

The description of the three-step addition which is controlled by the control signals T(1–3) is taken from statements (10.2), (10.4), (10.5), (10.14), and (10.15) where terminals C(4,2) are defined in terminal statement (10.3). Control signal T(1) is advanced to T(2), to T(3), and then back to T(0) by the incrementing-AC micro-operation if the condition DMR is not true. After the three-step addition, rule (1), rule (2a), and rule (2b) are implemented during DP(7), while rule (2c) is implemented during DP(6).

Register AE is conditionally complemented at DP(15). When it is complemented at this time, the next sequence will be the fetch sequence.

10.4.3 SUB Sequence

The subtraction called for by the SUB instruction is obtained by first complementing the sign of the addend and then performing an addition instead of a subtraction. Therefore, the SUB sequence is identical to the ADD sequence with two exceptions. First, terminal SUB instead of terminal ADD now becomes a part of the labels of the sequence. Second, the following execution statement to complement the sign bit X(0),

$$/SUB*DP(2)/ \quad X(0) ← X(0)' \qquad (10.17)$$

is added. This sign-complementing micro-operation is carried out after the addend has been read out of the memory but before the testing of the two signs. Notice that the micro-operation occurs at control signal DP(2).

10.5 OTHER SEQUENCES

The other sequences are the LDA, LDN, RSU, and RAU sequences for the LDA, LDN, RSU, and RAU instructions. While the ADD and SUB instructions involve two operands, these four instructions involve only one operand. The LDA and LDN sequences are almost identical to the ADD sequence. The RSU sequence needs some change from the ADD sequence. The RAU sequence is considerably different from the ADD sequence.

10.5.1 LDA Sequence

The LDA sequence or the load-accumulator sequence first clears the accumulator and then transfers an operand located in the memory to the accumulator. It can be regarded as the addition of the operand to zero in the accumulator. For this reason, the LDA instruction is often called CLA (clear add) instruction.

Because the LDA sequence performs an addition with the augend being zero, the sequence is identical to the ADD sequence with two exceptions. First, terminal LDA instead of terminal ADD now becomes a part of the labels of the sequence. Second, the following execution statement to put the number zero into the accumulator,

$$/LDA*DP(0)/ \quad A \leftarrow 0 \qquad\qquad (10.18)$$

is added. This micro-operation is carried out as the first step of the LDA sequence, as it occurs at control signal DP(0).

10.5.2 LDN Sequence

The LDN or load-accumulator-negative sequence first clears the accumulator and then transfers the number in the memory to the accumulator with the sign of the number complemented. It can be regarded as subtraction of the number in the memory from zero in the accumulator. For this reason, the LDN instruction is often called the CLS (clear subtract) instruction.

The LDN sequence is identical to the ADD sequence with two exceptions. First, terminal LDN instead of terminal ADD becomes a part of the labels of the sequence. Second, the following two execution statements are added,

$$/LDN*DP(0)/ \quad A \leftarrow 0$$
$$/LDN*DP(2)/ \quad X(0) \leftarrow X(0)' \qquad (10.19)$$

These two statements are the same as statements (10.17) and (10.18) except for the terminal name LDN being used here.

10.5.3 RSU Sequence

The RSU sequence or the replace-subtract-unity sequence subtracts one from a number in the memory and then stores the result into the same location of the memory. The RSU instruction enables the programmer to use any location of the memory as a 5-bit down-counter (a counter which decrements).

Since the subtraction in the RSU sequence can be regarded as the addition of -00001 to the number in the memory, this sequence is the same as the ADD sequence except for three changes. First, terminal RSU now becomes a part of the labels of the sequence. Second, the following two execution statements are added

$$
\begin{array}{lll}
/\text{RSU}*\text{DP}(0)/ & A \leftarrow 0 & \\
/\text{RSU}*\text{DP}(2)/ & A(0) \leftarrow 1, A(5) \leftarrow 1 & (10.20)
\end{array}
$$

to insert number -00001 to the accumulator. Third, the following three execution statements are added

$$
\begin{array}{lll}
/\text{RSU}*\text{DP}(8)/ & X \leftarrow A & \\
/\text{RSU}*\text{DP}(13)/ & \text{WRITE} \leftarrow 1 & (10.21) \\
/\Delta(\text{RSU}*\text{DP}(13))/ & \text{MEM}(M) \leftarrow X &
\end{array}
$$

to store the difference in the accumulator into the memory. Since the memory address has not been changed, the difference is stored at the same location. The delayed label $\Delta(\text{RSU}*\text{DP}(13))$ indicates that, after terminal WRITE is set to 1 at DP(13), the number in register X is stored into the memory 15 microseconds later.

10.5.4 RAU Sequence

The RAU sequence or the replace-add-unity sequence adds one to a number in the memory and then stores the result into the same location of the memory. The RAU instruction enables the programmer to use a location of the memory as an up-counter (a counter which increments); thus, this instruction is useful for counting or address indexing (see Chapter 7).

The memory address for an instruction address is six bits and that for an operand address is seven bits. In using the RAU instruction, the programmer should decide whether he needs a six-bit or a seven-bit counter. For a six-bit counter, any memory location can be used. For a seven-bit counter, the instruction RAU m where m is the memory address requires operand address m odd in order that the least significant bit of the location at memory address m − 1 becomes the most significant bit of the seven-bit counter. Since the parallel adder is a five-bit adder, the addition of one to an unsigned six-bit or seven-bit number makes the RAU sequence quite different from the ADD sequence.

Comment, RAU sequence begins here

/RAU∗DP(0)/	A ← 0	$clear register A
/RAU∗DP(1)/	X ← 0,	$clear register X
	READ ← 1	$initiate memory read
/Δ(RAU∗DP(1))/	X ← MEM(M)	$load addend to X
/RAU∗DP(2)/	A(5) ← 1	$load incremental bit
/RAU∗DP(5)/	IF (DMR=0) THEN (AC ← countup AC)	$start add subsequence
/RAU∗DP(6)/	IF (X(0)⊕OV=1) THEN (A(0) ← 1),	$insert the 6th bit
	IF (X(0)∗OV=1) THEN (SI ← 1)	$indicate 7th bit
/RAU∗DP(7)/	X ← 0	$clear register X
/RAU∗DP(8)/	X ← A	$transfer A to X
/RAU∗DP(9)/	WRITE ← 1	$initiate memory write
/Δ(RAU∗DP(9))/	MEM(M) ← X	$store X to memory
/RAU∗DP(10)/	M(0) ← 0	$change address to even
/RAU∗DP(11)/	X ← 0,	$clear register X
	READ ← 1	$initiate memory read
/Δ(RAU∗DP(11))/	X ← MEM(M)	$load to X
/RAU∗DP(12)/	IF (SI=1) THEN (X(5) ← 1)	$add the 7th bit
/RAU∗DP(13)/	WRITE ← 1	$initiate memory write
/Δ(RAU∗DP(13))/	MEM(M) ← X	$store X to memory

Comment, RAU sequence ends here

$$(10.22)$$

In the above description, the execution statements at DP(1) load the addend to register X, while the execution statements at DP(0) and DP(2) load the augend 000001 to the accumulator. The add subsequence is started by the execution statement at DP(5). The addition of the most significant bits (i.e., the sign bits) and the indication of the seventh bit take place in the execution statement at DP(6). (Notice that operator ⊕ in the condition of this statement gives the sum output of a single-bit half adder.) The execution statements at DP(7–9) store the sum in the accumulator into the same location of the memory. The execution statements at DP(10–13) perform the addition of the seventh bit in the case of a seven-bit counter. In this case, memory address m (which is odd) is changed to even by the micro-operation which resets M(0) to 0 at DP(10). The word at address (m–1) is read out at DP(11). The addition of the seventh bit (i.e., bit X(5)) is performed at DP(12); the sum in the accumulator is stored into the same location of the memory at DP(13).

It should be noted that, when memory address m is odd and the contents at address m are 111111, the contents at address m change into 000000 and the contents at address (m–1) becomes 000001 (assume that contents at address (m–1) are initially 000000). Also note that, when memory address m is even, the execution of the statements at DP(10–13), should not change the contents at address m except when the contents are 111111. Thus, it is important that the memory address of instruction RAU be odd in the case of a seven-bit counter.

PROBLEMS

10.1. Given the following pairs of signed binary numbers,
   (a) X=-10010, Y=-01010
   (b) X=+10101, Y=+01011
   (c) X=+10010, Y=-01100
   (d) X=-01100, Y=+10010
   (e) X=-10010, Y=+10010
   where X is the augend and Y the addend, perform additions of X and Y by using the rules of addition described in this chapter.

10.2. Do the following statement and statement(10.2) perform the same function?

$$/T(1)/ \quad A(4,5) \leftarrow A(4,5) \text{ add } X(4,5),$$
$$A(2,3) \leftarrow A(2,3) \text{ add } X(2,3), \qquad (10.23)$$
$$A(1) \leftarrow A(1) \text{ add } X(1)$$

Describe the differences if there are any.

10.3. Rewrite the micro-statements in statement (10.2) into one or more conditional micro-statements.

10.4. Rewrite the terminal statement (10.6) for G3 into one or more conditional micro-statements.

10.5. With respect to the ADD sequence, change micro-operation

$$A(M) \leftarrow countup \ A(M)$$

into a subsequence which performs the three-step addition.

10.6 If the two statements (10.20) are replaced by the following statement,

$$/RSU * DP(2)/ \quad A \leftarrow 100001 \hspace{3cm} (10.24)$$

what are the advantages and disadvantages?

10.7 Is overflow possible in the RSU sequence? If it is possible, illustrate the overflow by an example.

10.8 With respect to the RAU sequence (10.22), draw a truth table for the two variables OV and X(0), and explain by means of the truth table why the conditions
(a) $X(0) \oplus OV = 1$ and
(b) $X(0) * OV = 1$
are valid.

10.9 Given instruction RAU m where m is an even memory address, why will the execution of this instruction not change the contents at memory address m? What is the exception and what will be the result?

10.10 Replace the terminal statement which describes the carries for the parallel adder with the group carry in statements (10.1) by a terminal statement which describes a 5-bit parallel adder with the gated carry (see Chapter 3).

10.11 Replace the description of the three-step addition in the ADD sequence (10.16) by the description of addition using the parallel adder with the gated carry as described in Problem 10.10.

10.12 Are the micro-operations to reset registers OV, LZ, and SI at DP(14) in statement (10.16) needed? Why?

10.13 Write a program for testing the LDA, LDN, ADD, and SUB instructions by computing $-N+N$ (where N is a signed number) and determining whether the result is 0. Number N is to be manually loaded into the memory.

10.14 Write a program to test the RAU instruction by incrementing a count stored in a memory location. The count is initially set to 0 and the counting should be terminated when the count reaches 1111111.

10.15 Write a program to test whether the addition algorithm functions correctly.

10.16 Write a program to test whether the parallel adder functions correctly.

11

Multiplication

and Division

Sequences

This chapter presents the multiplication and division sequences for instructions MPY and DIV. Configurations for multiplication and division are first described; descriptions of these sequences then follow. As will be seen, the division sequence is more complex, partly because it is necessary to check division overflow and partly because of the use of the restoring method for comparing the divisor and the partial remainder in the division sequence. In both sequences, there is a loop for repeatedly performing the required addition or subtraction.

11.1 CONFIGURATION

The configuration for executing the multiplication and division sequences is identical to that described by statements (10.1) for the addition and subtraction sequences with the addition of the following elements:

```
Comment, configuration begins here
Register,      Q(0-5),                    $multiplier-quotient register
               C(6-0)                     $counter
               DV                         $division overflow indicator
Casregister,   AQ(0-10)=A-Q(M)            $AQ casregister                        (11.1)
Subregister,   Q(M)=Q(1-5),              $magnitude part of register Q
               AQ(M)=AQ(1-10)             $magnitude part of register AQ
Light,         LTDV(ON,OFF)               $division overflow light
```

As will be shown, register Q stores the multiplier or the quotient. The declaration of casregister AQ conveys the idea that the A register and the magnitude part of the Q register are regarded as one register. The magnitude part of the AQ register is capable of shifting to the right or left as if it were one register. There is a loop in both the multiplication and the division sequences. Counter C counts the number of iterations and controls the exit from the loop. Register DV and light LTDV indicate division overflow when it occurs. Although the same computer elements are used for multiplication and division, the functions of the X, A, and Q registers are different for each and are described below.

11.1.1 Multiplication Configuration

The functions of the X, A, and Q registers also change during execution of the multiplication sequence. These functions are illustrated in Figure 11.1. As shown in Figure 11.1(a) the multiplicand must be loaded into the A register by a LDA instruction (see Figure 7.1) before execution of the MPY instruction. When execution of the MPY instruction begins, the multiplier is taken out of the memory and temporarily stored in the X register as shown in Figure 11.1(b). The multiplier in the X(M) register is transferred to the Q(M) register, and the multiplicand in the A register is transferred to the X register, and the A register is cleared. This situation is shown in Figure 11.1(c) which also shows the register status at the true beginning of the multiplication steps. When the multiplication is completed, the multiplicand remains in the X register, but the multiplier in the Q(M) register is lost; instead, the product appears in the AQ(M) register. As shown in Figure 11.1(d), the most significant part of the product is in the A(M) register, while the least significant part is in the Q(M) part.

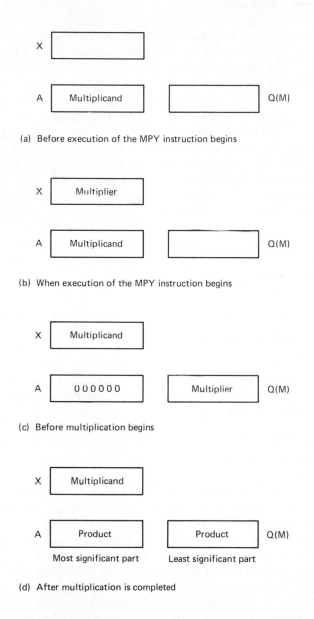

(a) Before execution of the MPY instruction begins

(b) When execution of the MPY instruction begins

(c) Before multiplication begins

(d) After multiplication is completed

Fig. 11.1 Functions of the X, A, and Q registers for the multiplication sequence

11.1.2 Division Configuration

The functions of the X, A, and Q registers also change during execution of the division sequence. These functions are illustrated in Figure 11.2. As shown in Figure 11.2(a), the dividend must be loaded into the AQ register by the LDA and sometimes SRE instruction (see Figure 7.1) before execution of the DIV instruction. When execution of the DIV instruction begins, the divisor is taken out of the memory and loaded into the X register as shown in Figure 11.2(b). Since the subtraction required by division is replaced by the addition of the 1's complement of the subtrahend, the divisor in the X(M) register is 1's complemented as shown in Figure 11.2(c). This situation represents the register status at the true beginning of the division steps. When the division is completed, the register status is as shown in Figure 11.2(d). The 1's complement of the divisor remains in the X(M) register, but the dividend in the AQ(M) register is lost. Instead, the quotient appears in the Q(M) register and the remainder in the A(M) register.

11.2 MULTIPLICATION SEQUENCE

The multiplication sequence is an execution sequence. The multiplication algorithm is first described, then the sequence chart, and finally the sequence itself.

11.2.1 Multiplication Algorithm

As mentioned in Chapter 1, the rules of the binary multiplication for numbers in the signed magnitude representation are the same as those for unsigned binary numbers (section 1.1.7 and example 1.11) except, in the case of signed binary numbers, the sign bit of the product must also be determined. The sign of the product is positive when the signs of the multiplicand and the multiplier are the same; otherwise, the sign is negative.

In Figure 11.3, an example is given to illustrate the application of the multiplication rules to sequential operations in the arithmetic registers. The multiplicand in the X register is 0.10001 and the multiplier in the Q register is 1.01001. The binary points of the multiplicand and the multiplier are both normally located. Since the contents of the X register do not change, the X register is shown only

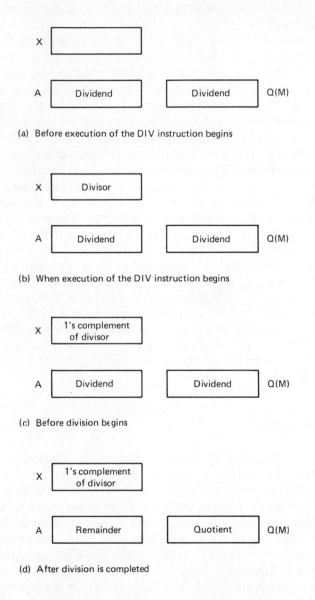

(a) Before execution of the DIV instruction begins

(b) When execution of the DIV instruction begins

(c) Before division begins

(d) After division is completed

Fig. 11.2 Functions of the X, A, and Q registers for the division sequence

once. Note the OV bit is placed to hold the carry from the most significant bit in the A(M) register; this carry is really not an overflow because the partial product is growing during each step of the multiplication.

　　　As shown in Figure 11.3, the A register is initially cleared. The least significant bit of the Q register, Q(5), is examined. If it is a 1, as in this case, the contents of the X(M) register are added to the contents of the A(M) register and the sum which is the partial product is left in the A(M) register. It is not the sum of the contents of the X and A registers because the sign bits are not involved in the addition, and these numbers are in the signed magnitude representation. If Q(5) is 0, there is no addition. The casregister AQ(M) is then shifted one bit to the right. Notice that the least significant bit of the multiplier is now lost, but it is no longer of any use. The contents of Q(5) are next examined again; at this time, it is the second least significant bit of the multiplier that is being examined. If Q(5) is 1, the contents of X(M) are added to the contents of the A(M); otherwise, there is no addition (i.e., addition of 0). This process of addition and right-shifting is repeated until all the multiplier bits are examined. The sign bit is now determined and inserted into the A(0) bit. The product is in the casregister AQ with the most significant part in the A(M) register and the least significant part in the Q(m) register. This example is the same as Example 1.11, and the product 1.0010011001 in this example agrees with that in Example 1.11, except for the presence of the sign bit and different location of the binary point.

11.2.2 Sequence Chart

　　　The MPY sequence implements the multiplication algorithm in the manner illustrated in Figure 11.3. Figure 11.4 shows the sequence chart of the MPY sequence. As shown, bit Q(0) is first reset to 0 and a memory read is initiated. After the multiplier is read into the X register, the contents of registers X, A, and Q are those shown in Figure 11.1(b). The sign bits X(0) and A(0) are compared; if they are not equal, register SI is set to 1. Later, sign bits Q(0) and A(0) are set to 1 when SI is 1. Counter C is set to 5. The multiplier is transferred to the Q(M) subregister from X(M). The multiplicand is transferred to the X register and the A register is cleared. At this time, the contents of registers X, A, and Q are those shown in Figure 11.1(c).

　　　The loop for multiplication, which consists of four steps, now begins. The first step counts down counter C. The second step

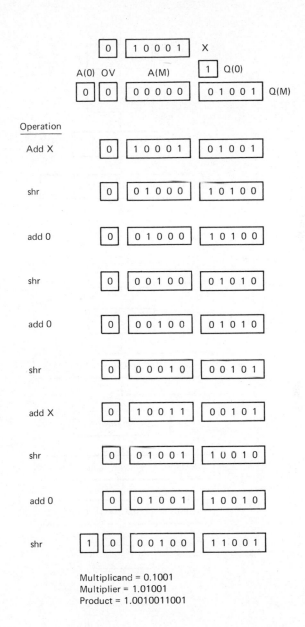

Fig. 11.3 Contents of the arithmetic registers during multiplication

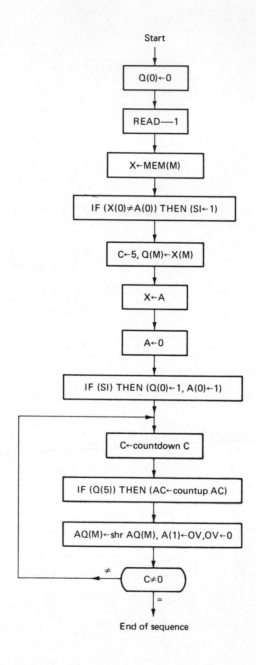

Fig. 11.4 Sequence chart for the multiplication sequence

initiates and carries out the addition of the multiplicand to form the partial product if Q(5) is 1. The third step shifts the contents of the AQ(M) register one bit to the right and the contents of bit OV are placed into bit A(1). The fourth step tests counter C to determine whether it has reached 0. If count C is not zero, the sequence repeats the four steps. When counter C reaches 0, the product is in the AQ register and the sequence ends. The contents of the X, A, and Q registers are those shown in Figure 11.1(d).

11.2.3 Sequence Description

The MPY sequence which is obtained from the sequence chart is now described.

Comment, MPY sequence begins here

/MPY∗DP(0)/	Q(0)←0	$clear Q(0)
/MPY∗DP(1)/	X←0,	$clear X
	READ←1	$initiate memory read
/Δ(MPY∗DP(1))/	X←MEM(M)	$load multiplier to X
/MPY∗DP(3)/	IF (A(0)≠X(0)) THEN (SI←1)	$set SI
/MPY∗DP(6)/	C←5,	$set C to 5
	Q(M)←X(M)	$transfer multiplier to Q
/MPY∗DP(7)/	X←0	$clear X
/MPY∗DP(8)/	X←A	$transfer multiplicand to X
/MPY∗DP(10)/	A←0	$clear A
/MPY∗DP(11)/	C←countdn C	$decrement C
/MPY∗DP(12)/	IF (Q(5)) THEN (AC←countup AC)	$start add subsequence

$$(11.2)$$

Comment, here the 3-step add subsequence occurs

/MPY∗DP(13)/	AQ(M)←shr AQ(M),	$shift AQ(M) right
	A(1)←OV	$transfer OV to A(1)
/2Δ(MPY∗DP(14))/	IF (C≠0) THEN (D←13)	$test for iteration

Comment, MPY sequence ends here

/DP(14)/	OV←0, LZ←0, SI←0	$clear OV, LZ, and SI
/DP(15)/	EL←0	$clear EL
	IF (AMER=0) THEN (AE←AE′)	$switch to fetch sequence
/TD/	IF (DMR=0) THEN (D←countup D)	$increment D

The sequence of the control and timing signals after timing signal DP(14) occurs requires explanation. Register D is incremented to 15_{10}. This occurs 15 microseconds after timing signal DP(14) occurs, but DP(15) does not occur until 50 microseconds after DP(14) occurs. However, control signal (2Δ(MPY∗DP(14))) occurs 30 microseconds after DP(14) occurs. If C is not zero when this control signal occurs, D is set to 13_{10} and the next timing signal will be DP(13) instead of DP(15). Thus, this sequence of control and timing signals is . . . . DP(14), TD, 2 Δ (MPY∗DP(14)), DP(13), . . . At the beginning of each iteration, registers OV, LZ, and SI are 0 because they were cleared at DP(14) of the previous sequence. Register AE was not complemented because DP(15) does not occur unless counter C reached 0.

11.3 DIVISION SEQUENCE

The division sequence is also an execution sequence. We first describe the division algorithm, then the division overflow, restoration of the partial remainder, the sequence chart, and finally the sequence itself.

11.3.1 Division Algorithm

As mentioned in Chapter 1, the rules of binary division for numbers in the signed magnitude representation are the same as those for unsigned binary numbers (section 1.1.8 and example 1.12) except the sign of the quotient must also be determined. The sign of the quotient is positive if the signs of the dividend and the divisor are the same; otherwise, the sign of the quotient is negative.

In Figure 11.5, an example is given to illustrate the application of the division rules to sequential operations of the arithmetic registers. The divisor is 0.10101. The 1's complement of the magnitude of the divisor, .01010, is in the X register because addition of 1's complement instead of subtraction is used. The dividend in the AQ register is 0.1000100000. The binary points of the dividend and the divisor are both normally located. Since the contents of the X register, which are the 1's complement of the divisor, do not change during the division, the X register in Figure 11.5 is shown only once. The OV bit is placed at the left of the A(1) bit to hold the leftmost bit of the AQ(M) register when this register is being left shifted.

Division begins by testing to see if there is an "overflow" (this will be discussed in the next section). When there is no overflow, the sign bit of the quotient is determined and stored in the Q(0) bit. Division now really begins by adding the contents of the X(M) register to the A(M) register. Because we are adding the 1's complement of the divisor, the result is actually a difference. At this

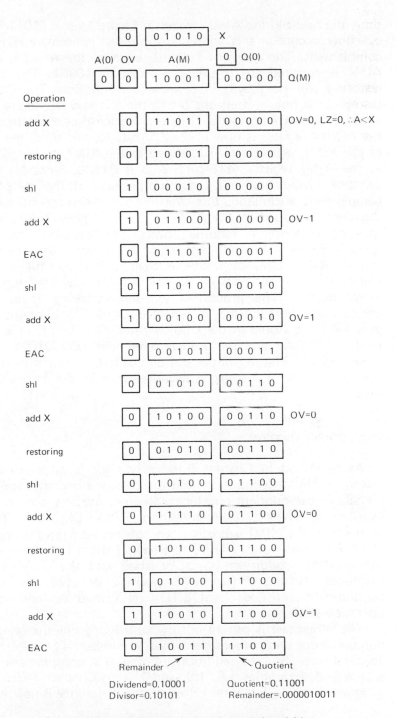

Fig. 11.5 Contents of the arithmetic registers during division

time, the result in the A(M) register in Figure 11.5 is 11011. Since no overflow occurs in this addition, the result is negative and is in 1's complement. The quotient bit is 0. Because the result is negative, A(M) is restored to its previous value of 10001. The details of restoring will be shown in a subsequent section. The OV-AQ(M) casregister is now shifted one bit to the left and the above quotient bit of 0 is inserted into the Q(5) bit. Notice that the leftmost bit of the AQ(M) register is now in the OV bit. At this time, the contents of the X(M) register are again added to the A(M) register. The result in the A(M) register in Figure 11.5 is 01100. Since bit OV now contains 1, overflow has occurred; because of the use of the 1's complement arithmetic, this overflow is an end-around carry, and this carry is added to the A(M) register. The result is positive and thus no restoring is required. Since overflow has occurred, the quotient bit is 1. The quotient bit of 1 is inserted into the Q(5) bit, and the OV-AQ(M) casregister is then shifted one bit to the left. Notice that the contents of the OV bit are now lost, but it is no longer needed. This process of addition, restoring (if no overflow occurs), and left-shifting is repeated until five quotient bits are generated and stored in the Q(M) register. Quotient 0.11001 is now in the Q register and the positive remainder .0000010011 is in the A(M) register. The remainder can be positive or negative, and in the case where the remainder is negative, it is in the 1's complement form.

11.3.2 Division Overflow

As described in Chapter 7, when divisor Y is too small with respect to the dividend X so that the quotient becomes too large to be held in the quotient register Q, division overflow occurs. Division overflow is tested by using condition (7.9) in Chapter 7. Thus, the contents in the X(M) subregister are subtracted from the contents in the A(M) register (not AQ(M) register). If the difference is negative, the overflow condition is not satisfied and the division process continues. If the difference is positive or zero, the overflow condition is satisfied; light LTDV is turned on and computer operation stops.

The above test is carried out by subtracting one unsigned binary number from another unsigned binary number. The subtraction is accomplished by the addition of the 1's complement of the subtrahend. Examples 1.8, 1.9, and 1.10 in Chapter 1 also serve as examples here. In Example 1.8 where the difference is positive, there is an addition of an end-around carry; register OV is set to 1 and register LZ is reset to 0. In Example 1.9 where the difference is negative, there is no end-around carry; the difference is in the 1's complement and registers OV and LZ are both reset to 0. In Example 1.10 where the magnitudes of the dividend and the divisor are the same, the difference consists entirely of 1's; it is a negative zero. Register OV is reset to 0 but register LZ is set to 1. Therefore, if either OV or LZ is 1 after the addition of the 1's complement of the subtrahend, division overflow occurs.

11.3.3 Restoring the Partial Remainder

As mentioned, if division overflow does not occur, the division may proceed. However, the negative difference from the division overflow test should first be restored to the value of the previous dividend. Similarly, if the partial remainder is negative after a subtraction in the division process, the partial remainder must be restored to its previous value. A three-step process to restore a negative number in the 1's complement to its original positive number is:

Step 1. Obtain the 1's complement of the difference (i.e., the 1's complement of A(M)).

Step 2. Add the 1's complement of the subtrahend (i.e., the divisor) to the result from step (1).

Step 3. Obtain the 1's complement of the result from step (2). This result is the original positive number.

As an example, consider Ex. 1.9 in Chapter 1 which shows binary subtraction by addition of the 1's complement of the subtrahend. The negative sum 10111, as shown in Ex. 1.9, is in the 1's complement form. The first step obtains the 1's complement of 10111; the result is 01000. The second step adds the result 01000 from step (1) to the 1's complement of the subtrahend 01110 (the addend in Ex. 1.9) as shown below,

$$
\begin{array}{r}
01000 \\
+01110 \\
\hline
10110
\end{array}
$$

Since no overflow occurs in the above addition, step (3) calls for obtaining the 1's complement of this sum; the result is 01001 which indeed is the augend in Ex. 1.9.

11.3.4 Sequence Chart

The DIV sequence implements the division algorithm in the manner illustrated in Fig. 11.5. The sequence chart for the DIV sequence is shown in Fig. 11.6. As shown, bit $Q(0)$ is first reset to 0 and a memory read is initiated. After the divisor is read into the X register, the contents of registers X, A, and Q are those shown in Fig. 11.2(b). The magnitude of the divisor is now 1's complemented, and the new contents of the X register remain unchanged during the entire division process. The sign of the quotient is determined and stored in register SI; it is later transferred to the $Q(0)$ bit. Counter C is set to 5. The test of division overflow now begins by performing the count-AC micro-operation to initiate the add subsequence. If the difference is positive (indicated by OV being 1) or zero (indicated by LZ being 1), register DV is set to 1 to indicate the division overflow. If switch ERRORSTOP is additionally at the NOBP or AVBP position, register RUN1 is set to 1 to stop computer operation. If the difference is negative (indicated by OV and LZ being both 0), the negative difference is restored to the original value of the dividend by the following three steps:

Step 1. IF $((OV + LZ) = 0)$ THEN $(A(M) \leftarrow A(M)')$
Step 2. AC $\leftarrow$ countup AC
Step 3. IF $(OV = 0)$ THEN $(A(M) \leftarrow (A(M)'))$

At this time, the contents of registers X, A, and Q are those shown in Fig. 11.2(c).

The loop for division now begins. Casregister OV-AQ(M) is shifted left one bit. A subtraction is next performed. Counter C is decremented by one. Register OV is set to 1 if the difference is positive, and is reset to 0 if the difference is negative. If the difference is zero, LZ is set to 1 and in turn OV is also set to 1. If OV is 0, the quotient bit is 0 and the three steps for restoring the partial remainder follow. If OV is 1 (this means that the difference is positive or zero), the quotient bit is 1, $Q(5)$ is set to 1, and the required addition of the end-around carry is performed by the count-A(M) micro-operation. At this point, counter C is tested for zero. If counter C is not zero, the sequence repeats the

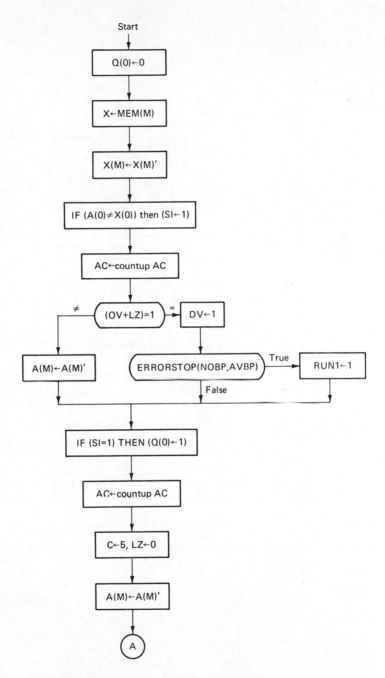

Fig. 11.6 Sequence chart for the division sequence

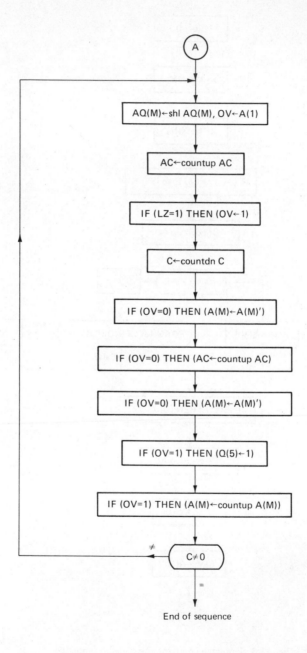

Fig. 11.6 (Continued)

micro-operations to shift casregister OV-AQ(M) left one bit, to perform the subtraction, to restore the partial remainder or to set Q(5) to 1, and to test counter C, until counter C reaches 0. At this time, the quotient is in the Q register and the remainder in the A(M) register as shown in Fig. 11.2(d).

11.3.5 Sequence Description

Comment, DIV sequence begins here		
/DIV*DP(0)/	Q(0)←0	$clear Q(0)
/DIV*DP(1)/	X←0,	$clear X
	READ←1	$initiate memory read
/Δ(DIV*DP(1))/	X←MEM(M)	$load divisor to X
/DIV*DP(2)/	X(M)←X(M)'	$complement divisor
/DIV*DP(3)/	IF (A(0)≠X(0)) THEN (SI←1),	$set SI
	IF (DMR=0) THEN (AC←countup AC)	$div overflow check begins
Comment, the 3-step add subsequence comes here		
/DIV*DP(4)/	IF (OV+LZ) THEN (DV←1,	$stops if overflows
	IF (ERRORSTOP(NOBP,AVBP) THEN (RUN 1←1)))	
	IF ((OV+LZ)=0) THEN (A(M)←A(M)'),	$first restoring step
	IF (SI=1) THEN (Q(0)←1)	$set quotient sign
/DIV*DP(5)/	IF (DMR=0) THEN (AC←countup AC)	$second restoring step
Comment, the 3-step add subsequence comes here		
/DIV*DP(6)/	C←5,	$set counter C to 5
	LZ←0,	$clear LZ
	A(M)←A(M)'	$third restoring step
/DIV*DP(7)/	AQ(M)←shl AQ(M),	$division begins here
	OV←A(1)	
/DIV*DP(8)/	IF (DMR=0) THEN (AC←countup AC)	$start add subsequence
Comment, the 3-step add subsequence comes here		
/DIV*DP(9)/	IF (LZ=1) THEN (OV←1)	$set OV
/DIV*DP(10)/	IF (OV=0) THEN (A(M)←A(M)'),	$first restoring step
	IF (OV=1) THEN (Q(5)←1)	$set quotient bit to 1
/DIV*DP(11)/	C←countdn C	$decrement C
/DIV*DP(12)/	IF (OV=0) THEN (AC←countup AC),	$second restoring step
	IF (OV=1) THEN (A(M)←countup A(M))	$add end-around carry
Comment, the 3-step add subsequence comes here		
/DIV*DP(13)/	IF (OV=0) THEN (A(M)←A(M)')	$third restoring step
/2Δ(DIV*DP(14))/	IF (C≠0) THEN (D←7)	$test for iteration
Comment, DIV sequence ends here		
/DP(14)/	OV←0, LZ←0, SI←0	$clear OV, LZ, and SI
/DP(15)/	EL←0,	$clear EL
	IF (AEMR=0) THEN (AE←AE')	$switch to fetch sequence
/TD/	IF (DMR=0) THEN (D←countup D)	$increment D

(11-3)

As in the description of the MPY sequence, the sequence of control and timing signals near the end of the DIV sequence is . . . , DP(14), TD, 2 (DIV∗DP(14)), DP(7),. . . . Only when counter C reaches zero does signal DP(15) occur. At that time, register AE is complemented and the next sequence is the fetch sequence.

PROBLEMS

11.1 Given the following pairs of signed binary numbers,
    (a) X = +10111   Y = −11101
    (b) X = −.10011,   Y = +.00111
    (c) X = +10.110,   Y = +110.01
    where X is the multiplicand and Y the multiplier, write a symbolic program to multiply X and Y, and show the execution of the MPY instruction in a manner as shown in Figure 11.3.

11.2 Given the following pairs of signed binary numbers,
    (a) X = +11111,   Y = −.00101
    (b) X = +.1101100111   Y = +.10001
    (c) X = +11.110   Y = −111.00
    where X is the dividend and Y the divisor, write a program to divide X by Y, and show the execution of the DIV instruction in a manner as shown in Figure 11.5.

11.3 Write a program for testing the MPY and DIV instructions by computing $(X \cdot X) \div X - X$ and determine whether the result is 0. Number X can be an integer or a fraction, and it is to be manually loaded into the memory.

11.4 Simplify the MPY sequence by reducing the micro-operations and execution statements if possible.

11.5 Simplify the DIV sequence by reducing the micro-operations and execution statements if possible.

11.6 Show an alternative way to restore the partial remainder in the DIV sequence.

11.7 Suggest a way that the delays in labels $\Delta(DP(15))$ and $2\Delta(MPY \ast DP(14))$ in the DIV sequence can be eliminated.

11.8 What micro-operations and control signals can be eliminated
    (a) if the MPY sequence is not implemented,
    (b) if the MPY and DIV sequences are both not implemented

12

Manual Controls

and

Input/output

Sequences

Many switches are used in this computer for manually controlling start, stop, loading, unloading, running, and the like. This chapter describes the logic of these switches, the logic of start-stop control, and the steps for loading and unloading. It also describes sequences for input and output data transfers either manually or by program control. These sequences implement instructions EXI, EXO, MNI, and MNO.

12.1 SWITCH LOGIC

The manual switches were described in Chapter 6. These switches set or reset registers and turn the lights on or off. The logic of these switches is described below.

12.1.1 CLEAR Switch Logic

Switch CLEAR, a single-position switch, is provided to clear all the registers and to turn their lights off. This "master-clearing" operation is described by the statements,

$$
\begin{array}{lll}
\text{Clock,} & \text{CP} & \\
\text{Switch,} & \text{CLEAR(ON)} & \\
\text{/CLEAR(ON)/} & \text{A} \leftarrow 0, & \text{LTA} \leftarrow \text{OFF,} \\
& \text{Q} \leftarrow 0, & \text{LTQ} \leftarrow \text{OFF,} \\
& \text{X} \leftarrow 0, & \text{LTX} \leftarrow \text{OFF,} \\
& \text{M} \leftarrow 0, & \text{LTM} \leftarrow \text{OFF,} \\
& \text{P} \leftarrow 0, & \text{LTP} \leftarrow \text{OFF,} \\
& \text{C} \leftarrow 0, & \text{LTC} \leftarrow \text{OFF,} \\
& \text{D} \leftarrow 0, & \text{LTD} \leftarrow \text{OFF,} \\
& \text{I} \leftarrow 0, & \text{LTI} \leftarrow \text{OFF,} \\
& \text{AE} \leftarrow 0, & \text{LTAE} \leftarrow \text{OFF,} \\
& \text{AV} \leftarrow 0, & \text{LTAV} \leftarrow \text{OFF,} \\
& \text{DV} \leftarrow 0, & \text{LTDV} \leftarrow \text{OFF,} \\
& \text{EL} \leftarrow 0, & \text{LTEL} \leftarrow \text{OFF,} \\
& \text{IE} \leftarrow 0, & \text{LTIE} \leftarrow \text{OFF,} \\
& \text{LZ} \leftarrow 0, & \text{LTLZ} \leftarrow \text{OFF,} \\
& \text{OV} \leftarrow 0, & \text{LTOV} \leftarrow \text{OFF,} \\
& \text{SI} \leftarrow 0, & \text{LTSI} \leftarrow \text{OFF,} \\
& \text{AC} \leftarrow 0, & \text{LTAC} \leftarrow \text{OFF,} \\
& \text{RUN1} \leftarrow 0, & \text{RUN2} \leftarrow 0,
\end{array}
\tag{12.1}
$$

The above registers and lights were described in Chapter 6 and shown in Figures 6.5 through 6.7. When registers RUN1 and RUN2 are both cleared to 0, light LTSTART will be turned off and light LTSTOP turned on as will be described in statement (12.5).

12.1.2 Light-switch Logic

Lights LTA(0–5), LTQ(0–5),....., LTIE described in statements (6.7) are associated respectively with switches SWA(0–5), SWQ(0–5),....., SWIE which are described in statements (6.5) and shown in Figures 6.6 and 6.7. Each pair of these switches and lights is implemented by a so-called light switch. A light switch has a translucent button which illuminates when the light is turned on by the switch. Each light can be turned on (i.e., luminating condition) by pressing the respective button. The logic for these switches and lights is described by the statements,

/SWA(0–5) (ON)/	A(0–5)← 1, LTA(0–5)← ON,
/SWQ(0–5) (ON)/	Q(0–5)← 1, LTQ(0–5)← ON,
/SWX(0–5) (ON)/	X(0–5)←1, LTX(0–5)← ON,
/SWM(6–0) (ON)/	M(6–0)←1, LTM(6–0)← ON,
/SWI(5–0) (ON)/	I(5–0)← 1, LTI(5–0)← ON,
/SWP(6–1) (ON)/	P(6–1)← 1, LTP(6–1)← ON,
/SWD(3–0) (ON)/	D(3–0)← 1, LTD(3–0)← ON,
/SWC(6–0) (OFF)/	C(6–0)← 0, LTC(6–0)← OFF, (12.2)
/SWAC(1–0) (ON)/	AC(1–0)← 1, LTAC(1–0)← ON,
/SWAE(ON)/	AE← 1, LTAE← ON,
/SWLZ(ON)/	LZ← 1, LTLZ← ON,
/SWOV(ON)/	OV← 1, LTOV← ON,
/SWSI(ON)/	SI← 1, LTSI← ON,
/SWDV(ON)/	DV← 1, LTDV← ON,
/SWAV(ON)/	AV← 1, LTAV← ON,
/SWIE(ON)/	IE← 1, LTIE← ON,

In the above conditional micro-statements, each has as many single-bit micro-statements as the number of subscripts. For example, the first conditional micro-statement means the following six micro-statements,

$$/SWA(0)\ (ON)/\quad A(0)← 1, LTA(0)← ON,$$
$$\text{- -} \qquad (12.3)$$
$$/SWA(5)\ (ON)/\quad A(5)← 1, LTA(5)← ON,$$

Furthermore, switches SWC(6– 0) function differently from the other switches as they set bits C(6– 0) to 0 (instead of 1) and lights LTC(6– 0) to OFF (instead of ON).

The above switches (except switches SWC) can turn the lights on but not off. There are other switches in statement (6.5) such as switches SWAM(OFF), SWQM(OFF),. . . . . . , SWDAI(OFF) which can turn the rows of lights collectively off. The logic for these switches is described by the statement,

/SWAM(OFF)/	A← 0, LTA ←OFF,
/SWQM(OFF)/	Q←0, LTQ← OFF,
/SWXM(OFF)/	X ←0, LTX ←OFF,
/SWMM(OFF)/	M← 0, LTM←OFF,
/SWIM(OFF)/	I← 0, LTI←OFF, (12.4)
/SWPM(OFF)/	P←0, LTP←OFF,
/SWDM(OFF)/	D←0, LTD←OFF,
/SWACM(OFF)/	AC←0, LTAC←OFF,
/SWCM(ON)/	C← 177, LTC←ON,

/SWAEM(OFF)/	AE←0, LTAE←OFF,
/SWLZM(OFF)/	LZ←0, LTLZ←OFF,
/SWOVM(OFF)/	OV←0, LTOV←OFF,
/SWSIM(OFF)/	SI←0, LTSI←OFF,
/SWDAI(OFF)/	DV←0, LTDV←OFF,
	AV←0, LTAV←OFF,
	IE←0, LTIE←OFF,

In the above statement, switch SWCM functions differently from the other switches as it sets register C to octal 177 (instead of 0) and it turns lights LTC off (instead of on). Registers DV, AV, and IE (and their lights) function as a group when they are reset to 0 by switch SWDAI.

12.1.3 Manual Start-stop Switch Logic

Switches START and STOP allow the operator to control the starting and stopping of the computer operation manually. The logic of these two switches is described below,

Switch,	START(ON),	
	STOP(ON),	
Light,	LTSTART(ON,OFF),	
	LTSTOP(ON,OFF)	(12.5)
/START(ON)/	LTSTART←ON, LTSTOP←OFF,	
/STOP(ON)/	LTSTOP←ON, LTSTART←OFF,	

When the START switch is turned to the ON position or when the computer is set to the *go state* (represented by RUN1' * RUN2 as will be described subsequently), light LTSTART is turned on and light LTSTOP is turned off. Similarly, when the STOP switch is turned to the ON position or when the computer is set to the *stop state* (represented by RUN1' * RUN2'), light LTSTOP is turned on and LTSTART is turned off. Note that RUN1' * RUN2' is set to 1 when switch CLEAR is turned on; therefore, the computer is in the stop state after switch CLEAR has been turned on.

12.1.4 Input-output Switch Logic

Switches INPUT and OUTPUT allow the operation to control input and output data transfers. The logic of these two switches is described below.

```
Switch,                 INPUT(ON),
                        OUTPUT(ON),
                        BII(ON),                                    (12.6)
/INPUT(ON)+BII(ON)/     AE←1, C←177, I(4)←1,
/OUTPUT(ON)/            AE←1, C←177, I(1)←1, I(4)←1,
```

To input data manually, switch CLEAR is first turned to the ON position. When switch INPUT or switch BII (to be described subsequently) is turned to the ON position, register AE is set to 1 to initiate an execution sequence, counter C is set to octal 177, and bit I(4) is set to 1. When bit I(4) is next set to 1, op-code 010000 of instruction MNI is now in register I(5–0). Similarly, when the OUTPUT switch is turned to the ON position, register AE is again set to 1, counter C to octal 177, and bits I(4) and I(1) to 1 to give op-code 01001 of instructin MNO.

12.1.5 Other Control Switch Logic

There are five other control switches, POWER, ERRORSTOP, MODE, MR, and JS and their associated lights. The logic of these switches is described below.

```
Switch,   POWER(ON,DC,MEM,ON),
          ERRORSTOP(NOBP,AVBP,BP),
          MODE(DM,AEM,IM,PM),
          MR(ON,OFF),
          JS(ON,OFF),
Light,    LTDC(ON,OFF),
          LTMEM(ON,OFF),
          LTDM(ON,OFF),
          LTAEM(ON,OFF),
          LTIM(ON,OFF),
          LTPM(ON,OFF),                                          (12.7)
          LTMR(ON,OFF),
          LTJS(ON,OFF),
/POWER(OFF)/    LTDC←OFF,LTMEM←OFF,
/POWER(DC)/     LTDC←ON, LTMEM←OFF,
/POWER(MEM)/    LTMEM←ON,LTDC←ON,
/POWER(ON)/     LTMEM←ON,LTDC←ON,
/MODE(DM)/      LTDM←ON,LTAEM←OFF,LTIM←OFF,LTPM←OFF,
/MODE(AEM)/     LTAEM←ON,LTDM←OFF,LTIM←OFF,LTPM←OFF,
/MODE(IM)/      LTIM←ON,LTDM←OFF,LTAEM←OFF,LTPM←OFF,
/MODE(PM)/      LTPM←ON,LTDM←OFF,LTAEM←OFF,LTIM←OFF,
```

/MR(ON)/	LTMR←ON,
/MR(OFF)/	LTMR←OFF,
/JS(ON)/	LTJS←ON,
/JS(OFF)/	LTJS←OFF,

When the POWER switch is at the DC position, all circuits except the memory are energized. When it is at the MEM position, all circuits as well as the memory are energized and the computer is ready for operation. When it is at the OFF position, the power is turned off. Lights LTDC and LTMEM indicate the states of the POWER switch. The ERRORSTOP switch has no associated light; its position is tested during the arithmetic sequences. The MODE switch has four positions and its states are indicated by lights LTDM, LTAEM, LTIM, and LTPM. Similarly, the MR and JS switches are indicated by lights LTMR and LTJS respectively.

12.2 START-STOP CONTROL

The logic for start-stop control of this computer is described below.

12.2.1 Configuration

The control for starting and stopping computer operation makes use of the following registers, switches, lights, and terminals,

Register,	RUN1,	
	RUN2,	
	EL,	
Switch,	POWER(DC,MEM,OFF),	
	START(ON),	
	STOP(ON),	(12.8)
	BIS(ON),	
	RCS(ON),	
Light,	LTSTART(ON,OFF),	
	LTSTOP(ON,OFF),	
	LTEL(ON,OFF),	

Terminal, GO=ST+EL*(IN+OUT),

ST=START(ON)+BIS(ON)+RCS(ON),

IN=EXI*DATAIN,

OUT=EXO*DATAOUT,

EXI=K(10)*AE,

EXO=K(11)*AE,

DATAIN,

DATAOUT,

In the above description, register RUN1 controls stopping and register RUN2 controls starting of the computer operation. Register EL indicates external data transfer. Switches START and STOP allow manual starting and stopping of computer operation respectively as has been discussed. Switch BIS allows starting from the bi-octal converter, an input device converting the input from an octal keyboard into binary signals. Switch RCS allows starting of computer operation remotely.

Terminals EXI and EXO, described in Chapter 8, are the command signals for the input and output instructions, respectively. Terminals DATAIN and DATAOUT are the command signals from an external device which requests the computer to accept the input data or to deliver the output data, respectively. Terminal IN is the command which occurs when both command signals DATAIN and EXI occur. Terminal OUT is the command which occurs when both command signals DATAOUT and EXO occur. Terminal ST is the command which occurs when switch START, BIS, or RCS is turned to the ON position. Terminal GO is the command to start computer operation as a result of the command from a manual switch or from the input or output instruction for data transfer.

12.2.2 Start Logic

When registers RUN1 and RUN2 are both 0, it is the *stop state* at which the computer stops operation. When register RUN1 is 0 and RUN2 is 1, it is the *go state* at which the computer executes sequence after sequence. These two states are shown in Figure 12.1. When register RUN1 is 1 and register RUN2 is 0 or when RUN1 and RUN2 are both 1, it is an intermediate state as will be shown.

As shown in Figure 8.1, register RUN2 controls starting because it controls clock CP. When RUN2 is 1, the clock signals CP1 and CP2

RUN1 RUN2

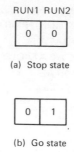

(a) Stop state

(b) Go state

Fig. 12.1 Stop and go states

described in statements (8.1) appear, and the control signals are in turn generated. Thus, to start computer operation, register RUN2 is set to 1; this changes the state from the stop state to the go state as illustrated in Figure 12.2.

RUN1 RUN2

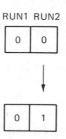

Fig. 12.2 From stop state to go state

The condition to set register RUN2 to 1 is when register RUN1 is 0 and terminal GO is 1, that is,

$$/GO/ \quad IF \quad (RUN1') \quad THEN \quad (RUN2 \leftarrow 1) \tag{12.9}$$

12.2.3 Stop Logic

As indicated in Figure 12.1, register RUN2 is changed from 1 to 0 in order to stop computer operation. However, instead of one step, this change actually takes three steps. As shown in Figure 12.3, during the first step, RUN1 is changed from 0 to 1. During the second step, RUN2 is changed from 1 to 0. And during the third step, RUN1 is changed from 1 to 0.

RUN1 RUN2

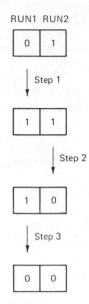

Fig. 12.3 From go state to stop state

The computer stops at many occasions. It stops when switch STOP is turned to the ON position, or

$$/STOP(ON)/ \quad RUN1 \leftarrow 1 \tag{12.10}$$

It also stops when switch MODE is at the DM position and switch MR is at the OFF position and register RUN2 is 1, or

$$/CP1/ \quad IF \; (MODE(DM)*MR(OFF)*RUN2) \; THEN \; (RUN1 \leftarrow 1) \tag{12.11}$$

Clock CP1 is used because the above statement should be conditionally executed at every clock period. It also stops at the end of a sequence when switch MODE is at position AEM or when switch MODE is at position IM and register AE is 1, if switch MR is at the OFF position and register RUN2 is 1, or

$$/DP(15)/ \quad IF \; ((MODE(AEM)+MODE(IM)*AR)*MR(OFF)*RUN2) \; THEN \; (RUN1 \leftarrow 1) \tag{12.12}$$

Timing signal DP(15) initiates the execution of the above statement because the stop should occur at the last step of every sequence.

As has been shown in statements (9.2), the computer stops when an illegal op-code occurs in the fetch sequence, namely,

$$(AE'*DP(4)/ \quad IF \ (DIE*ERRORSTOP(NOBP)) \ THEN \ (RUN1 \leftarrow 1)$$

As shown in statements (10.16), the computer stops when addition overflow occurs during the ADD sequence, namely,

```
/ADD*DP(7)/   IF (SI'*OV)  THEN (AV←1,
                            IF (ERRORSTOP(NOBP)) THEN (RUN1←1))
```

or during the SUB sequence, namely,

```
/SUB*DP(7)/   IF (SI'*OV)  THEN (AV←1,
                            IF (ERRORSTOP(NOBP)) THEN (RUN1←1))
```

or during the DIV sequence in statements (11.3) or,

```
/DIV*DP(7)/  IF (OV+LZ=0)  THEN (DV←1,
                              IF (ERRORSTOP(NOBP,AVBP)) THEN (RUN1←1))
```

As will be shown in statements (12.16) through (12.19), the computer stops in waiting for a signal from an input or an output device during an input or an output sequence, namely,

```
/EXI*DP(3)/   RUN1←1
/EXO*DP(3)/   RUN1←1
/MNI*DP(4)/   RUN1←1
/MNO*DP(4)/   RUN1←1
```

As will be shown in statements (13.1) through (13.14), the computer stops when the JS switch is at the ON position when executing a jump sequence or,

```
/UN*DP(4)/    IF (I(0)*JS(ON)) THEN (RUN1←1)
/SB*DP(4)/    IF (I(0)*JS(ON)) THEN (RUN1←1)
/NA*DP(4)/    IF (I(0)*JS(ON)) THEN (RUN1←1)
/NZ*DP(4)/    IF(I(0)*JS(ON)) THEN (RUN1←1)
```

Finally, the computer stops when executing the STP sequence as will be shown in statements (13.12) or,

$$\text{/STP*DP(4)/} \quad \text{RUN1} \leftarrow 1$$

The second step of changing RUN2 from 1 to 0 immediately follows the first step, or

$$\text{/CP2/} \quad \text{IF (RUN1) THEN (RUN2} \leftarrow 0) \qquad (12.13)$$

The third step immediately follows the second step, or

$$\text{/CP/} \quad \text{IF (RUN2}') \quad \text{THEN (RUN1} \leftarrow 0),$$
$$\text{IF (RUN1}'*\text{RUN 2}') \text{ THEN (LTSTOP} \leftarrow \text{ON,LTSTART} \leftarrow \text{OFF)} \qquad (12.14)$$

The third step is executed conditionally if terminal GO does not, in the meantime, become 1. Note that clock CP is used because clocks CP1 and CP2 cease to exist after the second step.

In short, after register RUN1 is set to 1, steps 2 and 3 automatically follow. If there is no signal in the meantime to start computer operation, registers RUN1 and RUN2 are both set to 0 and the computer is in the stop state.

12.3 INPUT AND OUTPUT SEQUENCES

Data can be transferred into the memory from an input device or transferred out of the memory to an output device. These transfers are carried out either by program control or manually. Sequences EXI and EXO transfer data by program control, while sequences MNI and MNO transfer data manually.

The configuration to accomplish these data transfers is described by the statements,

$$
\begin{aligned}
&\text{Memory,} && \text{MEM(M)=MEM(0-127,0-5),} \\
&\text{Register,} && \text{M(6-0),} \\
&&& \text{X(0-5),} \\
&&& \text{D(3-0),} \\
&&& \text{C(6-0),} \\
&&& \text{EL,} && (12.15) \\
&&& \text{RUN1,} \\
&\text{Switch,} && \text{INPUT(ON),} \\
&&& \text{OUTPUT(ON),} \\
&&& \text{START(ON),}
\end{aligned}
$$

Light,   LTEL,

Terminal,   READ,

WRITE,

E(0–5),

INPLEASE,

DATAIN,

OUTPLEASE,

DATAOUT,

In the above terminal statement terminals E(0–5) are the six input data lines, while the six output data lines are X(0–5) which are the outputs of register X. Terminal INPLEASE is a request signal from the computer to an input device signifying that the computer is ready to accept the input data, and terminal DATAIN is a reply signal from the input device to the computer that the input data is delivered. Terminal OUTPLEASE is a request signal from the computer to an output device signifying that the computer is ready to deliver the output data, and terminal DATAOUT is a reply signal from the output device to the computer that the output data is received. These terminals are illustrated in Figure 12.4.

12.3.1 Input Sequence EXI

The EXI sequence implements instruction EXI. During the execution of the sequence fetching the EXI instruction, the address of the first location of the block of memory locations into which the data are to be stored is placed into address register M. The EXI sequence begins by activating terminal INPLEASE. It then sets register EL to 1, turns light LTEL on, and stops computer operation. It waits for signal DATAIN from the input device. When the input device has the data ready at the six input lines E(0–5), it activates terminal DATAIN which starts computer operation. The sequence is now resumed. The data are first transferred to the X register from which the data are stored into the memory. Counter M(i.e., address register) is incremented by one, and counter C is decremented by one. These steps are repeated until counter C reaches zero.

The sequential operations described above are also shown in the sequence chart in Figure 12.5. The EXI sequence is described by the statements,

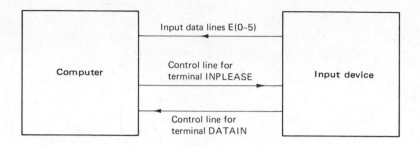

(a) Input data transfer

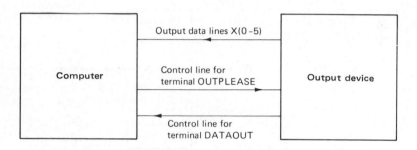

(b) Output data transfer

Fig. 12.4 External data transfers

Comment, EXI sequence begins here
/EXI∗DP(1)/	X←0,	$clear register X
/EXI∗DP(3)/	INPLEASE←1,	$initiate input transfer
	EL←1,	$set EL to 1
	LTEL←ON,	$indicate input transfer
	RUN1←1,	$initiate stop logic

Comment, computer is now waiting for signal DATAIN from the input device

(12.16)

/EXI∗DP(5)/	X←E,	$input external data
/EXI∗DP(9)/	WRITE←1,	$initiate memory write
/Δ(EXI∗DP(9))/	MEM(M)←X,	$store input data
/2Δ(EXI∗DP(10))/	IF (C=0) THEN (D←16_8)	$test counter C
/EXI∗DP(11)/	C←countdn C,	$decrement C
/EXI∗DP(12)/	M←countup M,	$increment M
/2Δ(EXI∗DP(13))/	D←0,	$repeat the sequence

Comment, EXI sequence ends here

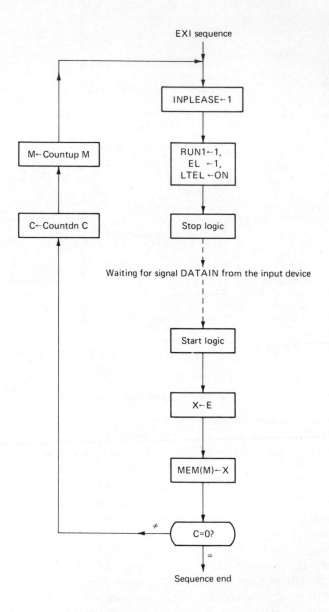

EXI sequence

INPLEASE←1

M←Countup M

RUN1←1,
EL ←1,
LTEL ←ON

C←Countdn C

Stop logic

Waiting for signal DATAIN from the input device

Start logic

X←E

MEM(M)←X

C=0?

Sequence end

Fig. 12.5 EXI sequence chart

In the above description, initiation of input transfer and initiation of stopping computer operation occur at DP(3). These two steps imply that signal DATAIN from the input device will not happen until after two clock periods. Label Δ (EXI*DP(9)) indicates that the actual storage of the data from register X into the memory occurs at 15 microseconds after the memory write is initiated. Notice that micro-operations D $\leftarrow$ 16_8 and D $\leftarrow$ 0 which set register D to a particular value occur at 30 microseconds after the occurrence of CP1 (i.e., after two deltas). This delay is provided so that these micro-operations occur neither at CP1 nor at CP2.

12.3.2 Output Sequence EXO

The EXO sequence implements instruction EXO. The sequential operations of the EXO sequence are similar to those of the EXI sequence except that terminal OUTPLEASE is activated by the computer to request the output device to accept the data in the X register. When the data is accepted, the output device activates terminal DATAOUT to resume computer operation. The EXO sequence is described by the statements,

```
Comment, EXO sequence begins here
/EXO*DP(1)/        X←0                         $clear register X
                   READ←1,                     $initiate memory read
/Δ(EXO*DP(1))/     X←MEM(M),                   $load data to register X
/EXO*DP(3)/        OUTPLEASE←1,                $initiate output transfer
                   EL←1,                       $set EL to 1
                   LTEL←ON,                    $indicate output transfer
                   RUN1←1                      $initiate stop logic
Comment, computer is now waiting for signal DATAOUT from the output device
/2Δ(EXO*DP(10))/ IF (C=0) THEN (D←16₈),  $test counter C
/EXO*DP(11)/       C←countdn C,                $decrement counter C
/EXO*DP(12)/       M←countup M,                $increment counter M
/2Δ(EXO*DP(13))/ D←0,                          $repeat the sequence
Comment, EXO sequence ends here
```

(12.17)

12.3.3 Manual Sequence MNI

The MNI sequence implements the manual input instruction MNI. It begins by turning on light LTEL and then stops computer operation. The operator then loads the data into register X by using the row of switches SWX(0-5) and then turns on the START switch. The MNI sequence now resumes and the data in the X register is stored into the memory. Counter C is decremented by one and counter M is incremented by one. These steps are now repeated until the desired number of words are stored.

The sequential operations of the MNI sequence are shown in the sequence chart in Figure 12.6. The MNI sequence is described by the statements,

Comment, MNI sequence begins here

/MNI∗DP(1)/	X←0,	$clear register X
	LTEL←ON,	$indicate input transfer
/MNI∗DP(4)/	RUN1←1,	$initiate stop logic

Comment, computer is now waiting for manual start signal

/MNI∗DP(9)/	WRITE←1,	$initiate memory write
/Δ(MNI∗DP(9))/	MEM(M)←X,	$store input data
/2Δ(MNI∗DP(10))/	IF (C=0) THEN (D←16_8)	$test counter C
/MNI∗DP(11)/	C←countdn C,	$decrement counter C
/MNI∗DP(12)/	M←countup M,	$increment counter M
/2Δ(MNI∗DP(13))/	D←0,	$repeat the sequence

$$(12.18)$$

Comment, MNI sequence ends here

12.3.4 Manual Sequence MNO

The MNO sequence implements manual output instruction MNO. Sequential operations of this sequence are similar to those of the MNI sequence. The MNO sequence is described by the statements

Comment, MNO sequence begins here

/MNO∗DP(1)/	X←0,	
	LTEL←ON,	
	READ←1,	
/Δ(MNO∗DP(1))/	X←MEM(M),	
/MNO∗DP(4)/	RUN1←1	

Comment, computer is now waiting for manual start signal

/2Δ(MNO∗DP(10))/	IF (C=0) THEN (D←16_8),	
/MNO∗DP(11)/	C←countdn C,	
/MNO∗DP(12)/	M←countup M,	
/2Δ(MNO∗DP(13))/	D←0,	

$$(12.19)$$

Comment, MNO sequence ends here

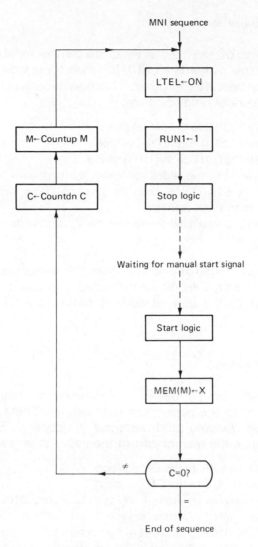

Fig. 12.6 MNI sequence chart

12.4 LOADING AND UNLOADING

When a program is prepared, it is manually loaded into the memory. After loading, the computer is set to run the program. The steps required for manual loading and running were enumerated in Chapter 7.

12.4.1 Manual Unloading

The contents of the memory words can be exhibited in the X register by the row of lights LTX(0-5) when these words are read out of the memory one after another. This operation is called *unloading*. The steps for manual unloading are:

Step 1. Set switch MODE to the PM position.

Step 2. Set switch CLEAR to the ON position.

Step 3. Set switch OUTPUT to the ON position.

Step 4. Set register M to the address at which the first word is to be unloaded.

Step 5. Set switch START to the ON position. (The first word is then transferred to the X register.)

Step 6. Repeat step 5 to unload the second, third, . . . words until all the words are unloaded.

The above steps unload the words from the consecutive locations of the memory. If words are to be unloaded nonconsecutively, register M must be set to the desired address before the START switch is turned on.

12.4.2 External Loading

The computer can be loaded from an external paper tape reader and unloaded onto the paper tape strip printer. These operations are called *external loading* and *external unloading*. The steps for externally loading the memory from the paper tape reader are:

Step 1. Set switch CLEAR to the ON position.

Step 2. Set switch INPUT to the ON position.

Step 3. The contents in register I at this time are 010000 (op-code of instruction MNI). Change register I manually by pressing switches SWI(0-5) to 010100 (op-code of instruction EXI).

Step 4. Set counter C to $n-1$, where n is the number of words to be loaded.

Step 5. Set register M to the address at which the first word should be loaded.

Step 6. (a) If the program is to be executed immediately after loading, set switch MODE to position PM and set register P to the first program address of the program to be executed.

(b) If the computer is to be stopped immediately after loading, set switch MODE to position IM.

Step 7. Set switch START to the ON position.

12.4.3 External Unloading

The steps for unloading the memory onto the paper tape strip printer are identical to the external loading steps except for two differences. The first is to set switch OUTPUT instead of INPUT in Step 2. The second is to change the contents of register I to 010110 instead of 010010 in Step 3, because 010110 is the op-code of instruction EXO.

12.4.4 Bi-octal Converter

When loading a program manually, the operator presses switches SWX(0–5). Instead of pressing these switches, the Bi-octal Converter is also available for loading. The converter which is connected to the computer by a short cable provides a matrix of 8 by 2 push-button switches. It accepts two octal digits (one in each column), converts them into 6 bits, and then enters the bits into register X. In addition, there are a start switch BIS, an input switch BII and a clear switch BIC. These switches and their logic are described in the statements,

```
Switch,   BIS(ON),                  $start switch
          BII(ON),                  $input switch
          BIC(ON),                  $clear switch
          BIOCT(1-2,0-7) (ON),      $a matrix of push-button switches
/BIOCT(1,0) (ON)/   X(0-2)← 0, LTX(0-2)← OFF,
/BIOCT(1,1) (ON)/   X(0-2)← 1, LTX(0-2)← OFF-OFF-ON,
/BIOCT(1,2) (ON)/   X(0-2)← 2, LTX(0-2)← OFF-ON-OFF,
/BIOCT(1,3) (ON)/   X(0-2)← 3, LTX(0-2)← OFF-ON-ON,
/BIOCT(1,4) (ON)/   X(0-2)← 4, LTX(0-2)← ON-OFF-OFF,
/BIOCT(1,5) (ON)/   X(0-2)← 5, LTX(0-2)← ON-OFF-ON,
/BIOCT(1,6) (ON)/   X(0-2)← 6, LTX(0-2)← ON-ON-OFF,
/BIOCT(1,7) (ON)/   X(0-2)← 7, LTX(0-2)← ON,
/BIOCT(2,0) (ON)/   X(3-5)← 0, LTX(3-5)← OFF,
/BIOCT(2,1) (ON)/   X(3-5)← 1, LTX(3-5)← OFF-OFF-ON,
/BIOCT(2,2) (ON)/   X(3-5)← 2, LTX(3-5)← OFF-ON-OFF
/BIOCT(2,3) (ON)/   X(3-5)← 3, LTX(3-5)← OFF-ON-ON,
/BIOCT(2,4) (ON)/   X(3-5)← 4, LTX(3-5)← ON-OFF-OFF,
/BIOCT(2,5) (ON)/   X(3-5)← 5, LTX(3-5)← ON-OFF-ON,
/BIOCT(2,5) (ON)/   X(3-5)← 6, LTX(3-5)← ON-ON-OFF,
/BIOCT(2,7) (ON)/   X(3-5)← 7, LTX(3-5)← ON,
```

(12.20)

The BIS switch functions as the START switch and the BII switch functions as the INPUT switch. The BIC switch clears the X register. Whenever one of the 16 BIOCT switches is pressed, three bits are entered in $X(0-2)$ or $X(3-5)$ and their respective lights are turned on. Loading is faster with Bi-octal Converter than with loading manually.

PROBLEMS

12.1 Draw a sequence chart for the EXO sequence.

12.2 Draw a sequence chart for the MNO sequence.

12.3 Explain why the following two micro-operations,

$$\text{IF } (C = 0) \text{ THEN } (D \leftarrow 16_8),$$

$$D \leftarrow 0,$$

in the description of the EXI, EXO, MNI, and MNO sequences should occur neither at CP1 nor at CP2, but after CP2 occurs.

12.4 Given register RUN(1-2), switch START(ON), switch STOP(ON), and clock P, when register RUN(1-2) contains 00 or 11, it is regarded as the stop or go state respectively. Describe the logic to change the state from the stop to go state and vice versa.

12.5 Describe the steps for manually loading a program into the memory by a sequence chart.

12.6 Describe the steps for manual unloading by a sequence chart.

12.7 Describe the steps for external loading by a sequence chart.

12.8 Describe the steps for external unloading by a sequence chart.

12.9 Write a sequence of no more than 8 steps to clear all words in the memory (i.e., to store 0's in all bits of the memory).

13

Other

Sequences

There are 24 sequences which implement the 30 instructions listed in Table 6.2. Sequences ADD, SUB, LDA, LDN, RAU, and RSU which implement respectively instructions ADD, SUB, LDA, LDN, RAU, and RSU were described in Chapter 10. Sequence MPY and DIV which implement respectively instructions MPY and DIV were described in Chapter 11. Sequences EXI, EXO, MNI, and MNO which implement respectively instructions EXI, EXO, MNI, and MNO were described in Chapter 12. This chapter describes the remaining 12 sequences for the remaining 18 instructions. In the following sections, address m in an instruction refers to a 7-bit operand address, while address n refers to a 6-bit instruction address in the instruction.

13.1 JUMP SEQUENCES

There are four jump sequences UN, SB, NA, and NZ which implement eight jump instructions UNE, UNO, SBE, SBO, NAE, NAO, NZE, and NZO. The first four are unconditional instructions, while the remaining four are conditional instructions. The format of these instructions is shown in Figure 6.11(b), and each consists of a 6-bit op-code and a 6-bit instruction address. As shown previously in the fetch sequence, the 6-bit instruction address n is converted into a 7-bit memory address. Except for the SB sequence, no memory access in these sequences is needed.

13.1.1 UN Sequences

This sequence implements the unconditional-jump instructions UNE and UNO. Instruction UNE ($I(0) = 0$) fetches the instruction at address n as the next instruction. Instruction UNO ($I(0) = 1$) is executed in the same way as instruction UNE if the JS switch is at the OFF position. If the JS switch is at the ON position, the computer operation stops; upon pressing the START switch to the ON position, instruction UNE is then executed.

Comment, UN sequence begins here

/UN∗DP(4)/	IF($I(0)$∗JS(ON)=1) THEN (RUN1←1)
/UN∗DP(5)/	P←0
/UN∗DP(6)/	P←X

Comment, UN sequence ends here

        (13.1)

The first statement states that if $I(0)$ is 1 and if switch JS is at the ON position, register RUN1 is set to 1 and computer operation stops. Register D is incremented to 5 just before the computer operation stops. When the START switch is next turned on, the sequence of the timing pulses resumes from DP(5). Micro-operation P←X transfers address n in the X register to program address register P.

13.1.2 SB Sequence

This sequence implements unconditional-jump instructions SBE and SBO. Instruction SBE ($I(0) = 0$) stores the address in register P into memory location at address 1 and then fetches the instruction at address n as the next instruction. Instruction SBO ($I(0) = 1$) is executed in the same way as instruction SBE if the JS switch is at the OFF position. If the JS switch is at the ON position, the computer operation stops; upon turning the START switch to the ON position, instruction SBE is then executed.

Comment, SB sequence begins here

/SB∗DP(0)/	M←0,
/Δ(SB∗DP(0))/	M(P)←P,
/SB∗DP(4)/	IF ($I(0)$∗JS(ON)=1) THEN (RUN1←1),
/SB∗DP(5)/	P←0,
/SB∗DP(6)/	P←X,
/SB∗DP(7)/	X←0,
/SB∗DP(8)/	X←M(P),
/SB∗DP(9)/	M←0,
/SB∗DP(10)/	M(0)←1,
/SB∗DP(13)/	WRITE←1,
/Δ(SB∗DP(13))/	MEM(M)←X,

Comment, SB sequence ends here

        (13.2)

The storing of the current instruction address in register P into the memory at address 1 is carried out first by storing it in subregister M(P), M(P) ← M, then by transferring it from subregister M(P) to register X, X ← M(P), and finally by storing it into the memory, MEM(M) ← X. The exchange of the current instruction address in register P and the jump address in register X needs a temporary storing at M(P). Address 0000001 is obtained by micro-operations M ← 0 and M(0) ← 1.

13.1.3 NA Sequence

This sequence implements conditional-jump instructions NAE and NAO. Instruction NAE (I(0) = 0) fetches the instruction at address n as the next instruction if the number in register A is negative. Instruction NAO(I(0) = 1) is executed in the same way as instruction NAE if the JS switch is at the OFF position. If the JS switch is at the ON position, the computer operation stops; upon pressing the START switch to the ON position, instruction NAE is executed.

Comment, NA sequence begins here

/NA*DP(4)/   IF (I(0)*JS(ON)) THEN (RUN1← 1),

/NA*DP(5)/   IF (A(0)*A(M)≠0) THEN (P←0),   (13.3)

/NA*DP(6)/   IF (A(0)*A(M)≠0) THEN (P←X),

Comment, NA sequence ends here

The above logic condition, $A(0) * A(M) \neq 0$, specifies all negative numbers in register A except negative zero. Micro-operation P ← X transfers jump address n in register X to program address register P.

13.1.4 NZ Sequence

This sequence implements conditional-jump instruction NZE and NZO. Instruction NZE (I(0) = 0) fetches the instruction at address n as the next instruction if the magnitude of the number in register A is not equal to zero. Instruction NZO(I(0) = 1) is executed in the same way as instruction NZE if the JS switch is at the OFF position. If the JS switch is at the ON position, the computer operation stops; upon pressing the START switch to the ON position, instruction NZE is executed.

Comment, NZ sequence begins here

/NZ*DP(4)/   IF (I(0)*JS(ON)) THEN (RUN1←1),

/NZ*DP(5)/   IF (A(M)≠0) THEN (P←0),   (13.4)

/NZ*DP(6)/   IF (A(M)≠0) THEN (P←X),

Comment, NZ sequence ends here

13.2 STORE SEQUENCES

There are two store sequences STA and STQ which implement two store instructions STA and STQ. The format of these instructions is shown in Figure 6.11(a); it consists of a 5-bit op-code and a 7-bit operand address. Each sequence requires one memory access.

13.2.1 STA Sequence

This sequence implements instruction STA. Instruction STA stores the contents of register A (i.e., accumulator) into the memory at address m. The contents of register A remain unchanged.

Comment, STA sequence begins here

/STA*DP(1)/	X←0,
/STA*DP(8)/	X←A,
/STA*DP(13)/	WRITE←1,
/Δ(STA*DP(13))/	MEM(M)←X,

(13.5)

Comment, STA sequence ends here

13.2.2 STQ Sequence

This sequence implements instruction STQ. Instruction STQ stores the contents of register Q into the memory at address m. The contents of register Q remains unchanged.

Comment, STQ sequence begins here

/STQ*DP(1)/	X←0,
/STQ*DO(10)/	X←Q,
/STQ*DP(13)/	WRITE←1,
/Δ(STQ*DP(13))/	MEM(M)←X,

(13.6)

Comment, STQ sequence ends here

13.3 SHIFT SEQUENCES

There are two shift sequences SR and SL which implement four shift instructions SRE, SRO, SLE, and SLO. The format of these instructions is shown in Figure 6.11(c); it consists of a 6-bit op-code and a 6-bit shift count k. No memory access is required in these sequences.

13.3.1 SR Sequence

This sequence implements instructions SRE and SRO. Instruction SRE (I(0) = 0) shifts the contents of subregister AQ(M) k bit-positions to the right. Instruction SRO (I(0) = 1) first resets register Q to 0 and then shifts the contents of subregister AQ(M) k bit-positions to the right.

Comment, SR sequence begins here		
/SR*DP(0)/	IF (I(0)=1) THEN (Q←0)	
/SR*DP(2)/	C(5–0)←X,	
	C(6)←0,	
/2Δ(SR*DP(10))/	IF (C=0) THEN (D←16$_8$),	(13.7)
/SR*DP(11)/	C←countdnC	
/SR*DP(13)/	AQ(M)←shrAQ(M),	
/2Δ(SR*DP(14))/	IF (C≠0) THEN (D←7),	
Comment, SR sequence ends here		

The last four execution statements in the above form a loop by which subregister AQ(M) is shifted as many times as that specified by counter C. There are two tests on counter C. The first test bypasses the remaining execution statements if shift count k is 0. The second test controls the termination of the loop. These tests occur at delayed control signals because of the setting-D-register micro-operations as explained previously.

13.3.2 SL Sequence

This sequence implements instructions SLE and SLO. Instruction SLE (I(0) = 0) shifts the contents of subregister AQ(M) k bit-positions to the left. Instruction SLO(I(0) = 1) not only shifts the contents of subregister AQ(M) k bit-positions to the left, but also transfers the contents of bit Q(0) (sign bit of register Q) to bit A(0) (sign bit of register A).

Comment, SL sequence begins here.		
/SL*DP(2)/	C(5–0)←X,	
	C(6)←0,	
	IF (I(0)) THEN (A(0)←Q(0)),	
/2Δ(SL*DP(10))/	IF (C=0) THEN (D←16$_8$),	(13.8)
/SL*DP(11)/	C←countdnC	
/SL*DP(12)/	AQ(M)←shlAQ(M),	
/2Δ(SL*DP(14))/	IF (C≠0) THEN (D←7),	
Comment, SL sequence ends here		

Again, the last four execution statements form a loop by which subregister AQ(M) is shifted. In comparison of the SR and SL sequences, the difference lies in the conditional resetting-Q-register micro-operation at DP(0) in the SR sequence and the conditional Q(0)-to-A(0) transfer micro-operation at DP(2) in the SL sequence.

13.4 MISCELLANEOUS SEQUENCES

There are four remaining sequences LDC, CAS, LCT, and STP which implement four instructions LDC, CAS, LCT, and STP.

13.4.1 LDC Sequence

This sequence implements instruction LDC which transfers the contents in the memory location at address m to the location at address (m + 1). It follows the format in Figure 6.11(a) which has a 5-bit op-code and a 7-bit operand address. It requires one memory access.

Comment, LDC sequence begins here

/LDS∗DP(1)/	X←0,
	READ←1,
/Δ(LDC∗DP(1))/	X←MEM(M),
/LDC∗DP(12)/	M←countupM
/LDC∗DP(13)/	WRITE←1,
/Δ(LDC∗DP(13))/	MEM(M)←X,

(13.9)

Comment, LDC sequence ends here

The above sequence first reads the word at address m out of the memory. It then increments the contents of memory address register M and finally stores the word in the X register back to the memory.

13.4.2 CAS Sequence

This sequence implements instruction CAS which complements the sign bit in the accumulator. The format was shown in Figure 6.11(b); it has only a 5-bit op-code. This instruction requires no memory access.

Comment, CAS sequence begins here

/CAS∗DP(6)/   A(0)←A(0)′   (13.10)

Comment, CAS sequence ends here

13.4.3 LCT Sequence

This sequence implements instruction LCT. The format for instruction LCT was shown in Figure 6.11(d); it has a 5-bit op-code and a 7-bit load count j. Instruction LCT loads count j into counter C. It is usually used in conjunction with input and output instructions. It requires no memory access.

Comment, LCT sequence begins here

/LCT*DP(2)/   C(6)←I(0),C(5-0)←X,   (13.11)

Comment, LCT sequence ends here

13.4.4 STP Sequence

This sequence implements instruction STP which stops computer operation; upon next pressing the START switch to the ON position, the computer resumes operation and fetches the instruction at address n as the next instruction. The format was shown in Figure 6.11(f); it consists of a 5-bit op-code and a 6-bit instruction address n. It requires no memory access.

Comment, STP sequence begins here

/STP*DP(4)/   RUN1←1,

/STP*DP(5)/   P←0,   (13.12)

/STP*DP(6)/   P←X,

Comment, STP sequence ends here

PROBLEMS

13.1 How can the 12 sequences in this chapter implement 18 instructions?

13.2 Draw sequence charts for the SR and SL sequences.

13.3 Write a symbolic program for this computer to test whether the SR and the SL sequences perform correctly.

13.4 Assume this computer consists of only these 18 instructions. How can the number of steps of the control sequence (i.e., the number of the labels) be reduced to improve the speed of the operation of the computer?

13.5 Describe a sequence for an instruction which performs the logical AND operation of the corresponding bits of the word in register A and the memory word at address m.

13.6 Describe a sequence for a store-zero instruction which inserts zero to all words of the memory.

13.7 Describe a sequence for a block-transfer instruction which transfers a fixed block of I6 memory words beginning at address m to another block beginning at the address which is stored in counter C by a prior LCT instruction.

13.8 Describe a sequence for a double-store instruction which stores the word in register A into the memory at address m and stores the word in register Q at address (m + 1).

13.9 Conceive a new instruction that would be useful to the programmer and specify a sequence to implement the instruction.

Appendix

Display of the

Fetch-sequence

Operation

This appendix presents a series of photos taken to show the conditions of the lights and the positions of the switches on the control panel at the end of each clock cycle of the fetch sequence. The instruction that is being fetched is 4014_8 (LDA 14_8), and is stored at memory locations 4 and 5. The first step of the series initializes the computer operation by turning switch POWER to position ON, switch MODE to position DM, and switch CLEAR to position ON. The second step sets the proper instruction address in register P. The fetch sequence begins at the third step and ends at the eighteenth step. Because switch MODE is at position DM, the computer stops after each step beginning from the third step. To resume operation after each stop, switch START is turned on; this is the manual operation required for the third through eighteenth steps. A detailed description of the switch logic and start-step logic is shown in Chapter 12.

There are three parts in each of the following steps. The first part describes the manual operations. The second part describes what the computer does as a result of the manual operations. And the third part shows the picture of the light conditions and the switch positions on the control panel as a result of the manual operations. As shown in Chapter 8, each clock cycle consists of two clock pulses CP1 and CP2. The steps of the fetch sequence are advanced by incrementing counter D; this incrementing is always activated by pulse TD. Pulse TD occurs when register AC is 0 and when clock CP2 occurs. During the last step, register AE is complemented to become 1 so that the next sequence will be an execution sequence.

STEP 1

(a) Manual operations

POWER ←ON,

MODE ←DM,

CLEAR ←ON.

Turn switch POWER to position called ON. Turn switch MODE to position DM (distributor mode). And turn switch CLEAR to position ON.

(b) Bi-tran-6 operations

/POWER(ON)/   LTMEM←ON,

LTDC←ON

When switch POWER is turned to position ON, lights LTMEM and LTDC are turned on.

/MODE(DM)/   LTDM←ON

When switch MODE is turned to position DM, light LTDM is turned on.

/CLEAR(ON)/   A←0, LTA←OFF,

- - - - - - - - - - - - - -

AC←0,LTAC←OFF,

RUN1←0, RUN2←0

When switch CLEAR is turned to position ON, all registers are reset to zero and their lights are turned off (see statement (12.1)).

/CP/   IF (RUN1'∗RUN2') THEN

(LTSTOP←ON,LTSTART←OFF)

When registers RUN1 and RUN2 are both zero, light LTSTOP is on and light LTSTART is off.

(c) Display

STEP 2

(a) Manual operation

SWP (2)←ON

In order to set Program Address Register P(6–1) to 000010 (P(0) is dummy), only switch SWP(2) needs to be turned on. (Note P has been set to 0 in Step 1.)

(b) Bi-tran-6 operations

/SWP(2)(ON)/ P(2)←1,
LTP(2)←ON.

When SWP(2) is turned on, only P(2) bit of Program Address Register is set to 1, and light LTP(2) is turned on. Lights LTP (6–3,1–0) remain off.

(c) Display

STEP 3

(a) Manual operation

START←ON

Turn switch START to position ON.

(b) Bi-tran-6 operations

/AE'*DP(0)/M←0

Register AE is 0 when it is in the fetch sequence. Pulse DP(0) occurs when Register D contains 0 and when the clock is CP1. When AE' * DP(0) becomes 1, Memory Address Register M is cleared.

/Δ(AE'*DP(0))/ M(6–1)←P(6–1)

Pulse Δ(AE'*DP(0)) occurs (i.e., 1) at 15 microsec. after pulse (AE'* DP(0)) occurs. When Δ(AE'*DP(0)) becomes 1, the contents of P(6–1) are transferred to M(6–1).

/TD/ IF(DMR') THEN (D←countup D)

When pulse TD occurs, counter D is incremented if DMR' is 1. DMR' is 1 when either switch MODE is not at position DM, or switch MR is not at position ON. D contains 0001 after this step.

(c) Display

STEP 4

(a) Manual operation

START←ON

Turn switch START to position ON.

(b) Bi-tran-6 operations

/AE′*DP(1)/ READ←1,
X←0

Pulse DP(1) occurs when Register D contains 1 and the clock is CP1. When AE′*DP(1) becomes 1, Register X is cleared and terminal READ is set to 1 to initiate memory read.

/Δ(AE′*DP(1))/ X←MEM(M)

Pulse Δ(AE′*DP(1)) occurs at 15 microsec. after pulse (AE′*DP(1)) occurs. When Δ(AE′*DP(1)) becomes 1, the memory word in location M (which is 0000100) is read into Register X (which is 100000).

/TD/ IF (DMR′) THEN (D←countup D)

Explained in Step 3. D contains 0010 after this step.

(c) Display

STEP 5

(a) Manual operation

  START←ON   Turn switch START to position ON.

(b) Bi-tran-6 operations

  /AE′*DP(2)/ 1←0,   When AE′*DP(2) becomes 1, Instruc-
      IE←0   tion register I and register IE are both
                 cleared. Explained in Step 3.

  /TD/ IF(DMR′) THEN (D←countup D)   D contains 0011 after this step.

(c) Display

STEP 6

(a) Manual operation

START←ON

Turn switch START to position ON.

(b) Bi-tran-6 operations

/AE′*DP(3)/ I←X

When AE′*DP(3) becomes 1, the contents of register X are transferred to register I (i.e., op-code is now in register I). Register I should now contain 100000 because the instruction is LDA.

/TD/ IF(DMR′) THEN (D←countup D)

Explained in Step 3. D contains 0100 after this step.

(c) Display

STEP 7

(a) Manual operation

START←ON	Turn switch START to position ON.

(b) Bi-tran-6 operations

/AE′∗DP(4)/ IF(DIE) THEN (IE←1), IF (DIE∗ERRORSTOP(NOBP)) THEN (RUN1←1)	When AE′∗DP(4) becomes 1, terminal DIE is sensed for 1. If DIE is 1, it indicates an illegal op-code; Instruction Error Register IE is set to 1. If DIE is 1 and switch ERROR-STOP is at position NOBP (no by-pass), register RUN1 is turned on to stop computer operation. Here, DIE is 0 because the op-code 100000 is LDA, and IE thus remains 0.
/TD/ IF(DMR′) THEN (D←countup D)	Explained in Step 3. D contains 0101 after this step.

(c) Display

STEP 8

(a) Manual operation

START←ON

Turn switch START to position ON.

(b) Bi-tran-6 operations

/AE'∗DP(5)/ IF (AEMR'∗IMR')

   THEN (P←countup P)

AEMR' denotes that either MODE switch is *not* at AEM position or switch MR is *not* at ON position.

IMR' denotes that either MODE switch is *not* at IM (instruction mode) position or switch MR is *not* at ON position. When AE'∗DP(5) becomes 1 and, if both AEMR' and IMR' are true, then Counter P(6 − 1) counts one up (P(0) is dummy).

/TD/ IF(DMR') THEN (D←countup D)

Explained in Step 3. D contains 0110 after this stop.

(c) Display

STEP 9

(a) Manual operation

    START←ON   Turn switch START to position ON.

(b) Bi-tran-6 operations

    /AE′∗DP(6)/   No micro-operation occurs.

    /TD/ IF(DMR′) THEN (D←countup D)   Explained in Step 3. D contains 0111
                                                  after this step.

(c) Display

STEP 10

(a) Manual operation

START←ON   Turn switch START to position ON.

(b) Bi-tran-6 operations

/AE$'$*DP(7)/   No micro-operation occurs.

/TD/ IF(DMR$'$) THEN (D←countup D)   Explained in Step 3. D contains 1000 after this step.

(c) Display

STEP 11

(a) Manual operation

    START←ON   Turn switch START to position ON.

(b) Bi-tran-6 operations

    /AE'*DP(8)/   No micro-operation occurs.

    /TD/ IF(DMR') THEN (D←countup D)   Explained in Step 3. D contains 1001
                                          after this step.

(c) Display

STEP 12

(a) Manual operation

START'ON   Turn switch START to position ON.

(b) Bi-tran-6 operations

/AE'*DP(9)/   No micro-operation occurs.

/TD/ IF(DMR') THEN (D←countup D)   Explained in Step 3. D contains 1010
                                   after this step.

(c) Display

STEP 13

(a) Manual operation

    START←ON

(b) Bi-tran-6 operations

    /AE′*DP(10)/ M(0)←1

    /TD/ IF (DMR′) THEN (D←countup D)

Turn switch START to position ON.

When AE′*DP(10) becomes 1, bit M(0) of Memory Address Register M is set to 1 for fetching the second memory word of the instruction.

Explained in Step 3. D contains **1011** after this step.

(c) Display

STEP 14

(a) Manual operation

START←ON

Turn switch START to position ON.

(b) Bi-tran-6 operations

/AE'∗DP(11)/ READ←1,
      X←0

When AE'∗DP(11) becomes 1, register X is cleared and Memory Read is initiated.

/Δ(AE'∗DP(11))/ X←MEM(M)

When the delayed pulse (AE'∗DP(11)) occurs, the operand in the memory located by M (i.e., 0000101) is read into Register X.

/TD/ IF (DMR') THEN (D←countup D)

Explained in Step 3. D contains 1100 after this step.

(c) Display

STEP 15

(a) Manual operation

START←ON   Turn switch START to position ON.

(b) Bi-tran-6 operations

/AE'∗DP(12)/   No micro-operation occurs.

/TD/ IF(DMR') THEN (D←countup D)   Explained in Step 3. D contains 1101 after this step.

(c) Display

STEP 16

(a) Manual operation

START← ON   Turn switch START to position ON.

(b) Bi-tran-6 operations

/AE'∗DP(13)/   No micro-operation occurs.

/TD/ IF(DMR') THEN (D←countup D)   Explained in Step 3. D contains **1110** after this step.

(c) Display

STEP 17

(a) Manual operation

    START←ON   Turn switch START to position ON.

(b) Bi-tran-6 operations

    /DP(14) OV←0,   When pulse DP(14) occurs, registers
            LZ←0,   OV, LZ, and SI are reset to zero. Note
            SI←0,   there is no AE$'$ in the label; this
                                          means that these micro-operations
                                          occur at every fetch or execution
                                          sequence.

    /TD/ IF (DMR$'$) THEN (D←countup D)   Explained in Step 3. D contains 1111
                                          after this step.

(c) Display

STEP 18

(a) Manual operation

START←ON

Turn switch START to position ON.

(b) Bi-tran-6 operations

/AE'∗DP(15)/ M←0

When pulse AE'∗DP(15) becomes 1, register M is cleared.

/Δ(AE'∗DP(15))/ M(5-0)←X,
M(6)←I(0)

When the delayed pulse AE'∗ DP(15) becomes 1, the contents of the X register are transferred to sub-register M(5-0), and bit I(0) is transferred to bit M(6). Register M then contains the operand address.

/DP(15)/EL←0,
IF (AEMR') THEN (AE←AE')

At DP(15) register EL is set to 0. And if AEMR' (see Step 8) is true, the contents of register AE are complemented.

/TD/ IF(DMR') THEN (D←countup D)

Explained in Step 3. D contains 0000 after this step.

(c) Display

References

1. Burks, A. W., Goldstine, H. H., and von Neumann, J., "Preliminary Discussion of the Logical Design of an Electronic Computing Instrument," Part I, *Datamation,* Vol. 8, No. 9, pp. 24-31, September, 1962
2. Burks, A. W., Goldstine, H. H., and von Neumann, J., "Preliminary Discussion of the Logical Design of an Electronic Computing Instrument," Part II, *Datamation,* Vol. 8, No. 10, pp. 36-41, October, 1962.
3. Chu, Y., "Digital Computer Design Fundamentals," McGraw-Hill Book Co., 1962.
4. Iverson, K. E., "A Programming Language," John Wiley & Sons, N.Y., 1962.
5. Schorr, H., "A Register Transfer Language to Describe Digital Systems," Technical Report No. 30, Digital Systems Laboratory, Department of Electrical Engineering, Princeton University, September, 1962.
6. Schwarz, H. R., "An Introduction to Algol 60," *Comm. ACM,* Feb. 1962, pp. 82-95.
7. Goldstine, H. H., and von Neumann, J., "On the Principles of Large Scale Computing Machines," *John von Neumann Collected Works,* Vol. V, Pergamon Press, pp. 1-32, 1963.
8. Braun, E. L., "Digital Computer Design," Academic Press, 1963.
9. Organick, E. I., "A MAD Primer," Ulrich's Book Store, Ann Arbor, Michigan, 1964.
10. "IBM 7090/7094 IBSYS Operating System, version 13, Fortran IV Language," File No. 7090-25, Form C28-6390-3, IBM Corporation.
11. Falkoff, A. D., and Iverson, K. E., "A Formal Description of System/360," *IBM Systems Journal,* Vol. 3, No. 3, 1964.
12. Schlaeppi, H. P., "A Formal Language for Describing Machine Logic, Timing and Sequencing (LOTIS)," *IEEE Trans. on Electronic Computers,* August, 1964, pp. 439-448.

13. Mullery, A. P., "A Procedure Oriented Machine Language," *IEEE Trans. on Electronic Computers,* August, 1964, pp. 449-455.
14. Chu, Y., "An Algol-like Computer Design Language," *Comm. of ACM,* October, 1965, pp. 607-615.
15. "Technical Operational Manual for the Bi-Tran Six Digital Trainer," Vol. 1 and 2, Fabri-Tek, Inc., Hopkins, Minnesota, 1965.
16. Bartee, T. C., "Digital Computer Fundamentals," Second edition, McGraw-Hill Book Co., 1966.
17. Arden, B. W., "Michigan Algorithm Decoder," Computer Center, University of Michigan, Ann Arbor, Michigan, August, 1966.
18. Organick, E. I., "A Fortran IV Primer," Addison-Wesley Publishing Co., Inc. 1966.
19. "Program Library for Bi-Tran Six Computer," Fabri-Tek, Inc., Hopkins, Minnesota, 1966.
20. Parnas, D. L., "A Language for Describing the Function of Synchronous Systems," *Comm. of ACM,* February, 1966, pp. 72-76.
21. Wilber, J. A., "A Language for Describing Digital Computer," *Report No. 197,* Department of Computer Science, University of Illinois, February 15, 1966.
22. Giese, A., "Hargol—A Hardware Oriented Algol Language," *Internal Report* No. VA5, August, 1966, A/S Regnecentralen, Copenhagen, Denmark.
23. Metze, G., and Seshu, S., "A Proposal for a Computer Compiler," *Proc. of the SFCC Conference,* 1966, pp. 253-263.
24. Zucker, M. S., "LOCS: An EDP Machines Logic and Control Simulator," *International Convention Record,* Part 3, 1965, pp. 28-50.
25. Breuer, M. A., "General Survey of Design Automation of Digital Computer," *Proc. of the IEEE,* Vol. 54, No. 12, December, 1966, pp. 1708-1721.
26. Chu, Y., and Frank, A., "Symbolic Design of Bi-Tran Six Computer," *Tech. Report,* TR-66-36, Computer Science Center, University of Maryland, November, 1966.
27. Sardarian, G., "Symbolic Design for the CDC 1700 Computer Logic," *Thesis,* Department of Electrical Engineering, University of Maryland, January, 1967.
28. Mesztenyi, C. K., "Translator and Simulator for the Computer Design and Simulation Program," *Tech. Report TR-67-48,* Computer Science Center, University of Maryland, May, 1967.
29. Gschwind, H. W., *Design of Digital Computers,* Springer-Verlag, New York, 1967.

30. Flores, I., "Computer Design," Prentice-Hall, Inc., 1967.
31. Hellerman, H., "Digital Computer System Principles," McGraw-Hill Book Co., 1967.
32. Clark, W. A., "Macromodular Computer Systems," *AFIPS* Spring Joint Computer Conference, Vol. 30, pp. 335-336, 1967.
33. Ornstein, S. M., Stucki, M. J., and Clark, W. A., "A Functional Description of Macromodules," *AFIPS* Spring Joint Computer Conference, Vol. 30, pp. 337-364, 1967.
34. Mesztenyi, C. K., "Computer Design Language, Simulation and Boolean Translation," *Technical Report 68-72,* Computer Science Center, University of Maryland, June, 1968.
35. Lecht, C. P., "The Programmer's PL/1," McGraw-Hill Book Co., 1968.
36. Frederick, D. M., "Simulation of a Large-Scale General-Purpose Computer," *Master Thesis,* Department of Electrical Engineering, University of Maryland, June, 1968.
37. Maisel, H., "Introduction to Electronic Digital Computers," McGraw-Hill Book Co., 1969.
38. Murrill, P. W., and C. L. Smith, "Fortran IV Programming for Engineers and Scientists," International Textbook Company, 1968.

Index